The Laser Printer Reference

Peter Randall

New York   London   Toronto   Sydney   Tokyo   Singapore

Credits

Publisher
Michael Violano

Managing Editor
Kelly D. Dobbs

Editor
Susan Hunt

Production Editor
Bettina A. Versaci

Developmental Editor
Perry King

Editorial Assistant
Lisa Rose

Book Designer
Michele Laseau

Cover Designer
HUB Graphics

Production Team
Katy Bodenmiller, Michelle Cleary, Terri Edwards, Mitzi Gianakos,
Howard Jones, John Kane, Loren Malloy, Roger S. Morgan,
Linda Quigley, Michelle M. Self, Greg Simsic, Suzanne Tully

About the Author

Peter Randall is President of Ariel Enterprises, Inc., a software development and consulting firm. He has written more than 30 major applications for use in business. He has co-authored more than 15 books, including *The Lotus Guide to 1-2-3 Release 2.2*, *The Lotus Guide to Release 3.4+*, and *WordPerfect 5.1 Power Pack*.

Overview

Contents

Part II Operating, Maintaining, and Selecting Your Laser Printer

PART V Appendices

INTRODUCTION

An Evolutionary Leap in Printing Technology

The New Office Standard

In 1983, a Hewlett-Packard LaserJet was the ultimate status symbol of the modern office. It not only cranked out pages faster than just about any other kind of output device, it did so with magnificent quality, and with virtually no noise.

Today, the HP's LaserJet 4 is turning heads (see Figure I.1). It is not so much the printer—which, based on a new Canon engine, is similar in performance to the LaserJet III—but rather the quality of the output. Following the lead of the competition and the success of its own enhanced-resolution LaserJet III, Hewlett-Packard has advanced the quality of its output to a true 600 dots per inch (dpi). To this Hewlett-Packard adds the extremely successful Resolution Enhancement Technology (RET), first introduced with the LaserJet III, which enables the laser to position and resize dots so that the final output smooths jagged edges and avoids *staircasing* (see Chapter 1 for details). That means your lines and curves will be considerably smoother, serifs will have crisper edges, and line intersections will be sharper.

In addition to improved resolution, the LaserJet 4 is smarter and faster than its predecessors. The printer uses a new RISC-based processor and includes two megabytes of user-memory. For Windows users, the LaserJet 4 includes a TrueType rasterizer and ten TrueType fonts built-in to provide exceptional speed and accuracy when printing Windows documents. Add to this the standard 35 scalable Intellifonts and you have font capability usually associated only with PostScript-based printers. To deal with its multiple personalities, the LaserJet 4 introduces a new level of printer control called Printer Job Language (PJL), which permits explicit-language switching as well as automatic-language switching, based on the content of the print job. The combination of PJL and further enhancements to PCL 5 enables the printer to communicate with the computer, updating it with the printer's status. The printer reports to the computer which page of the print job it is currently printing, whether it needs paper or toner, and many other useful facts. Other new features include PostScript Level 2 support built into the LaserJet 4M, or as a well-integrated upgrade for the standard LaserJet 4. Finally, the LaserJet 4 enables you to connect more than one I/O—for example, parallel and serial ports—and to switch between them as print jobs are presented.

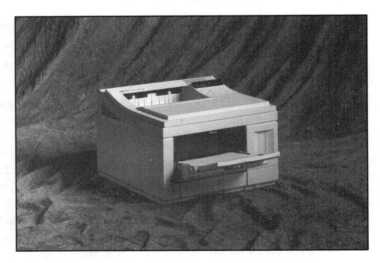

Figure I.1. The Hewlett-Packard LaserJet 4, introduced in 1992.

When Hewlett-Packard was busy developing its latest printing wonder, the competition was not sitting idly by. They came up with new features and enhancements: Industry leader Compaq introduced a line of high-end printers under the Pagemarq moniker; IBM continued to push the very successful Lexmark brand of printers; Apple Computer has held onto its printer niche in the PostScript-only market; and, as anticipated, the Japanese have flooded the market with big brand-name products and no-name clones. Panasonic, Okidata, NEC, C. Itoh, Fujitsu, and Epson have all introduced new and competitive products.

Competition is great news for the consumer. Not only do you have the opportunity to pick and choose a printer that has exactly the features you need or want, but a printer will probably cost significantly less than it did last year. The only downside to all of this innovation is that it has made the process of selecting a printer far more complicated. As in all such decisions, information is your strongest ally. This book will provide you with an understanding of how a laser printer works and how to get the most from it. Chapter 7 specifically discusses how to wade through the sea of confusing features and prices when buying your next printer.

A Book for the Laser Printer User

Beyond helping you to buy your new laser printer, this book is designed to make printing with your laser printer easier by explaining a number of key issues, as follows:

➤ How a laser printer works

➤ How to install and transport your laser printer

➤ How to use the various functions such as the menu control panel

➤ Selecting the right paper

➤ Maintaining your laser printer

➤ How to diagnose and correct problems

➤ Understanding fonts

➤ Programming with PCL-5

➤ Selecting hardware and software options

You can use *The Laser Printer Reference* in one of two ways. First, you can read through Sections I and II, by using your printer and exploring under the hood as you read along. This will give you an in-depth understanding of how your printer works, how to maintain it, and what can go wrong with it. You can then use the book as a trouble-shooting guide should you have problems in the future.

Second, you can read all of the basic materials and tackle the advanced topics as well. You will find a complete primer if you have the background and inclination to do some PCL programming. You need to do this because you can then write your own PCL commands and execute them from DOS. This will enable you to get the full benefit of your laser printer even with programs that don't explicitly support the printer.

Finally, make sure you look at Chapter 16 to learn about important hardware and software enhancements that can augment your reports and presentations.

Who This Book Is For

This book is for the following people:

➤ People who are contemplating buying a laser printer and want to learn how it works and what it can do. Later on, this book will become a trusted reference guide.

➤ People who have purchased a new laser printer for personal or business use, or whose departments have just acquired a laser printer, and want to learn how they can get the most out of the printer.

➤ People who share a laser printer with other users and do not have immediate access to the documentation.

Although much of the discussion and many of the examples utilize one or more of Hewlett-Packard's successful LaserJet models, this book is not limited in applicability to those models. Hewlett-Packard has always been at the forefront of laser printer designs, and provides an excellent baseline for a comparison of features and price. Hewlett-Packard has developed and maintained the PCL standard control language emulated by so many of the compatibles, and Hewlett-Packard uses the standard Canon engines that are the basis for most of its competition. This is why many of the software and control examples are shown with Hewlett-Packard's current LaserJet 4, and the older LaserJet III is used for many of the maintenance discussions. The former was chosen because it represents the state of the art for printer control and the latter because it is based on the Canon SX engine (see Figure I.2) common to many different manufacturers.

Figure I.2. Hewlett-Packard LaserJet III, The standard of Canon SX-based printers.

When you are using a Hewlett-Packard-compatible, some of the hardware and control panel discussions may not apply directly, but probably will apply in concept. The discussion of printing partial pages, or manually ejecting the page by pressing the Form Feed button applies to your printer because it will have the same sort of problems and you will need to provide the same kind of solutions, although they may appear under different names.

Whatever your printing needs or choice of printer, laser printers are an invaluable technological boost to your arsenal of computing tools. This book will help you take advantage of the tremendous printing capabilities sitting at the end of your parallel or serial cable. The power is now in your hands.

PART

Getting Started with Laser Printing

The Fundamentals of Laser Printing

Although laser printers are commonplace in most offices today, many people still are unsure about how they work. Some people assume that the laser literally etches words on the paper; for others, a laser printer is a mysterious black box.

You do not need to know how a laser printer works in order to use it—most software today supports laser printers, and software support staffs can answer many technical questions. However, if you do understand the basics of your printer, you will never be baffled when nothing happens after you have issued a print screen command. As you will learn below, laser printers are *page printers*, meaning that they wait until they receive a full page of data or a page eject command before printing a page. Pressing a form feed button on your laser printer will solve the problem, as will issuing a manual page eject command from your software, or another print screen command from DOS. This is only one instance where understanding how your printer works can save you frustration and wasted effort.

Understanding how your laser printer functions will also help you to make the right *care and feeding decisions*. You will understand how a build-up of toner on the corona wire can cause imaging problems, and how the wrong kind of paper will lead to poor quality imaging.

At the very least, read the following explanation of what happens under your laser printer's hood after you have issued a print command. When your curiosity is whetted, read the next section, which gives a detailed account of the process of laser printing.

In Brief: The Laser Printing Process

When you issue a print command, the following steps occur:

1. A data signal representing what you see on the screen is converted into an electronic image.

2. The electronic image is transmitted to a laser that bounces off of a rotating mirror onto a negatively charged rotating drum in the toner cartridge.

3. Wherever the laser strikes the drum, the drum loses its charge. The discharged areas represent the form of characters, numbers, and graphic elements.

4. The toner in the cartridge sticks to the discharged areas of the drum and is repelled from the charged areas.

5. A sheet of paper is fed into the printer and given a positive charge that pulls the toner from the drum, still in the pattern of characters, numbers, and graphic elements.

6. A set of fuser rollers melts the toner onto the paper.

7. The paper is ejected from the printer.

From Computer to Laser Printer

Print commands issued via a serial, parallel, or Specialty I/O port (see Chapter 2) consist of a mixture of ASCII characters and command characters. ASCII characters are the binary computer code consisting of zeros and ones that represent the letters, numbers, or special symbols that you want to print. The command characters tell the printer how to print characters, where to place characters, what font to select, and what spacing to use. These formatting instructions constitute Hewlett-Packard's Printer Command Language (PCL 5) or Adobe's PostScript page description language

After the data signal enters the printer, it passes into a portion of the printer memory called the Input/Output (I/O) buffer where it is stored temporarily. When it is in the I/O buffer, the data is analyzed by the printer's internal microprocessor to identify PCL 5 commands and to separate them from the ASCII characters through a process called *parsing*. The PCL 5 commands and ASCII text are then moved to another area of memory called the *page intermediate*. After the PCL 5 commands are in the page intermediate, they are executed—for example, underlining, italicizing, and shading. The ASCII data is sorted according to its relative position on the page as created by your computer, not in the order in which it is received by the printer.

For example, when you are transmitting a three-column page to the printer, the top line of the second column is transmitted by the software after the bottom line of the first column in the logical sequence of the file containing the text; however, because the printer lays down the page line by line as the page roles through the paper path, the top of the second column must be printed immediately after the top of the first column. In a similar fashion, figures and graphic elements such as lines, shading, and boxes are positioned and even overlaid in the page intermediate.

You can picture the page intermediate as an electronic replica of the page as it will be printed on paper, with each line of text and each graphic element positioned in its correct location. Before this electronic image can be printed it must be converted into a bit-mapped format. A bit-mapped image is a string of zeros and ones, with ones representing the dots of toner required to form a character or graphic element, and zeros representing white space around the characters or graphic elements. (See Figure 1.1.)

Graphic data in the page intermediate is stored in bit-mapped format, and therefore requires considerable amounts of memory. This is why the size of graphic images that can be output by a particular laser printer is limited by the amount of memory available. When you attempt to load more graphic data than can be held in the page intermediate memory, the page will eject partially printed, and the printer will display an 020 Memory Overflow Error (see Chapter 10).

In contrast to graphic data, text data is stored as ASCII characters in the page intermediate and is not converted to bit-mapped form until it is moved to the strip buffer, in order to conserve memory space.

Dot Row	Bit Map
01	00000000 11111100 00001111 1100000
02	00000111 11111111 00011111 1110000
03	00001111 11111111 10011111 1100000
04	00111111 11010111 11011110 0000000
05	00111110 00000001 11111110 0000000
06	01111100 00000000 01111110 0000000
07	01111000 00000000 01111110 0000000
08	11110000 00000000 00111110 0000000
09	11110000 00000000 00111110 0000000
10	11110000 00000000 00011110 0000000
11	11110000 00000000 00011110 0000000
12	11110000 00000000 00011110 0000000
13	11110000 00000000 00011110 0000000
14	11110000 00000000 00111110 0000000
15	01111000 00000000 00111110 0000000
16	01111000 00000000 01111110 0000000
17	01111100 00000000 11111110 0000000
18	00111110 00000001 11111110 0000000
19	00011111 11010111 11011110 0000000
20	00001111 11111111 10011110 0000000
21	00000111 11111111 00011110 0000000
22	00000000 10101000 00011110 0000000
23	00000000 00000000 00011110 0000000
24	00000000 00000000 00011110 0000000
25	00000000 00000000 00011110 0000000
26	00000000 00000000 00111110 0000000
27	00000000 00000000 00111100 0000000
28	00000000 00000000 01111100 0000000
29	00000000 00000001 11111000 0000000
30	00000001 11111111 11110000 0000000
31	00000011 11111111 11100000 0000000
32	00000001 11111111 10000000 0000000

Figure 1.1. The bit-map concept: Ones correspond to white areas, and zeros correspond to dark areas.

Graphic and text data remain in the page intermediate area until a complete page of information is ready to be printed. Consequently, laser printers are considered page printers rather than line printers, which lay down one line of text at a time. This is also why you must give a laser printer a form feed instruction when you transmit less than a full page of text—such as a short worksheet or a screen print.

After the page intermediate is completely filled with a page worth of data, the ASCII text and the bit-mapped graphics are passed to another area of memory called the strip buffer, which arranges the data in sequential horizontal lines. At this point the text characters are converted into lines of dots corresponding to their bit-mapped image, as specified by the PCL 5 font commands sent with the text.

By now you can appreciate the complex task that the laser printer's microprocessor must perform. As the microprocessor prepares data in the strip buffer, it must look up each ASCII character in its memory to find the right bit-mapped dot pattern for the font selected. That is why PCL printers must have the bit-mapped image of all the fonts to be used on a page stored in internal memory either as a resident font on an external ROM cartridge, or in temporary RAM as a soft font.

With scalable fonts, the bit-mapped image is created at the time that the font is selected by scaling the font outline to the designated point size. The bit-mapped image is stored in the printer's RAM memory in the same fashion as a bit-mapped soft font.

Page description systems, such as PostScript, carry the process one step further. They contain only the outlines of the families of fonts in internal RAM or ROM memory. The various point sizes, stroke angles, and stroke weights required by a particular font are created as needed by a dedicated microprocessor that mathematically manipulates the outline. The microprocessor scales the outlines up or down to create a particular point size.

Whether the bit-mapped image was transmitted by the computer, looked up in the printer's memory, or created by a PostScript processor, it is sent to one of three strips in the strip buffer. A strip is an electronic image that composes a tiny slice of a line of text or graphic characters. To visualize a strip, imagine taking this page and cutting it horizontally into hundreds of pieces. Each piece would only represent a small, undecipherable portion of each letter. But as you laid them down in the right order, the type would gradually become recognizable. The strip buffers work the same way; after a strip of data is filled with dots, the image is transmitted to the laser engine—the drum and laser imaging assembly—for printing.

When a strip of data is completely transmitted to the engine, the strip buffer is cleared in preparation for receiving the next strip of data from the page intermediate. Meanwhile, another strip representing the next slice of the page, is already filled with dots and ready for transmission to the laser.

Three strip buffers are used sequentially so that one can be created when another is being printed, and the third waits to be reloaded. By using three strip buffers, the printer can prepare the strip data at a pace determined by the complexity of the data, while the laser and the print engine can operate at the constant speed required by the printing process. The three buffers provide the slack needed when these speeds are different.

If the preparation process moves faster than the print process, it can be temporarily halted by the printer software. However, when the preparation process falls behind the print process so that all three strip buffers are completely drained—usually caused by extremely dense, small type or complex graphics—the printer will terminate the printing process and report an 021 Print Overrun Error on its display panel (see Chapter 10).

The data from the strip buffer is sent to a solid state laser in the form of "on/off" codes. The codes correspond to the individual dots and the white space between them. Next, the Resolution Enhancement Technology offered on some Hewlett-Packard models takes the binary code from the strip buffer and processes it through an Application Specific Integrated Circuit (ASIC). The ASIC uses pattern recognition techniques to determine where individual dots should be optimally placed and sized to smooth staircasing. The ASIC controls the size of the dots by manipulating the duration of the laser pulses (longer pulses create bigger dots), and the position of the dots by controlling the timing of an individual pulse (shortening the period between one dot and the next will move the dots closer together, while lengthening the duration has the opposite effect).

The laser does not shoot directly at the paper, it bounces off a rotating mirror assembly that causes the beam to scan horizontally across a rotating drum in the toner cartridge. This begins the actual printing process.

Drum Roll

The action takes place within the toner cartridge, technically known as an EP for electrophotographic cartridge. The cartridge contains the following main components (see Figure 1.2):

➤ A photosensitive drum protected by shutters that open when the cartridge is inserted into the printer.

➤ A gear assembly that turns the drum.

➤ A supply of toner, that consists of tiny black, thermoplastic particles impregnated with bits of iron.

➤ Two cleaning blades that remove excess toner from the drum before recharging the drum.

➤ A high-voltage primary corona wire (so named because it generates a high voltage electric charge that ionizes the adjacent air or corona and imparts a static electricity charge to nearby objects) (see Figure 1.3).

Because of the special properties of the photoreceptor material covering the drum, the charge will be removed from any point on the drum struck by light. Therefore, as the laser is scanned across the drum by the rotating mirror and pulsed on and off according to the bit-mapped image in the strip buffer, it causes the drum to lose the electrical charge in all areas that correspond to printed dots. The invisible pattern of charges corresponding to the intended characters and graphics is called the electrostatic image. The electrostatic image is converted to a visible image through a developing process.

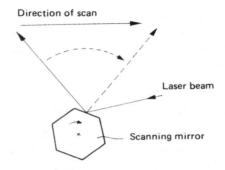

Figure 1.2. Cross-section of a toner cartridge.

During developing, the photosensitive drum rotates in close proximity to the developing, cylinder (see Figure 1.2), which rotates in the opposite direction of the drum. The developing cylinder is used to transfer toner particles from the toner bin to the photosensitive drum. The cylinder picks up a uniform layer of toner particles by using an internal magnet to attract the iron in the particles. The particles are given a negative surface charge when they rub against the developing cylinder, which also carries a negative charge.

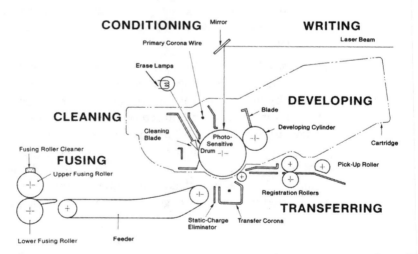

Figure 1.3. The transfer corona is used to place a charge on a paper that will attract the toner particles.

As the photosensitive drum and the developing cylinder rotate together, the negatively charged toner particles are repelled by the negative charge of the unexposed areas of the photosensitive drum and are attracted to the exposed areas. The toner particles *jump* from the developing cylinder to the exposed areas, creating a visible image. Because the toner only sticks to the areas struck by the laser beam, this system is called a *black-write* system. Some laser engines, such as that made by Ricoh, use the reverse process by charging the drum and the toner particles in a fashion that causes the toner particles to stick to the unexposed areas of the drum. These systems are called *white-write* systems.

Because the drum has as a circumference smaller than the length of the paper, it must rotate several times to print a complete page. It must transfer the first part of the page to the paper and erase itself by means of a series of erase lamps that discharge the entire drum; it then must be recharged by the primary corona wire before forming the next part of the image.

The Paper Mill

The next step in the printing process is for the electrostatic image to be transferred to the paper. When the image begins to form on the drum, the microprocessor activates the paper feed mechanism which carries a piece of paper in a path adjacent to the drum. The paper is given a positive charge by a transfer corona wire. The positive charge on the paper is stronger than the attraction of the drum, so it pulls the negatively charged toner particles from the drum to the paper in a position identical to that on the drum. The ability of the paper to hold a charge is critical to the successful transfer of the toner. Choosing paper with the proper electrical qualities is discussed in Chapter 4.

At this point, the toner particles are only held to the paper by gravity. To permanently affix the toner, the laser printer passes the paper through a set of high temperature (400 degrees Fahrenheit) nonstick fuser rollers that melt the toner particles onto the paper surface. The paper is ejected from the printer and you have a finished page.

Unpacking, Setting Up, and Shipping Your Laser Printer

You need to review the setup procedure before you plug in your laser printer. This will ensure proper installation and minimize problems if you decide to sell and ship the machine, or move to another office.

When you purchase your laser printer, the manufacturer provides detailed instructions for getting the printer from the box to your desk or work table. When you don't have the instructional literature, the procedure is as follows:

1. Make sure you have the following items along with the printer: the power cord, paper tray, cartridge, and cleaning bar—a piece of plastic approximately nine inches long and a half-inch wide with two handles in the middle (see Figure 2.1).

2. Place the laser printer on a sturdy desk or table in a sufficiently well-ventilated space.

3. Remove all of the packing spacers and tape.

4. Before inserting the toner cartridge, rock it back and forth 45 degrees; break the plastic tab on the side and pull out the plastic divider strip. Insert the cartridge into the printer.

5. Plug the power cord into the printer. Connect the cord to a surge suppressor that is connected to an outlet with sufficient current.

6. Install any font cartridges—maximum of two for most printers.

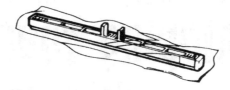

Figure 2.1. The cleaning bar is used to remove excess toner from the fuser rollers.

7. Connect a cable from the printer to the computer; when you use a serial connection, you may have to specifically select the serial settings on the menu panel.

8. Load paper into the paper tray and conduct a self-test.

9. Configure your software for your new printer.

Although some of the preceding steps are obvious, several require amplification and are discussed below.

Selecting a Site

Your laser printer can be placed anywhere in your office. However there are two constraints. First, although the printer contains an ozone filter, you should avoid operating it in a very small room with little or no ventilation. For some people, ozone can be irritating to the eyes, nose, throat, and other mucous membranes. This is important if the printer will see heavy duty use and the filter is not changed at the proper maintenance intervals (see Chapter 5). Also, multiple printers in a small area can raise ozone levels to higher-than-recommended levels.

Second, avoid using the printer in very hot or humid work environments. This can cause excessive paper jams and imaging problems. Extremely low humidity environments can also cause certain imaging problems (see Chapter 4).

Uncrating Your Printer

Your laser printer will be shipped with various pieces of tape and foam that protect vital parts of the printer during shipping. The printer will not function properly when the tape and foam are not removed. You can open the hood and remove all of the spacers, tape, and styrofoam.

TIP

When you work in a large corporation that trashes its equipment boxes, consider storing the packing foam and spacers in your desk or take the whole box home. This will ensure that you have a box of the right size for shipping.

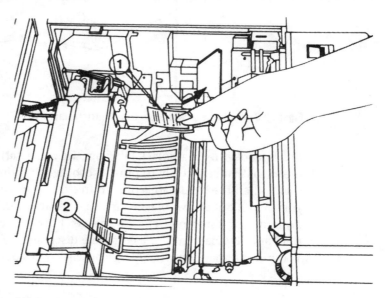

Figure 2.2. Packing spacers around the fuser assembly on a Canon SX engine-based laser printer. Remove them before you use the printer.

Installing a Toner Cartridge

Toner cartridge installation is well documented in the instructions that accompany each cartridge. The procedure entails pulling the tape, rocking the cartridge to disperse any clumped toner, opening the printer, inserting the cartridge into the guides, inserting the cleaning bar on some models, and closing the hood. When you install a new toner cartridge, you should keep two key points in mind—rocking the toner cartridge and breaking the small tab off of the cartridge.

You need to gently rock the toner cartridge several times to distribute the toner evenly. This step might seem unnecessary, but it can have a major impact on the print quality and life of the cartridge. Figure 2.3 shows the proper technique for rocking a cartridge.

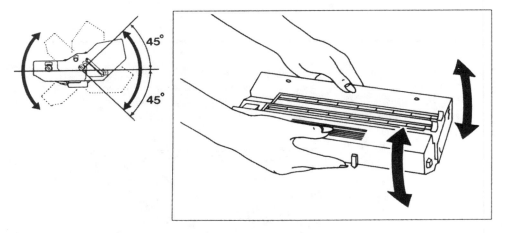

Figure 2.3. Rocking a cartridge before installation.

Breaking off the small black tab from the toner cartridge does not mean that you are ready to print. Nothing will print if you do only that. When the black tab is broken free from the cartridge, it enables you to pull out a clear plastic tape that separates the toner from the drum during shipping (refer to Chapter 1 for a description and illustration, and to Chapter 6 for a complete discussion of toner cartridges). You can pull hard on the tape because it comes out easiest with one quick tug.

If the tape breaks from the plastic tab and you can see an edge, carefully try to pull out the remainder with a pliers. If that does not work, you will have to get another cartridge. (Should the tape break, contact your supplier because he may be able to get a replacement.)

After the the tape has been pulled and the cartridge is seated, the last step is to install the cleaning bar on some models. Lift the fuser roller cover and drop in the cleaning bar. The bar sits in a well under the cover (see Figure 2.4). After doing so, you will notice that the top of the fuser assembly does not close tightly. The printer is designed so that the cover of the fuser assembly presses the cleaning bar against the fuser roller with spring pressure. The spring action prevents the fuser assembly cover from closing tightly. Many users call Hewlett-Packard's technical service department when they reach that phase of the setup because they suspect that something is wrong with their printer.

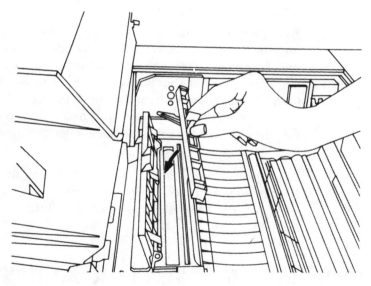

Figure 2.4. Cleaning bar assembly, with the cover open.

Providing Adequate Power

Inadequate power is a common problem you will encounter with a laser printer, especially when you use the laser printer in a home setting.

Laser printers draw a fair amount of current—7.6 amps, more than half of a standard 15-amp circuit. Do not plug into a socket or surge protector with a computer, other peripherals, copiers, or high-current machines unless you are sure that you are within the 15-amp limit.

If the lights dim when your laser printer produces a page—the fuser element that bonds the toner to the page draws most of the juice— too much current is being drawn on the outlet to which the printer is connected. Plug the laser printer into another outlet, preferably one that is connected directly to the main circuit breaker or fuse box. Be aware that continual use with inadequate current can damage the printer's power supply.

You need to make sure that you use a surge protector to guard against spikes or higher-than-normal jolts of electricity. The electronic components of a printer are every bit as susceptible as a computer to damage from electrical spikes. Due to the complex electronics of a laser printer, damage can be very expensive.

You might be able to run your laser printer—or computer—without a surge protector for years and never experience a problem. However, the next time you flip on your gear, an irregularity in the power line might cause a spike that burns out the power supply or I/O chips and leaves you with dead equipment and a big repair bill. You need to run all of your computing equipment through surge protectors designed to prevent spikes and overloads—use a separate surge protector for your laser printer.

When your power is *dirty* because of electromagnetic interference (EMI) from radio transmitters or other electronic gear, purchase a surge protector with EMI reduction/filter capabilities. The extra cost is minimal.

Installing One or Two Font Cartridges

A major problem that new laser printer users report is that they cannot access their plug-in font cartridges. Although there are many software explanations, the obvious problem may be that the cartridge is not plugged in all the way. When you look at the open end of a font cartridge, you will notice a row of metal contacts. These must be *grabbed* by a very tight plug at the end of the slot. When you insert the font cartridge into a slot, it will slide in easily and seem to hit a wall. When this happens, firmly push it until you feel metal contacts seat in the plug. You should be able to hear a distinct click. The cartridge is correctly installed.

WARNING

When you use the PostScript cartridge or other add-on cartridges, make sure you turn off the power before inserting it into a cartridge slot. After you install the cartridge and turn on the power, your printer will print out the test page shown in Figure 2.5. Some special purpose cartridges—such as the Printer Fac cartridge from Moonlight Computer Products—must be placed in a specific slot and do not work on all laser printer models.

Selecting Parallel or Serial Connections

Most laser printers have a parallel port and a serial port. With a serial connection, data is transmitted sequentially as a series of eight bits for each character, one bit after the other. In a parallel mode, the eight data bits are transmitted simultaneously. Parallel data transmission is approximately three times faster for transmitting soft fonts and graphics.

Although using the parallel port is faster, using the serial port can also be beneficial. For example, your printer might be tied into a printer sharing device that requires a serial connection or your computer may only have one parallel port that is already in use with another device. Another point for you to consider is how far away from your computer your printer will be. Technically, parallel cables should not be more than 10 feet long, although you might be able to use one up to 20 feet. You will notice the greatest problems with graphics programs because they may print with difficulty when your cable is beyond the maximum length. Serial cables can be as long as 50 feet for RS-232 cables, and up to 500 feet for RS-422 cables.

Figure 2.5. Test sheet generated by PostScript cartridge.

When you have the choice of using a parallel or serial connection, use the parallel option. All you have to do is strap on a standard parallel cable and the printer defaults to parallel mode.

When you opt for a serial connection, you may have to change the menu setting on the printer and add a line to your AUTOEXEC.BAT file or use a batch file at the DOS prompt to tell your computer where to direct print signals. The LaserJet 4 and its compatibles have automatic I/O switching that enables the parallel and serial port to be active by switching between them. When your printer has this feature, you still need to set the serial communication parameters on your computer.

Whether you are using a parallel or serial cable, keep the length as short as possible; the longer the cable, the more susceptible the data is to interference from power cords, especially when the cable is not properly shielded. The best way for you to check for shielding is to examine the ends of the cable and see whether any of the braided or smooth metal surrounding the individual wires is exposed.

The quality of the cable is important, therfore you should not economize in this area. Purchase a cable from a reputable manufacturer rather than from a discount distributor to ensure unimpeded data transfer.

One of the leading causes of printer failure is loose or disconnected cables. You need to bolt down or clip the cable firmly onto the plugs on the computer and the printer.

Another cabling consideration is the use of a switch box. Switch boxes can allow several computers to share the same laser printer. Unfortunately, rotary mechanical types function by rubbing metal contacts across each other and that process can create small spikes of electricity that can damage the I/O chip in your printer.

Many of the newer mechanical switches are buffered—their mechanical contacts are isolated electronically from the data line, eliminating the possibility of a spike. Therefore, when you decide to use a mechanical switch, make sure it is buffered. When in doubt, check with the manufacturer or don't take a chance with it. Electronic or smart-switches are safe and they are available in a variety of configurations from many vendors.

Setting Your Computer for Serial Mode

After you have decided the mode in which you will operate your printer, you must communicate that information to the printer and the computer each time you start up your system. You can do this through batch files that are designed to execute a sequence of commands when you type their name and press Enter.

Batch files can be used in two ways to set up your laser printer. The first involves creating an AUTOEXEC.BAT batch file if you don't have one, or by modifying an existing version. An AUTOEXEC.BAT file is a special kind of batch file that is run each time you turn on your computer; you don't have to type AUTOEXEC.BAT, the computer finds and runs it. You can take advantage of this automatic feature and insert a MODE command into your AUTOEXEC.BAT file, that instructs DOS to direct print output to the proper port in the right format. After it is in the AUTOEXEC.BAT file, the MODE command will be read every time you start up your computer and output will be sent to the printer via the parallel or serial port—whichever you selected.

The alternative is for you to create a specific batch file that tells the computer you are using a serial printer—the computer defaults to the parallel port. This is useful when you have a dot matrix or other type of printer already connected to your parallel port and want to alternate between the two without using a switch box (see below). Instructions for creating and modifying the AUTOEXEC.BAT batch file and for creating specific batch files for your laser and dot matrix printer, are described below.

When you are using WordPerfect, Word, Lotus 1-2-3, or other software that has drivers (software settings) for serial laser printers, the following batch files may be superfluous. You can still create them, because without the MODE commands, you will not be able to print from DOS (see your DOS manual for screen prints and echo printing of directories) or other print tasks from programs without port-specific drivers.

Creating an AUTOEXEC.BAT File for a Serial Laser Printer Installation

Floppy disk users: Make sure you have an A prompt. This procedure must be carried out with each bootable floppy disk.

Hard disk users: Make sure you have a C prompt and are in the root directory.

1. Type the following, and press Enter.

   ```
   copy con:autoexec.bat
   ```

2. Type the following, and press Enter.

   ```
   mode com1:9600,n,8,1,p
   ```

3. Type the following, and press the F6 key.

   ```
   mode lpt1:=com1:
   ```

The characters ^Z will appear on the screen, signaling the end of the batch file.

4. Press Enter and the system will display the following:

   ```
   1 file copied
   ```

Reboot your computer. Each time you turn on your computer, all printer output will be shifted to the laser printer connected to serial port COM1:.

NOTE

When COM1: is not available because it is connected to an external modem, a mouse, or some other device, you can connect the laser printer to COM2: and change the mode command in step 2 to read as follows:

```
mode com2:9600,n,8,1,p

mode lpt1:=com2:
```

29

Using a Dot-Matrix Printer with Your Laser Printer

When you have a dot-matrix printer connected to your parallel port (LPT1:) and you use it occasionally instead of your laser printer, your computer defaults to LPT1:. Unless your computer is instructed otherwise, all print output will be sent to parallel port one. By using the AUTOEXEC.BAT file created above, the computer will redirect all output intended for LPT1: to COM1: and will not send any output to LPT1: unless you change the instructions. The following batch file will do just that from the root directory,

1. Type the following and press Enter.

    ```
    copy con:matrix.bat
    ```

2. Type the following and press the F6 key.

    ```
    mode LPT1:
    ```

The characters ^Z will appear on the screen, signaling the end of the batch file.

3. Press Enter and the system will display the following:

    ```
    1 file copied
    ```

When you want to use your dot-matrix printer connected to LPT1:, type the following from the A prompt on your floppy disk or the C prompt on your hard disk—no need to type "bat." Output will once again be directed to LPT1:

```
matrix
```

To return the output to your laser printer, you will need to redirect the output to COM1:. Use the following to create the necessary batch file.

1. From the root directory, type the following and press Enter.

    ```
    copy con:laser.bat
    ```

2. Type the following, and press Enter.

    ```
    mode com1:9600,n,8,1,p
    ```

3. Type the following, and press the F6 key.

    ```
    mode lpt1:=com1:
    ```

The characters ^Z will appear on the screen, signaling the end of the batch file.

4. Press Enter and the system will display the following:

```
1 file copied
```

Type the following from the A prompt with your floppy system, or the C prompt with your hard disk system to restore control to the LaserJet.

```
laser
```

By toggling back and forth, you can easily use your dot-matrix and laser printer.

Creating an AUTOEXEC.BAT File for a Parallel Laser Printer

Although you do not need to issue a mode command when you are using a laser printer connected to a parallel port, it can eliminate certain problems that may occur with some software programs. To create an AUTOEXEC.BAT file for a parallel laser printer, use the following instructions.

Floppy disk users: Make sure you have an A prompt. This procedure must be carried out with each bootable floppy disk.

Hard disk users: Make sure you have a C prompt and are in the root directory.

1. Type the following, and press enter.

```
copy con:autoexec.bat
```

2. Type the following, and press the F6 key.

```
mode LPT1: ,,P
```

The characters ^Z will appear on the screen, signaling the end of the batch file.

3. Press Enter. The system will prompt you with the following:

```
1 file copied
```

You issue the mode command with a parallel laser printer because it will eliminate possible printer time-out problems, in which the printer fails to respond within the time limits enabled by DOS. By using the mode command, you increase the time that DOS will wait before it issues the time-out error.

Modifying an Existing AUTOEXEC.BAT File

When your computer has an AUTOEXEC.BAT file, you can modify it to include a mode command by using the text editor supplied with DOS versions 5.0 and higher—called EDIT—or your word processor. See Options 1 and 2 above for the exact syntax of the mode command for parallel and serial printers. When you are using your own word processor, you need to save the file as an ASCII or text file not as a formatted word processing file.

Using EDIT To Modify AUTOEXEC.BAT

Floppy disk users: Make sure EDIT.COM is on the disk containing your AUTOEXEC.BAT file. When you have multiple disks that you need to start the computer, use the following procedure to modify the AUTOEXEC.BAT file on one disk and copy it to each of your other program disks.

Hard disk users: Make sure that the file EDIT.COM is in your root directory. Alternately, the computer can be pathed to the directory containing EDIT.ROM—see your DOS manual for information about the path command:

1. Type the following:

   ```
   edit autoexec.bat
   ```

2. The screen will display your current AUTOEXEC.BAT file as follows:

   ```
   path=c:\dos;c:\wp51;c:\dbase4;c:\batch;c:\

   prompt $p$g

   menu
   ```

NOTE

Your AUTOEXEC.BAT file will probably be different. The file listing is provided only for illustrative purposes.

3. Insert the mode command at the point that you want—avoid the first and last line. In the preceding example, move the cursor to line two. Press Enter to insert a new line. When you want to insert a mode command for a serial laser printer, type the following and press Enter.

```
mode com1:9600,n,8,1,p
```

4. You can examine the contents of your batch file. The screen should appear as follows:

```
path=c:\dos;c:\wp;c:\dbase;c: \batch;c:\

mode com1:9600,n,8,1,p

mode lpt1:=com1:

prompt $p$g

menu
```

5. To save your modified AUTOEXEC.BAT file, press Alt-F and select Save followed by Alt-F, Exit.

   Your new AUTOEXEC.BAT file will be saved, and the DOS prompt will return to the screen.

Using a Word Processor to Modify AUTOEXEC.BAT

When you use a word processor instead of EDIT, you need to retrieve the AUTOEXEC.BAT file as an ASCII or DOS text file— the AUTOEXEC.BAT file is written without any control codes. Consult your word processor manual if you are not sure about how to do this. You insert the appropriate mode command as discussed in Options 1 and 2, and save the file in ASCII or DOS format; if you save it in your word processor's format, DOS will not be able to read it.

When your AUTOEXEC.BAT file has lines beyond 80 characters, they will scroll off the screen and wrap to the next line—possibly making it confusing as to where new lines start. Before modifying the file, you might want to set your right margin for the maximum number of characters or the widest landscape orientation to keep any lines from wrapping.

WARNING

Any changes made to your AUTOEXEC.BAT file will not take effect until you restart your computer, soft boot—by simultaneously pressing Alt - Ctrl - Delete—or by manually executing the AUTOEXEC.BAT file by typing the following and pressing Enter.

```
autoexec
```

Setting Your Printer for Serial Mode

Most laser printers default to parallel mode, so once you have set the MODE command you don't have to touch the menu panel when you are using a parallel connection. For a serial connection, however, you may have to manually select the serial port. Some laser printers are autosensing—such as the LaserJet 4—and can switch automatically between parallel and serial ports. The following steps can be used to select the serial mode on a LaserJet III printer.

1. Turn on the printer with the rocker switch on the back.

2. Press the On-Line button. The light above the button will turn off.

3. Press the MENU button and hold it down until AUTO CONT=OFF* appears. This might take five seconds. When you release the button too soon, the display will say COPIES=1. Press the On-Line key to exit the setup menu, then repeat the procedure starting with step 2. Pressing and releasing the MENU button causes one set of options, and pressing and holding the MENU button causes a second set to appear.

4. Press the MENU button again. The words I/O=PARALLEL will appear in the display.

5. Now press the plus (+) or minus (–) key so that I/O=SERIAL is displayed in the LCD screen.

6. Press the ENTER/RESET MENU button. An asterisk will appear after the words I/O=SERIAL, indicating that the selection will be saved in the printer's memory.

7. To save the changes and exit the menu mode, press the On-Line button. Then press and hold the CONTINUE/RESET button until the 07 RESET message appears. The new changes will be in effect once the printer is on-line.

NOTE

You can fine-tune the serial specifications—set a faster baud or transmission rate. The serial defaults, however, will work for most software programs. The other options are described in the chapter that describes the menu panel.

Testing the Communication Link

To ensure that you are connected to your computer, press Shift-Print Screen. The form feed light on your laser printer should be lit, and the green Ready light should blink. Take the printer off line and press FORM FEED. The page should eject with whatever was on your screen when you initiated the print screen.

Running a Self-Test

Once your printer is connected to your computer, you should run a self-test by carrying out the following procedure. The LaserJet III menu is used in this example.

1. Press the On-Line button and the light above the button will go off.

2. Press and release the PRINT FONTS/TEST key for several seconds, until the words 05 SELF TEST appear in the LCD display. The pattern shown in Figure 2.6 will be printed after about a 30-second delay.

NOTE

If you hold the key down until the words 04 SELF TEST *appear, your laser printer will continuously churn out the test pattern until you press the On-Line button again.*

3. Examine the test pattern sheet. If nothing prints, you have probably forgotten to remove the plastic strip in the toner cartridge. Pull out the strip and repeat the test. If your printer still won't generate the test pattern, contact your dealer or call the manufacturer's technical support line.

Repacking and Transporting Your Laser Printer

When you are moving the printer from one table or desk to another, there is no reason to repack it, although you should remove the toner cartridge before moving the machine. However, when you are going to transport it by car or truck to another office, you have to repack it. This is why you should save the original carton and packing materials from your laser printer. The packing material and spacers are designed to protect sensitive parts from getting damaged.

It is especially important for you to repack the piece of packing foam that fits in the engine cavity. The mirror assembly of most laser printers moves a small distance when the cover is closed to achieve the proper angle of deflection for the laser beam (see Chapter 1). Without that packing foam, the metal clip holding the mirror may move and cause it to go out of alignment or break off completely. The packing foam will prevent this from happening. If you have lost the styrofoam piece, make one yourself or use a piece of strapping tape to hold the mirror assembly in place. Another reason for you to save the boxes and packing material has to do with resale—the original boxes and packing material can make a deal more attractive.

Always remove the toner cartridge before you pack your laser printer or the toner will spill. Because toner particles can slip through the filter of home vacuum cleaners you need to call a professional to service your printer.

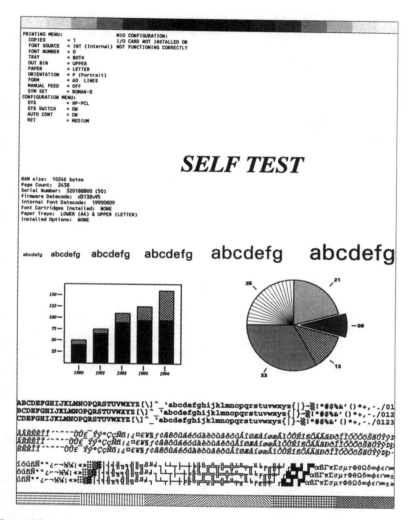

Figure 2.6. Built-in test from a LaserJet III.

When you follow these procedures, you minimize the chances of damaging your laser printer during transit and ensure the quality of your copies.

Using the LaserJet 4 Menu Panel

The LaserJet 4 enables you to control many aspects of the printer by pressing the buttons on the front panel (see Figure 3.1). This enables you to control certain printer parameters when your software does not have built-in LaserJet support—such as selecting an internal font, the number of copies, and other important printer functions.

As useful as the menu system is, if you are only using software programs such as WordPerfect or Microsoft Word, which offer complete LaserJet 4 control, you may never have to touch the menu system. In fact, unless your software cannot control the LaserJet 4 printer, you can set the menu and forget it; most application software does have the ability to drive LaserJet printers, and will override any instructions that you have entered in the menu panel system. For example, if you set the LaserJet to print three copies of each page, and your word processor issues a print command for one page, your LaserJet will only print one copy.

Nevertheless, when you want to run the printer from DOS, or use an application package that does not support the LaserJet or compatible, the menu panel can save you a great deal of time and effort. The menu provides access to many of the key functions you need when running non-LaserJet supported software—font choices from the built-in fonts or, in the case of the LaserJet 4, the new scalable fonts; interline spacing—lines per inch; number of copies to be printed; and symbol set—special characters and symbols, such as foreign characters with accents and special legal symbols required for some word processing applications.

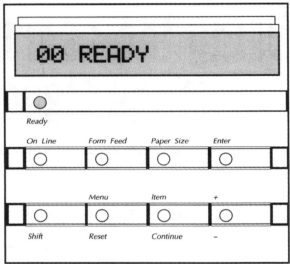

Figure 3.1. LaserJet 4 Menu panel.

The alternative to using the menu is for you to learn the PCL printer control language and write your own command strings. See Chapters 14 and 15 for a complete course in writing and using PCL commands. When you understand the PCL printer language, you can control features not accessible through the menu panel system—such as margins and page size—and can introduce hundreds of individual fonts to your printing efforts.

An alternative is for you to start with the menu and get comfortable with the capabilities of the printer, and then introduce some of your own PCL printer commands. In this chapter you will learn everything you need to know about the LaserJet 4 menu panel system. If you have an earlier model LaserJet or compatible, the operation of the menu panel is similar, although the specific options and command sequences will vary. First, a discussion about the other functions supported by the buttons on the panel.

Tour of the Menu Panel

The menu panel consists of eight buttons, which allow you to control your printer and to select settings from a built-in menu. The menu options appear on an illuminated display. The display also shows you the status of the printer and error conditions. (The bulk of the chapter is devoted to the menu system; the last section describes the status indicators.) Below the display is the green Ready light (see Figure 3.1), that glows after the printer has warmed up or recovered from an error situation. The bottom of the panel contains the following eight buttons:

On-Line	Form Feed	Paper Size	Enter
Shift	Menu/Reset	Item/Continue	+/-

Some buttons perform dual functions separated by a slash in the button name, as in Item/Continue, which accesses the Item switching command if pressed alone or the Continue command if pressed in combination with the Shift key. Each button and its functions is described in the following sections.

Several buttons (On-Line, Form Feed, Continue, and Reset) have an immediate impact on the current print job. The other buttons are tied to a sophisticated menu system that is accessed by pressing the Menu button—each press of the button will switch to another major menu. The Item button enables you to cycle through the various items on a particular menu, while the Plus (+) and Minus (-) buttons are used to shift the setting of a particular item.

On-Line Mode

When your LaserJet 4 is on-line, it is ready to receive data from the computer. You don't have to set the printer on-line yourself—it defaults to the on-line mode when you turn on the power, following a brief diagnostic routine that checks the integrity of the memory chips and various electronic assemblies. When you first turn on the printer, the display will read the following as the circuits are being checked.

```
05 SELF TEST
```

When the self test is successful, the orange light below the On-Line button will glow, indicating that the printer is ready to accept data, and the display will read as follows:

```
00 READY
```

To take the printer off-line, press the On-Line button and the orange light will go out. You would need to take the printer off-line in the following circumstances:

1. You want to issue a Form Feed to manually eject a page (see Form Feed, below).

2. You want to perform a printer test or print the Typeface List.

3. You wish to change fonts or other cartridges.

4. You wish to insert a different size paper tray or insert the envelope tray.

5. You want to access the menu system.

6. You need to reset the printer.

To return the printer on-line, press the On-Line button. You can also return the printer to on-line by pressing the Continue button when you have received a warning message or when you want to override a paper selection or feed request. Pressing Reset will also return the printer on-line, although it will abandon all data that resides in the printer buffer. It is roughly equivalent to turning the printer off and on again.

Form Feed

The Form Feed button sends a manual page eject command to the printer. It is used when the printer's buffer contains less than a full page of data. Like all LaserJets, the LaserJet 4 prints only when it has a full page stored in memory or is issued a form feed. A DOS screen print—Shift-Print Screen keys—is only 25 lines long and will not send enough lines to cause a page eject.

The partial page will sit in the printer's memory (as indicated by the glowing light over the Form Feed button) until you press the Form Feed button or issue an eject from your software. Alternatively, you can wait until you send enough additional data to the printer to fill the rest of the page.

To issue a form feed, take the printer off-line and press the Form Feed button once. Whatever data is in the printer's memory will be printed, and the page will eject. Make sure you return the printer on-line by pressing the On-Line button.

Paper Size

The HP LaserJet 4 contains two internal paper sources: the Paper Cassette Tray, which is located at the bottom of the standard configuration and can hold 250 sheets of 20 pound paper; and the Multi-Purpose (MP) Paper Tray, which folds out from the front of the printer. The paper cassette operates in the same fashion as the 8½-by-11-inch tray of the Series II, III and compatibles, except it requires that you place letterhead or other preprinted paper face down and the top pointing towards you—the opposite of the previous models. The standard Cassette Tray handles only 8½-by-11-inch letter-sized paper. You must purchase optional trays for legal and other sized paper. If you occassionally want to use non-letter sized paper or want to load more than 250 sheets, you can use the MP tray in cassette mode. In this mode the MP tray acts as though it were another paper tray with a continuous supply of paper—up to 100 sheets. The only problem with this concept is that the MP tray is not capable of detecting what sized paper you feeding to it. To ensure proper feeding and processing, the LaserJet 4 requires that you indicate the size of the paper you are feeding the MP tray by selecting the size from the menu displayed when you press the Paper Size button. To select a particular size, press the Paper Size button and press the Plus (+) or Minus (-) button until the paper size you want is displayed. Press Enter to save the new setting, and On-Line or Reset to return to printing. If you press Reset, any data in the print buffer will be lost, but the saved change will immediately become effective. If you select Enter, the printer will return on-line and continue to print, but the saved change will not become effective until the next print job.

The Enter Button

The Enter button is used to save a changed menu setting to the printer's *permanent* memory. When you turn on or Reset the printer, the saved setting will be used as the default. You first must select your menu option—paper size, serial port settings, default font, and so on—and then rotate through the various settings for that option by pressing the Plus or Minus keys. When the setting that you want is displayed, press Enter to store it to the printer's memory. If there is no data in the printer's buffer, the printer will reset when you leave the menus. When there is data stored in the print buffer, the printer will display the message:

```
10 Reset to Save
```

You can choose Reset and that will abandon the data in the print buffer and immediately reset the environment to the new setting. Choosing On-Line will return you to the current print job without adopting the new setting and assumes the new setting for the next print job; or choose Continue and that enables you to return to the menus.

The Shift Button

The Shift button works like the shift button on your keyboard — it assigns a second function or value to one of the primary keys. To access the second function, press and hold the Shift key while pressing the desired key. On the LaserJet 4, three keys have dual functions that are accessed by the Shift key, as follows:

Unshifted	Shifted
Menu	Reset
Item	Continue
Plus (+)	Minus (-)

The Menu Key

The Menu key shifts between the seven primary menus and the Ready mode. Pressing the Menu key rotates through the titles of the following seven menus:

Printing Menu

PCL Menu

Job Menu

Config Menu

Parallel Menu

Serial Menu

Test Menu

If you have installed PostScript on another I/O device, its menu will be added to the sequence. Each of the seven primary menus will be discussed later in this chapter.

The Reset (Shift-Menu) Button

The Reset button is roughly the equivalent of turning the printer off and on again. When you press Reset, the page buffer is purged, all temporary typefaces and macros are deleted, and the printer is reset to the user defined defaults. In addition, the input buffer of the current I/O is purged. It is possible to change the degree of reset performed by accessing the Menu of Resets by pressing and holding Reset (Shift-Menu) for 10 seconds. The three degrees of reset are as follows:

Menu	(described in the preceding section)
Active I/O	Clears the page buffer, temporary typefaces and macros and the I/O buffers for the current I/O port only.
All I/O	Clears the page buffer, temporary typefaces and macros and the I/O buffers for all I/O ports.

The Item Button

The Item button enables you to rotate among the various items on each of the seven primary menus. For example, the Printing Menu contains the following items which can be accessed in turn by pressing the Item button after selecting the Printer Menu with the Menu button.

Copies

Paper

Orientation

Form

Manual Feed

Resolution Enhancement (RET)

The Continue Button

The Continue button returns the printer on-line after it has issued a warning or prompt that you want to ignore. You will occasionally need to instruct the LaserJet 4 to continue printing after it was interrupted. This will be necessary under the following circumstances:

➤ When you have stopped printing by taking it off-line—for example, you might want to suspend printing to make sure that you are printing the correct version of a document.

➤ When the printer encounters a paper jam or an error condition—for example, a memory overflow caused by a graphic image with too many points for the LaserJet's microprocessor to interpret.

➤ When the printer calls for an alternate paper size—an envelope or legal size—but you do not have the required paper or the right size tray and you want to print on the current paper stock. By pressing Continue, the page will print out on whatever paper is installed, although you may lose a portion of data if the requested paper was larger than the installed paper.

TIP

This situation would most likely occur when you are trying to set up margins for an envelope or odd sized piece of paper. Rather than running envelope after envelope through the printer, you can see exactly where the address is falling on the logical page by printing it on an 8½-by-11-inch sheet of paper and making appropriate adjustments.

The Plus/Minus (+/-) Keys

The Plus and Minus keys are used to change the settings for each of the items on each of the primary menus. When there are a limited number of options for a setting, the buttons will rotate among them in a forward direction (Plus) or backward direction (Minus). When the setting is a value such as the number of copies, the Plus button increases the value, while the minus key decreases it. If you want to make large changes in a setting's value, you can press and hold the Plus or Minus button, thereby increasing or decreasing the value in increments of 10.

Using the LaserJet 4 Menu System

You can specify a number of different values for your LaserJet 4, such as the number of copies to be printed, the internal font to be used as a default font, the orientation, etc. These values or settings are stored in the printer's memory and will remain in force until they are altered. In other words, after you set three copies, the printer will continue to print three copies of each sheet until you instruct it to change to a different number of copies. This is also true for font, page length, and so on. The entire group of parameters in temporary or volatile memory is called the Current Printer Environment.

The parameters of the Current Printer Environment are constantly changing as your software sends commands for margins, type fonts, page lengths, and so on. Because the Current Printer Environment parameters are stored in volatile memory, they are lost each time the printer is turned off or reset.

A second set of parameters is called the User Default Environment. The User Default Environment can be altered easily through the menu panel system. Each time the printer is turned on or reset, the User Default Environment parameters are copied to the Current Printer Environment. This establishes the Current Printer Environment's initial parameters for the printing session.

Values in the User Default Environment are stored in a nonvolatile random access memory. This means that they are stored even if the printer is turned off. When you change parameters through the control panel menu system, they remain until you explicitly change them via the menu system.

A third set of parameters is contained in the Factory Default Environment. Factory Defaults are located in read-only memory (ROM), which means that they can be used, but not altered. When you first install your LaserJet 4 printer, the parameters in the User Default Environment and the Factory Default Environment are identical. They can only be changed as you changed the User Default Environment parameters, by means of the menu system.

In summary, the LaserJet 4 has three sets of parameters: the temporary Current Printer Environment; the permanent but alterable User Defaults Environment, and the permanent Factory Default Environment.

The three environments form a natural hierarchy regarding changes (see Figure 3.2). At the top, the Current Printer Environment constantly changes as the page changes. Next, there is the User Default Environment, that only changes via the control panel menu system. At the bottom, the Factory Default Environment never changes. You can reset the Current Printer Environment to the User Default Environment by pressing Reset or by turning the printer off and on. You can reset the User Default Environment to the Factory Default Environment by turning the printer off, pressing and holding the On-Line button while turning the printer back on. This step is called a cold reset.

In many ways, the LaserJet 4's menu system is easier to use than previous models' menus. It consists of seven or more primary menus (if you add optional personalities or I/O ports, their menus are added to the basic seven). Each of these primary menus contains several items, each of which can be assigned two or more settings. Some items are set to On or Off, others can be assigned a range of specific settings, such as paper sizes, and still others are assigned a numeric value such as the number of copies. As described above, you access the primary menus by pressing the Menu button, the items on a menu by pressing the Item button and the settings for an item by pressing the Plus or Minus buttons. Following is a brief discussion of the menus, items and settings.

Current Default Environment
- Always changing
- Uses volatile RAM memory
- Changes input via PCL commands

Reset Button
Copies User Default
to Current Default

User Default Environment
- Stable but changeable
- Uses nonvolatile RAM memory
- Changes input via Menu System

Cold Reset
Copies Factory Defaults
to User Defaults

Factory Default Environment
- Unchangeable
- Use permanent ROM memory

Figure 3.2. The hierarchy of printer environments.

Printing Menu

Copies

Copies can be set to any value from 1 to 999, with 1 being the default. To change by increments of 1, press the Plus or Minus buttons. To change by increments of 10, press and hold the Plus or Minus buttons.

Paper/Envelope

You can select paper sizes of Letter (the default), Legal, A4, and Executive; or envelope sizes of COM10, Monarch, C5, DL, B5.

Orientation

Portrait or Landscape. The Portrait mode is used for normal settings and the Landscape mode is used for sideways printing.

Form

Form sets the vertical spacing based on the default paper size and the number of lines per page. The default is 60 lines per page, which on 8½-by-11-inch paper with 1/2-inch top and bottom margins, yields 6 lines per inch.

Manual Feed

When turned On, Manual Feed causes the printer to prompt you to feed paper via the MP tray, regardless of the software specifications. When you are ready to print, press On-Line. To override the manual feed request, press Continue.

RET

RET sets the degree of Resolution Enhancement, or turns it off entirely. To set the RET value, print the self-test sheet (see the following) and look at the RET block sample. For optimum results, the RET sample should be uniform. If the sample has dark vertical lines between the shaded blocks, the RET is set too high and should be reduced. If there are clear spaces between the shaded blocks, RET is set too low and should be raised. The RET is affected by the Print Density setting described under the Config Menu below. It is best to set the desired overall density first and then the RET.

PCL Menu

Font Source

Font Source determines where the PCL command processor looks for the default font. It can be set to any of the following selections:

I   Internal

C   Cartridge

S   Soft Font

Mn SIMM memory module where n = the slot number of the module

Font Number

Font Number selects a font from the designated source. The font numbers of all fonts available on your printer can be determined by printing the PCL Typeface List from the Test menu described below.

Pitch or Point Size

Pitch and Point Size select either the pitch (for fixed pitch fonts) or point size of the default front. Point sizes range from .44 to 99.99.

Symbol Set

Symbol set selects the character set to be used with the default font. Because the printer is shipped with the Roman-8 symbol set as the default, many users find it advantageous to change this setting to PC-8, which exchanges many of the seldom used foreign characters for the PC line draw characters used to display lines and boxes on character based displays and reports.

Job Menu

PageProtect

PageProtect is used to assign more memory to the page imaging process. If you receive the dreaded 021-Print Overrun error message often, you should experiment with setting page protection on. Although this will reduce performance in other areas, it will prevent the 021 error. The printer will warn you when you do not have enough memory installed to implement page protection.

Resolution

Resolution enables you to select between the 600 dpi default resolution and 300 dpi. You generally will want to leave the printer set for 600 dpi as that will produce the best results. You may want to select 300 dpi if you are printing graphics specifically designed to print at 300 dpi, and if the software does not have a LaserJet 4 driver.

Personality

Personality enables you to select the printer control language (PCL, PostScript, Auto or Other). When set to Auto, the LaserJet 4 can detect and switch between PostScript and PCL. This is the best option unless you know that you will only be using one or the other. If you add a different printer language, you may need to set the language via this option. If you do set a specific personality as the default, the printer can still be switched to an alternate personality via software using the appropriate PJL command (see Chapter 12).

Timeout

The LaserJet 4 is able to work with multiple I/O ports simultaneously. This means that you could attach one computer or network to the parallel port, and another to the serial or optional I/O port. The LaserJet 4 will listen to each of them and will switch between them after print jobs. In order to accomplish this, the printer needs to be able to conclude a print job that does not provide an explicit end-of-job signal (see Chapter 12 on PJL). Like most network queues, the LaserJet 4 uses a timing logic to make this determination. If it does not hear anything from the active port for a specified time period—the default is 15 seconds—the printer concludes that the job is finished and it terminates the current print job so that it can go on to the next. The wait time is specified, in seconds, by the Timeout. If your slow printing jobs are getting interrupted prematurely, you may wish to raise the Timeout setting. When you are printing from a network, you should try adjusting the network's print job Timeout setting first, because this is probably the cause of your problem.

Configuration Menu

MP Tray

The MP tray can be configured to operate in three different modes. In Cassette mode it emulates a paper cassette and feeds paper continuously. In Manual mode it operates as a source for manually inserted paper only. The user must press On-Line each time the printer prompts for more paper. Finally, in First mode the MP tray emulates a cassette tray from which paper will be drawn—before the standard or optional cassette—only when the specified MP paper size (see Paper Size Button described above) matches that requested by the software. If the size does not match or the MP tray is empty, the printer will switch to the next available cassette with the correct paper size.

Lock

The lock option enables you to prevent one or more of the paper sources from being used accidently when the default tray runs out of paper. The number and combinations of lock options will depend on the setting of the MP tray and the installation of the optional 500 sheet lower cassette. After a paper source is locked out, it will not be selected when the primary paper source runs out. The locked-out paper source still can be selected explicitly by software. This option is particularly important when you want to place letterhead or other special paper in one tray, and plain paper in the other. By locking the tray containing the letterhead, it will not accidently be used to print a report when the plain paper tray runs dry.

Clr Warn

The LaserJet 4 uses a high level of logic for processing complex pages that may exceed its processing capacity. Rather than refusing to print part of the page as with most previous LaserJets and compatibles, the LaserJet 4 will try to work around the problem first by reducing resolution, then by reducing page protection, and finally by compressing the data. When performing such an alteration to your print request, the printer will display a warning message in place of the Ready display. The setting of the Clr Warn item determines if the message is displayed until it is manually cleared by pressing the Continue button (On, the default), or until the next print job (Job).

AutoCont

The Auto Continue setting determines whether the printer halts until you press the Continue button after experiencing a nonfatal error, or resumes processing after displaying an error message for 10 seconds. By default, Auto Continue is set Off, requiring manual intervention. If you are using the printer on a network, you may want to set it On.

Density

Density sets the relative darkness of the image from 1 to 5, with 3 being the default. If a particular image appears too light, you need to increase the density. If you want to reduce toner consumption for draft printing, you can set it to a lower density. Remember to reset it after you are finished. Also, note that the Density setting will impact the RET setting on the Printer Menu.

Toner Low

Running out of toner in the middle of a report or print job, may or may not be critical depending on what you are printing. The LaserJet 4 will warn you of low toner by displaying a warning. The Toner Low setting determines whether the printer will stop until you explicitly restart it by pressing the Continue button. Setting Toner Low to On will cause the printer to warn but not stop. Setting Toner Low to Off will cause it to warn and stop.

Parallel Menu

High Speed

Determines whether the printer should accept data at high speed. The default setting of Yes is best for most computers. You should select No only if you suspect that you are getting transmission errors due to the slow speed of an older computer.

Advanced Functions

The Advanced Functions option enables your computer and Laser-Jet 4 to communicate back and forth. This means that the printer can send important data messages back to the computer, as well as receive print commands from the computer. This should be left On unless you experience problems with your software.

Serial Menu

Serial

Serial determines which of the two standards for serial communications is being used: RS-232 or RS-422. The default is set to the more common RS-232. RS-422 is generally used when the serial cables must be fairly long and requires special cables and connectors.

Pacing

The LaserJet 4 supports two standards for controlling the pace of information flow between the computer and the printer. The default, DTR/DSR, requires that the computer support hardware flow control as most computers now do. The option, XON/XOFF, relies on software-based flow control and does not support the printer sending status messages back to the computer.

Baud Rate

Baud rate determines the speed of serial transmissions between the computer and the printer. The default of 9,600 baud is appropriate for most situations. If your computer's serial port supports higher rates and the environment is electronically clean, you may get better performance by setting a high baud rate. The printer and the computer must be set to the same baud rate. If you are experiencing transmission errors and are working in an electronically dirty environment—lots of high powered electrical equipment nearby—you may want to try lowering your baud rate. Again, your computer and printer must be set to the same rate.

Robust On

The Robust On/Off is only appropriate if the printer is set to XON/XOFF pacing. It determines which signal is associated with XON state. By default it is set On.

DTR Polarity

DTR polarity sets the logic associated with the DTR signal. By default it is set to Hi.

Test Menu

Self-Test

By selecting the self-test option from this menu, you will initiate a single cycle of the printer self-test culminating in the printing of the self-test page. (See Figure 3.3.) This page contains a wealth of information about your printer, including all the settings of the menu items, the page count, the hardware and software options installed and the RET test block. If you are experiencing problems with your laser printer, you should first print a copy of the self-test sheet to see if any other user has accidently changed a critical setting. This review is much easier if you save a copy of the working settings for comparison.

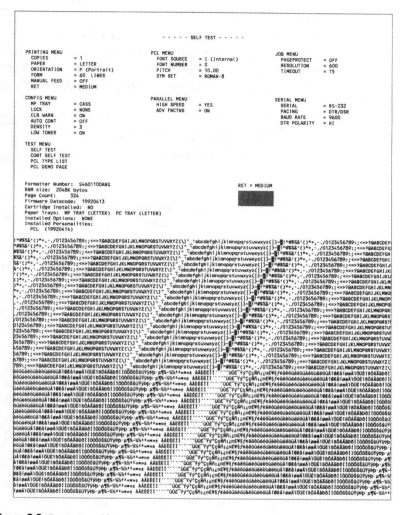

Figure 3.3. Printer self-test.

Continuous Self-Test

This option cycles through the self-test logic and report continuously until you press Continue or On-Line.

PCL Type List

The PCL type list prints a sample of all available PCL typefaces, their assigned number and the Escape sequence that can be used to call a particular face. (See Figure 3.4.) The typeface list is an excellent tool for selecting the best font for a particular piece of text.

HEWLETT PACKARD

HP LaserJet 4 Printer
PCL Typeface List

Internal Scalable Typefaces and Bitmapped Fonts

Typeface	Pitch/Point	Escape Sequence	Font #	Font ID
Courier	Scale	<esc>(□)<esc>(s0p██h0s0b4099T	I 000	
CG Times	Scale	<esc>(□)<esc>(s1p██v0s0b4101T	I 001	
CG Times Bold	Scale	<esc>(□)<esc>(s1p██v0s3b4101T	I 002	
CG Times Italic	Scale	<esc>(□)<esc>(s1p██v1s0b4101T	I 003	
CG Times Bold Italic	Scale	<esc>(□)<esc>(s1p██v1s3b4101T	I 004	
CG Omega	Scale	<esc>(□)<esc>(s1p██v0s0b4113T	I 005	
CG Omega Bold	Scale	<esc>(□)<esc>(s1p██v0s3b4113T	I 006	
CG Omega Italic	Scale	<esc>(□)<esc>(s1p██v1s0b4113T	I 007	
CG Omega Bold Italic	Scale	<esc>(□)<esc>(s1p██v1s3b4113T	I 008	
Coronet	Scale	<esc>(□)<esc>(s1p██v1s0b4116T	I 009	
Clarendon Condensed	Scale	<esc>(□)<esc>(s1p██v4s3b4140T	I 010	
Univers Medium	Scale	<esc>(□)<esc>(s1p██v0s0b4148T	I 011	
Univers Bold	Scale	<esc>(□)<esc>(s1p██v0s3b4148T	I 012	
Univers Medium Italic	Scale	<esc>(□)<esc>(s1p██v1s0b4148T	I 013	
Univers Bold Italic	Scale	<esc>(□)<esc>(s1p██v1s3b4148T	I 014	
Univers Medium Condensed	Scale	<esc>(□)<esc>(s1p██v4s0b4148T	I 015	
Univers Bold Condensed	Scale	<esc>(□)<esc>(s1p██v4s3b4148T	I 016	
Univers Medium Condensed Italic	Scale	<esc>(□)<esc>(s1p██v5s0b4148T	I 017	
Univers Bold Condensed Italic	Scale	<esc>(□)<esc>(s1p██v5s3b4148T	I 018	
Antique Olive	Scale	<esc>(□)<esc>(s1p██v0s0b4168T	I 019	
Antique Olive Bold	Scale	<esc>(□)<esc>(s1p██v0s3b4168T	I 020	
Antique Olive Italic	Scale	<esc>(□)<esc>(s1p██v1s0b4168T	I 021	
Garamond Antiqua	Scale	<esc>(□)<esc>(s1p██v0s0b4197T	I 022	
Garamond Halbfett	Scale	<esc>(□)<esc>(s1p██v0s3b4197T	I 023	

██Pitch: .10 - 576   □Symbol set   ██Point size: .25 - 999.75
See your HP LaserJet 4 Printer User's Manual for more information.

Figure 3.4. PCL typeface list.

PCL Demo Page

The demo page not only demonstrates the capabilities of the printer using the PCL language and available fonts, but it also clearly demonstrates that the language processor is operating correctly. (See Figure 3.5.)

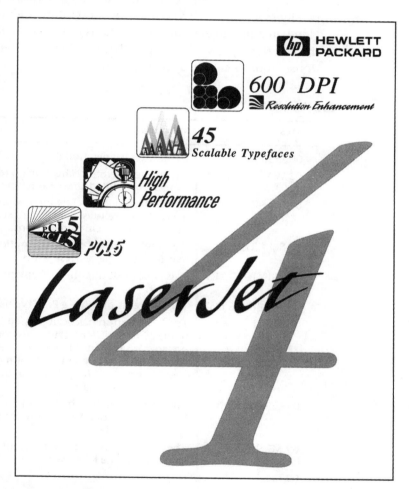

Figure 3.5. PCL demo page.

Summary of Display Status Indicators and Prompts

By now you have seen several of the messages that appear in the display panel. The following list recaps those items, and lists other possible messages that you may encounter during a printing session. Numbered messages under 10 are status indicators, telling you what the LaserJet 4 printer is doing. Other numbers represent error conditions. Prompts call for specific actions.

STATUS INDICATORS

Message	Meaning
00 READY	The printer is operational.
02 WARMING UP	The fusing assembly is heating up to the proper temperature (400 degrees Fahrenheit).
04 SELF-TEST	The Continuous Self-Test menu option has been selected. The self-tests print until stopped by pressing the Continue or On-Line buttons.
05 SELF-TEST	The single page self-test menu option has been selected. A single self-test prints.
06 PRINTING TEST	This appears during the printing process of the self-test.
06 TYPEFACE LIST	The printer is printing a PCL Typeface list.
07 RESET	The Reset button has been pressed. All menu items returned to the User Default Environment settings previously saved in the printer's memory. Reset also clears any *temporary* soft fonts or macros that have been downloaded from the computer, and clears any page data in the buffer.
08 COLD RESET	The user held down the On-Line button when turning the printer on. All menu settings will be returned to the factory defaults.
09 MENU RESET	The 09 messages are three different levels of reset available via the Reset Menu.
09 RESET ACTIVE I/O	
09 RESET ALL I/O	

Message	Meaning
10 RESET TO SAVE	You changed one or more settings via the configuration menus while there was data in the printer buffer. If you press the Continue or On-Line buttons, your changes will be recorded, but will not become effective until the next print job. If you press Reset, the change will become effective immediately, but you will lose all data in the buffer, including print data, temporary soft fonts and temporary macros.
12 PRINTER OPEN	The top cover of the printer is not closed.
13 PAPER JAM	The printer has sensed a paper jam.
14 NO EP CART	There is no toner cartridge loaded in the printer.
16 TONER LOW	The toner cartridge is almost out of toner. Rock the cartridge back and forth and replace it. If the message goes off, you are fine for a while. If the message persists, you are really close, so you better have a spare.

PROMPTS
PAPER-RELATED

Prompt	Required Action
ME FEED	The printer is waiting for you to insert an envelope into the MP tray. If you want to print on paper from the cassette tray instead, press the Continue button. The size of the envelope will be specified as in: ME FEED COM-10 for commercial #10 envelopes: (4⅛-by-9½ inches); ME FEED MONARC when the command is for a a Monarch size envelope (3⅞-by-7½ inches).
MF FEED	The printer is waiting for a single sheet of paper (odd size or regular) to be placed into the MP tray. You can print on paper from the installed paper cassette if you press the Continue button. The size of the paper requested will follow the command. If the printer receives a command for legal size paper (8-½-by 14 inches), the message will read: MF FEED LEGAL

continues

FONT-CARTRIDGE-RELATED

Prompt	Required Action
MC/PC/LC LOAD	The LaserJet is waiting for the correct size paper cassette to be inserted into the paper cassette slot. Or the correct paper size to be specified for the MP tray. Remember, each cassette has a series of projections that allow the printer to sense what size paper cassette is currently in use. The size of the paper requested will follow the message as in: PC LOAD LETTER or: MC LOAD LEGAL Insert the requested cassette and the printer will resume operation or press Continue to use the paper in the installed cassette.

FONT-CARTRIDGE-RELATED

Prompt	Required Action
FE CARTRIDGE	The font cartridge was removed when the printer was on-line. The only solution is to turn the power off, then back on again. This wipes out the printer's memory, so any page data in the buffer will have to be retransmitted, and any soft fonts or macros that were in memory must be downloaded again. The moral? Don't remove a font cartridge while the printer is on-line. If you're using the PostScript or other processor-based cartridge, make sure that the power is off before you insert or remove the cartridge; otherwise, you may damage the cartridge.
FI CARTRIDGE	An accessory cartridge was removed when the printer was displaying an error message. The printer cannot clear the error without the cartridge present, so reinsert the cartridge, clear the error and then remove the cartridge.
FR CARTRIDGE	An accessory cartridge was inserted when the printer was displaying an error message. The printer cannot clear the error while the cartridge is present, so remove the cartridge, clear the error and then reinsert the cartridge.

PART

Operating, Maintaining, and Selecting Your Laser Printer

Selecting Paper for Your Laser Printer

Laser printers accept a variety of paper types, but you will get better results with some paper types than others. Although some papers will cause minimal wear and tear on your printer, other papers can damage your machine with repeated use. Some preprinted forms will look like a million dollars when you have finished printing on them; some preprinted forms won't be worth a cent because their inks have run during the printing process. Although some mailing labels work well, others cause jams and emit toxic gases when they pass through the hot fuser rollers.

Although a complete discussion of paper chemistry and physics could fill a book or two, there are several key concepts you need to know to get the best results from your printing efforts and to avoid needless jams or repair bills. This chapter covers those concepts and provides specific guidelines to help you select the best paper for your printer.

A Crash Course in Paper Making

There are different types of textures, surfaces, colors, and weights of paper for you to choose from. There are papers for just about every purpose imaginable. Paper is primarily composed of fiber and water, although various fillers are added to alter brightness, opacity, stiffness, and other characteristics. The fiber in most paper is cellulose—derived from wood. Fine papers often use cellulose derived from cotton or rags sold by textile and garment makers. (Hence the term rag content as a measure of the quality of cotton bond.)

There are different ways to extract cellulose fibers used for paper. The process in which wood, rags, or other materials are converted into usable forms is called *pulping*. Mechanical wood pulp is made by crushing the wood into fibers. This process is the least expensive, but the paper is weak and has contaminants that cause yellowing with age—newsprint is about 80 percent mechanical pulp with 20 percent chemical pulp added for strength.

Chemical wood pulp is made by cooking the wood in solutions that dissolve the contaminants and leave the cellulose fiber. Papers made with chemical wood pulp are clean and strong, and are the best types of paper for you to use in LaserJet printers. Other methods of pulping use combinations or variations of the above processes.

There are more steps that a paper manufacturer takes to refine the pulp—bleaching, washing, and beating. The more steps a manufacturer takes to refine the pulp, the more expensive it becomes. A variety of chemicals, fillers, and other additives are mixed with the pulp—and water—to make the slurry that flows onto the paper machine. This slurry is about 99.5 percent water and flows out of a slit onto a moving mesh screen called a wire. The water drains out through the wire, sometimes with the aid of suction. After traveling along the wire for about 20 yards, enough water has been removed so that the sheet can be lifted off the wire and enter the press section for drying. Before leaving the wire, a dandy roller may be used to imprint a design or watermark into the fibers. The watermark, that can be seen if you hold a sheet of paper up to the light, is like a coat of arms of the manufacturer.

Effects of Different Papers on Laser Printer Performance

There is tremendous variability within the process of making paper. The paper from two manufacturers can have quite different electrical properties that are critical to the laser imaging process, and physical properties that are critical to the paper-handling mechanism. Two grades of paper from the same manufacturer can also have different properties, as can two batches of the same grade from the same manufacturer made at different times or at different plants. These differences are significant in a laser printer because the toner image is transferred to the paper when the printer gives the paper a positive charge that pulls the toner particles from the photosensitive drum. Various additives, along with moisture content, affect the ability of the paper to hold a uniform electrical charge. Whenever the charge is not uniform or within the required voltage range, the quality of the image is affected.

The degree in which moisture is removed from the paper determines whether it curls when it is passed through a laser printer. The fuser rollers of the printer, which can reach nearly 400 degrees Fahrenheit, drive off some of the moisture in the paper—similar to an iron drying out a wet piece of fabric. The instant drying of paper can result in extreme curling that can cause a jam or leave you with an unacceptable finished product. All of the paper types can develop curling problems if you store them improperly.

When paper is made, the fibers line up with the moving wire and give the paper a grain direction. Paper can be cut long grain—with the grain, or short grain—across the grain. For best results with printing on letter or legal size paper, Hewlett-Packard and other manufacturers recommend that you use a long grain stock.

Most cut-sheet paper that you buy off the shelf is cut at the paper mill where it is manufactured. Grain direction is marked on the ream label. You can test grain direction by wetting one side of a sheet of paper; the paper curls parallel to the long grain.

Paper Classifications

When you visit a paper dealer, you will be surprised at the vast selection of paper types and grades. The following categories are pertinent to you.

Bond

Bond refers to paper generally using 100 percent chemical wood or cotton pulp. In contrast, newspaper grade paper contains more lignin (wood fibers) and other contaminants that affect the laser printer's operation. Two types of bond are described below.

> **Xerographic Bond**. Xerography or electrophotography—on which laser printing is based—requires a controlled electrical surface and accurately cut sheets for consistent performance. Xerographic bond paper is manufactured to meet these requirements. There are no industry standards for xerographic paper. Because fillers are cheaper than fiber, less expensive xerographic papers may use more filler that results in higher *dusting* and lower performance. Therefore, inexpensive xerographic papers that perform poorly and contaminate the printer may not be such a bargain.

> **Cotton Bond**. Cotton bond is used for letterhead stationery. Makers of cotton bond do not pay as much attention to the electrical properties of the paper or precision machining. Paper manufacturers have introduced cotton bonds that you can use in laser printers or photocopy machines.

Offset

Offset papers are designed to work with sticky inks that have a high surface tension. Offset paper manufacturers are not concerned with the electrical properties of the paper, so their stock may not provide a consistently good image with laser printers.

Selecting Standard (Letter and Legal) Sized Papers

Xerographic Bond Papers

Xerographic bond papers are the best choice for laser printers. Within the xerographic family, you can select papers from 16 to 36 pounds. Pound is the measure used by the paper industry to indicate the thickness of the paper. Technically, a 20-pound paper (indicated as

20#) means that 500 sheets of standard size paper (17-by-22 inches) weighs 20 pounds. The higher the weight, the thicker the feel of the paper and the more opaque (less transparent) it will be. For most general printing applications, 20-pound paper is an appropriate weight.

You do not need to know the electrical resistivity, ash content, and acid content of a brand of paper before you make a purchase of xerographic paper. When it falls within the weight range for your printer, test a batch to see whether it works well, and under what conditions it fails. If you want to keep a formal record, use the form shown in Figure 4.1 to track your experimentation.

Printer			Page Count		
Paper Manufacturer		Product #	Lot #		Basis Weight
Date		Amount Printed		Price	

RESULTS:

	excellent	very good	good	acceptable	poor	very poor	not-acceptable
Background?							
Quality?							
Density?							
Smearing?							
Streaks?							

	NO	YES
Multiple Feed? Number of occurrences		
Jams? Number of occurrences		
Curling?		
Sample Attached?		

NOTES:

Initials:

Figure 4.1. Model form for tracking paper lots.

Cotton Bond Papers

When Hewlett-Packard developed the original LaserJet printer, it was assumed that users would be content to use the xerographic paper recommended for the machine. But users had become accustomed to the finer finish and richer feeling of cotton bond letterhead, and used it instead of the cheaper-feeling xerographic stock. Although the image quality is adequate—and some brands work well—many makes of cotton bond cause excessive jams and premature wear of key parts of the machine. This occurs because they are coated to increase stiffness and the coating tends to cause dusting that can be abrasive. Some low-quality xerographic bonds can also generate harmful dust and cause problems.

With the knowledge that users preferred cotton bond, Hewlett-Packard designed the LaserJet Series II so that it would eliminate some of the wear problems and accommodate the stiffer cotton papers. The LaserJet III uses the same paper path mechanism as the Series II and can use cotton papers. The LaserJet 4 uses a more convoluted paper path than the Series II or III. When you have difficulty with stiff paper, try using the MP tray. Although some cotton bond papers work better than others, if you use cotton bond regularly, increase your cleaning maintenance to remove the cotton dust that will inevitably shake free from the paper as it is manipulated by the feed mechanism.

General Problems with Bond Papers

Running heavier bond paper weights may cause an imaging problem called *background*. When this occurs the whole sheet of paper appears grey or dingy. This problem is prevalent with users on the East coast during the late fall and winter months as humidity drops and stored paper drys out. For background problems, increasing the density dial—1 maximum, 9 minimum—will decrease background. Storing paper properly will help you to keep it from drying out.

Areas of high humidity experience a different problem with heavier bond called drop out, that peaks during the summer months. Certain circular or oblong areas of the paper absorb excessive moisture which changes the electrical resistivity so that the toner does not fully transfer from the EP drum to the paper. This leaves an area that is lighter than the rest of the page or is dropped out (see Figure 4.2). Again, proper storage can help cure the problem.

```
"#$%&'()*+,-./0123456789:;<=
#$%&'()*+,-./0123456789:;<=>
$%&'()*+,-./0123456789:;<=>?
%&'()*+,-./0123456789:;<=>?@
&'()*+,-./0123456789:;<=>?@A
'()*+,-./0123456789:;<=>?@AB
()*+,-./0123456789:;<=>?@ABC
)*+,-./0123456789:;<=>?@ABCD
*+,-./0123456789:;<=>?@ABCDE
+,-./0123456789:;<=>?@ABCDEF
,-./0123456789:;<=>?@ABCDEFG
-./0123456789:;<=>?@ABCDEFGH
./0123456789:;<=     .BCDEFGHI
****************.......********
```

Figure 4.2. Sample of a drop out.

Recommendations for Using High Dusting Bond

When you do run cotton bond or low-quality xerographic bond through your laser printer, you are reducing the mean time between failure (MTBF), depending on the that model you are using. You can minimize the excess wear, however, by thoroughly cleaning the inside of your machine with a rag and a vacuum.

When you run paper through a laser printer, the dust collects around the shiny registration roller at the front of the paper path (see Figure 4.3). Although the dust will not harm the roller, it can easily spread to other parts of the machine where it can cause problems with imaging and premature wear. When you frequently use paper that causes excessive dust, open the top of the printer at the end the day and vacuum along the registration roller to pick up the dust. You cannot overclean your printer because the more dust-free you keep it, the longer you will have a trouble-free machine.

When you are selecting a new cotton bond, use the following guidelines:

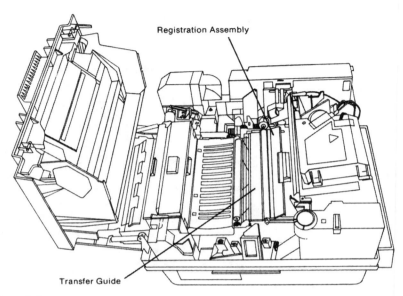

Figure 4.3. Registration roller, LaserJet III.

1. Stick with smooth finishes. Papers with *cockle* finishes (small pock marks) or *laid* finishes (rows of small horizontal indentations) will yield a poorer image because the rougher surface does not have close contact with the EP drum. The nonsmooth surfaces are also more prone to paper misfeeds and jams.

2. Be a cautious pioneer. Buy new types of paper one ream at a time. When you are satisfied with a paper and have run *several* reams through your printer, purchase the stock in bulk. The same brand purchased at different times can vary dramatically in performance because of fluctuations in the paper manufacturing process and the effects of storage. So never get talked into purchasing an 18-wheeler's worth of cotton stock just because it says specially designed for laser printers. Use the paper testing checklist shown in Figure 4.1 to monitor each brand you test.

Paper Stock To Be Avoided

The following types of stock should not be used in a laser printer:

➤ Preprinted forms. Do not use preprinted forms unless you are certain that the ink on the form can withstand 400 degrees Fahrenheit for 0.1 second without breaking down and emitting toxic gases. The ink must also not react to the resins in the toner. When the ink does meet the heat and reaction requirements, you need to make sure that it is completely dry on the forms before you print or you will have a problem called *offset*—ink from the forms is transferred to the imaging drum and rollers of the laser printer—resulting in damage to the imaging assembly. With preprinted forms, ink can build up on the cleaning bar pad and you will have to replace the pad more often.

➤ Glossy paper. Do not use glossy paper because it contains a clay coating and the toner does not stick well to the coating.

➤ Colored papers. Do not use colored papers unless the dyes are heat resistant.

➤ Multipart forms. Do not use multipart forms because they can tear and jam the machine. Also, carbonless paper contains chemicals that may not be safe when passing through the fusing assembly.

➤ Papers with perforations that run widthwise—at right angles to the paper path. Do not use paper with width perforations because it tends to cause excessive jamming and misfeeds when the paper bends at the perforation. Lengthwise perforations may also cause problems if the perforations are not precisely cut.

➤ Stock with holes in it. Do not use prepunched paper or paper with cutouts for spiral comb binding because it is likely to cause jams. The toner may also pass through the holes and begin to accumulate in the printer.

Recycled paper also may be problematic for laser printers because there are no uniform specifications for its production as of the time of this writing. Consistency can also be a problem because some batches may be fine while others may cause imaging or jamming problems. Also, most recycled paper is short fiber and tends to dust more, so you will need to do additional cleaning if you use recycled stock.

Selecting Envelopes

You need to avoid certain types of envelopes because they can cause jamming or misfeeds, including the following:

➤ Metal clasps or tie strings—metal clasps can destroy the fuser mechanism and scratch the photosensitive drum in the toner cartridge

➤ Double flaps or double-sided seams

➤ Expansion folds or gussets

➤ Embossed areas

In addition, avoid the following:

➤ Envelopes made from Tyvek and other shiny surfaces that may jam, melt, and/or cause poor imaging

➤ Envelopes made from recycled paper because they contain contaminants from the recycling process

When you use envelopes made from xerographic or cotton bond stock, check the glue on the envelope tongue. Some glues break down under the high heat of the fuser rollers (400 degrees Fahrenheit). The glue can release toxic fumes and may be rendered ineffective. Check with your envelope vendor to make sure that your envelope stock can withstand the heat of the fuser assembly.

You should never use envelopes with self-sealing adhesive strips because they will catch in the paper path mechanism. Also, when the protective coating gets removed, the glue will be exposed to the rollers and it might release harmful gases or leave a residue in the fuser assembly. Never use window envelopes because the plastic film used for the window may melt when heated in the fuser mechanism.

You should not attempt to run wrinkled, creased, or damaged envelopes through your laser printer because they will cause a jam and never make it to the imaging/fusing assembly. When an envelope does jam, do not reload it into the envelope tray or attempt to print it through the manual paper feed mechanism.

Using Mailing Labels

You can run pressure-sensitive mailing labels through your laser printer although they present numerous opportunities for jamming as well as potential environmental hazards if you choose the wrong stock.

The glue used to hold labels can emit toxic gases when heated to 400 degrees Fahrenheit. Acrylic-based adhesives tend to be safer at the fusing temperature. You need to check with the label manufacturer to ensure that the glue can withstand the temperatures encountered in your laser printer. When you are printing labels, always use label stock in well-ventilated areas.

You can purchase labels that can be safely run through a laser printer directly from Hewlett-Packard or from major manufacturers such as Avery and 3M. Your office supplier should be able to sell you name brand labels designed for use with laser printers.

In addition to the issue of adhesive safety, you need to observe the following guidelines when you are seeking a brand of labels for your laser printer:

1. Never use label sheets that have spaces between the labels. These labels are more prone to peeling off during the printing process and can lead to serious repeated jams.

2. Do not use labels in which the glue oozes out the edges when pressure is applied. You can test a sheet by pressing it with a board and then placing a sheet of xerographic or cotton bond paper on top of it. When the paper sticks to the labels, glue will be extruded during the printing process and come in contact with the rollers and/or the toner drum, causing a messy problem and future jams.

3. The labels should be made of xerographic bond stock for best imaging and fewest dust problems.

4. Open the rear output door if available. That will enable the label sheets to travel a straight path rather than curl around and eject through the top. The less curling of the label sheets, the less the likelihood of a label jamming in the fuser rollers and causing significant damage.

Using Transparencies

The key to successfully using overhead transparencies is to find stock that won't melt at 400 degrees Fahrenheit. Transparencies that melt in the fuser roller will cause serious jams and may emit hazardous gases. You can purchase laser-safe transparency sheets from major office suppliers. For best results with transparencies, you can use the rear exit (if available) on your laser printer to minimize curl and the possibility of jamming.

Manually Feeding Paper

The laser printer enables you to print odd size or heavy weight paper by manually feeding the stock. You should feed paper above 24 pounds through the manual feed system rather than the paper tray.

Whenever you insert a piece of paper into the manual feed system, it trips a photosensor flag and tells the printer that the manual feed mechanism is ready to feed paper. A carefully positioned protrusion on the front edge of your paper tray activates a series of micro switches that tells the printer what size paper tray you are using—legal, letter, A3, or envelope.

The manual feed slot, however, cannot distinguish what size paper you have inserted. When the printer calls for you to manually feed a particular size, it assumes that you have inserted the correct size. When you insert the wrong size, it can cause a jam when the printer senses paper in an unexpected location later in the print process. For example, when the printer calls for legal size paper and you manually feed letter size—or press the Continue button with the letter paper tray inserted—the printer will sense the trailing edge of the shorter paper before it is expected and will assume that the cause must be a paper jam. The printer will then terminate the print process and require manual clearing. In the case of an MP tray, the paper size is set via the menu.

TIP

The manual feed mechanism requires paper at least 7½ inches in length. It is possible, however, to print on small sheets—such as postcards—by attaching them to a piece of 8½-by-11-inch paper with tape that can withstand high temperatures. Fold the top of the 8½-by-11-inch page over the tape to keep it from peeling off or extruding adhesive on the fuser rollers, and insert the whole assembly through the manual feed slot.

Storing Paper

You can use all of the preceding information to make the best paper selection, but when you store the stock improperly, you may still experience poor imaging, a high rate of jams or multiple feeds, and unacceptably curled output. This problem is reported to be prevalent with the new Hewlett-Packard LaserJet 4. Hewlett-Packard suggests the following paper storage precautions and practices to reduce curling problems.

1. Rewrap reams after you open them. This will prevent excess moisture from building up in the paper.

2. The optimal temperature range for storing paper is 63 to 73 degrees Fahrenheit. Relative humidity should be 40 to 50 percent.

3. Do not store cartons or reams of paper directly on the floor because they will accumulate dust that can be transferred to the printer.

4. Do not store heavy objects on top of reams of paper because it may lead to creasing.

5. Avoid excessively dusty storage areas because the dust may find its way into the printer.

6. Allow paper to take on the temperature of the room in which the laser printer will be operated before unwrapping it. Rapidly changing temperatures can lead to curling in the paper tray, causing misfeeds or jamming.

7. Keep unwrapped paper away from direct sunlight because that tends to cause curling due to uneven heating and drying.

When you follow the above procedures and precautions, you will minimize the second major cause of imaging problems with laser printers—improper storage. Poor paper selection is the prime cause. Although it is impossible to guarantee perfect operation throughout the life of the printer, be assured that if you pay attention to the details discussed in this chapter, the likelihood is greater that you will have consistent and trouble-free laser printing.

5

Routine Maintenance Tips

Performing Regular Maintenance

Laser printers are easy-to-maintain machines; with a few routine, simple maintenance actions, you can keep a laser printer in peak operating condition. When you use lower grade papers or ones that create excessive dust, you will have to do some extra maintenance. There are three tasks that should be part of your regular maintenance efforts—cleaning the paper path, cleaning the corona wires, and cleaning the fuser assembly.

WARNING

Turn off your laser printer before you do any maintenance inside the printer. Use only a slightly damp cloth for cleaning, unless directed otherwise. Although the specific steps and location of parts will vary for different models of laser printers, the methods discussed for maintaining a LaserJet III will apply to compatible printers.

Cleaning the Paper Path

Once a month, use a soft, damp cloth to wipe dust and dirt from all of the metal surfaces and rollers in the paper path. You can also use a regular household vacuum to remove paper dust; however, it is not recommended for toner spills.

You also need to wipe up or vacuum paper dust on the shiny metal registration roller located inside the printer near the front of the machine (see Figure 5.1). To clean the metal surfaces, you can pick up the metal registration assembly cover where the roller is affixed, by pulling the green plastic handle upward. Make sure you close the registration assembly when you are finished.

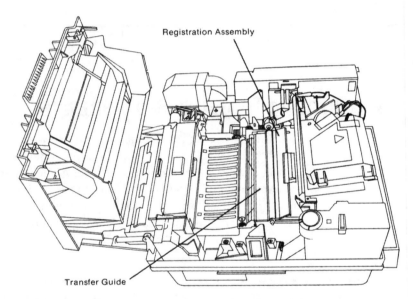

Figure 5.1. Registration assembly area of a Hewlett-Packard LaserJet III.

You need to clean the four plastic *separation pawls* that peel the paper off the fuser roller. The fuser pawls are located in the rear of the printer behind the fuser assembly. Behind the cleaning bar cover, you will notice a green, felt-covered cover with a handle. Push the handle back and the four pawls will be exposed (see Figure 5.2). Clean them with a damp cloth periodically.

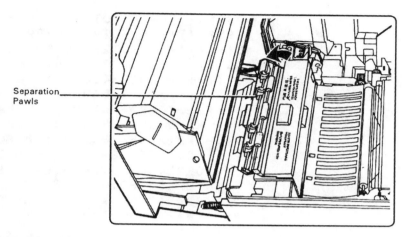

Figure 5.2. Fuser assembly separation pawls.

Cleaning the Corona Wires

Cleaning the transfer corona wire is a critical part of the maintenance program. You must keep the transfer corona wire clean so it will put a uniform charge on the paper; when the charge is not uniform, the print output will be uneven (see Figure 5.3). As described in Chapter 1, the transfer corona wire is used to give the paper a positive charge. Because the toner is negatively charged, it is attracted to the positively charged paper. The transfer corona wire retains a positive charge and it naturally attracts loose toner. When the transfer corona wire gets coated with loose toner, it can no longer generate a uniform charge, and the toner does not stick to the paper properly giving you an uneven image.

There is a build-up of toner on the transfer corona wire after running a large batch of envelopes, because only a portion of the transfer corona wire is shielded from loose toner. The Hewlett-Packard service center frequently receives calls from users who have just run a large number of envelopes and find uneven toner distribution on subsequently printed full sheets of paper.

```
"#$%&'()*+,-./0123456789:;<=
#$%&'()*+,-./0123456789:;<=>
$%&'()*+,-./0123456789:;<=>?
%&'()*+,-./0123456789:;<=>?@
&'()*+,-./0123456789:;<=>?@A
'()*+,-./0123456789:;<=>?@AB
()*+,-./0123456789:;<=>?@ABC
)*+,-./0123456789:;<=>?@ABCD
*+,-./0123456789:;<=>?@ABCDE
+,-./0123456789:;<=>?@ABCDEF
,-./0123456789:;<=>?@ABCDEFG
-./0123456789:;<=>?@ABCDEFGH
./0123456789:;<       ABCDEFGHI
********************* . . . . . ********
```

Figure 5.3. Poor printing because of dirty transfer corona wire.

The crisscross wire in front of the plastic guide is not the transfer corona wire. The transfer corona wire is a straight piece of wire that lies in a recessed cavity (see Figure 5.4). The crisscross wire assembly keeps the paper from falling into the transfer corona wire cavity.

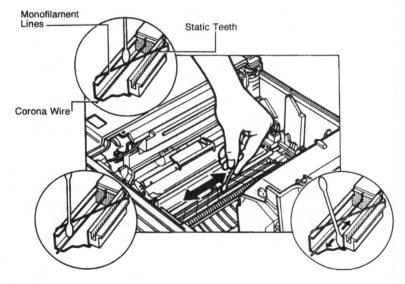

Figure 5.4. Crisscross and corona wires.

To clean the corona wire, you gently wipe it with a soft cotton swab dipped in isopropyl alcohol to remove any toner. Be careful not to stretch or break the corona or protective crisscross wires.

You need to clean the groove behind the corona wire cavity periodically with the cleaning brush supplied with your printer. The cleaning brush, which has a green plastic handle and a felt cleaning pad, sits on the left side of the printer in a recessed cavity (see Figure 5.5).

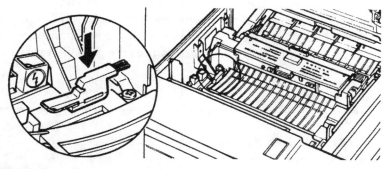

Figure 5.5. Location of the cleaning brush.

You insert the bristles into the groove and move the brush sideways, hopping over the crisscross wires. When you are finished, put the brush back inside the printer so you will always know where it is.

The primary corona wire in your EP cartridge also needs routine maintenance (see Chapter 6 for a technical explanation). You can also do this with the cleaning brush. You need to remove the cartridge and insert the handle into the slot on the cartridge (see Figure 5.5). Move the brush side to side several times. This will remove any excess toner and assure optimum imaging capabilities (see Figure 5.6).

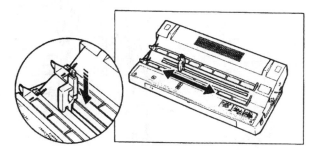

Figure 5.6. The technique for cleaning a primary corona wire.

Cleaning the Fuser Assembly

You need to change the fuser roller cleaning pad every time you change the EP cartridge. You can improve the print quality and reduce wear on the machine by regularly removing the paper dust and toner debris from the fuser roller, and by cleaning the bar during routine maintenance.

First, you need to wait until the fuser assembly has cooled. Lift the green cover of the fuser assembly (see Figure 5.7) and remove the cleaning bar, exposing the fuser roller. Run a clean cloth over the entire length of roller—do not use water, alcohol, solvents, or detergents. You can manually turn the gears that rotate the roller to clean the entire surface.

WARNING

When you finish cleaning the fuser roller, check the cleaning pad. When the pad has a build-up of paper dust and excess toner, it won't effectively clean the roller. Lightly scrape off the dust and toner by running the back of an ordinary hair comb over the cleaning pad; you will extend the cleaning pad's ability to do its job.

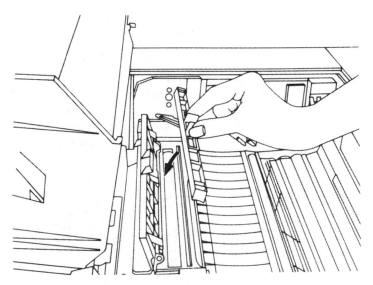

Figure 5.7. A fuser assembly with its cover open.

On the rest of the printer, clean any place you can reach with a rag—try not to disturb the places you cannot reach. Do not remove any of the screwed-in parts to clean the printer.

Establishing a Laser Printer Maintenance Schedule

Table 5.1 shows some general guidelines about how often you should clean the printer.

TABLE 5.1. CLEANING GUIDELINES FOR PRINTER USE

Printer Use	Cleaning Frequency
Large quantities of cotton bond paper	Daily
Moderate use with xerographic bonds	Weekly
Light use with a mix of papers	Monthly

When you follow the proper cleaning and maintenance procedures, your laser printer will last longer. Hewlett-Packard and other printer manufacturers recommend that—at the minimum—you should carry out routine maintenance every time you change your EP cartridge. However, frequent cleaning will keep your laser engine running more smoothly.

Rather than performing maintenance activities when it is convenient, you should incorporate them into your office routines. This will ensure that the necessary jobs are done at the correct intervals.

Removing Toner Deposits

Excess toner deposits should be vacuumed out by an authorized service representative. You cannot use an ordinary household vacuum for the job, because the toner particles are so fine that they will slip through the vacuum's filter and be forced out of the exhaust. You will be transferring the toner problem from your printer to your carpeting, walls, or clothes.

An excess of toner can result from transporting your printer with the EP cartridge in place, or from using a lot of punched paper that enables the toner from the photosensitive drum to fall through instead of sticking to the page. When you run your finger across any metallic portion and find a black residue that won't come off with a dry cloth, it is time for a professional cleaning. You will need to contact your service representative for help.

Changing the Ozone Filter

Many people are concerned about emissions from laser printers. Laser printers and personal copiers do emit ozone. The charge generated by the corona wires splits oxygen (O_2) molecules apart. The loose oxygen atoms can combine with regular oxygen to create ozone (O_3) molecules. The ozone molecules eventually divide and return to O_2 as they hit other objects.

Under normal circumstances, ozone is harmless in the office. But some people are especially sensitive to it and may experience irritation of the eyes, nose, and throat, as well as a slight headache. The following problems lead to ozone emissions from laser printers.

1. The printer is used in a small, poorly ventilated area.

2. Several printers (or copiers) are operating at the same time in a small area.

3. The ozone filter (see below) is no longer effective.

4. Humidity is very low.

To reduce ozone emissions, your LaserJet III is equipped with a special filter that accelerates the conversion of the O_2 molecules to their regular O_3 form. When the page count on your self tests is creeping towards the 50,000 mark, you need to change the filter.

NOTE:

Although the filter is designed to last 50,000 pages, dust particles can render it ineffective much earlier. When you work in a dusty environment, you need to change the filter more frequently.

When you replace the filter, turn off the printer and open the hood. You need to open the filter cover to remove the filter (see Figure 5.8) by pulling on the clear plastic tab and inserting the replacement filter. When you are finished, close the filter compartment door and shut the hood of the printer; you are ready for approximately 50,000 more pages.

Figure 5.8. Replacement of a LaserJet III ozone filter.

Getting the Most Out of the Toner Cartridge

The toner cartridge works with the laser imaging system to print a page. This chapter explains the various components of the electro-photosensitive (EP) cartridge and how they function. When you understand how toner cartridges work, you will be able to solve problems and maintain consistent, high-quality imaging.

Different models of laser printers require different EP cartridges. Although they may vary in size and shape, they all contain the same or similar elements. The following discussion of the EP cartridge for a Canon SX engine-based printer covers most Hewlett-Packard models and compatibles.

The Inner Workings of a Toner Cartridge

When the cartridge is inserted into the printer, a metal shutter opens and exposes an internal electrophotosensitive (EP) drum to a laser beam in the printer. The laser beam forms an image on the drum that attracts the toner. The toner is transferred to the paper and permanently affixed by a high-temperature fuser roller (see Chapter 1 for details of the laser printing process). An EP cartridge contains the components such as those shown in Figure 6.1.

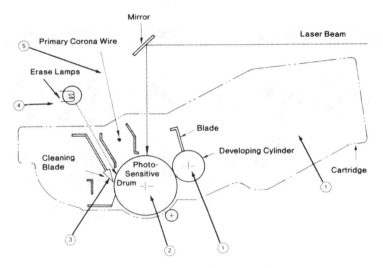

Figure 6.1. Cross-section of a toner cartridge.

The Toner Reservoir

The toner reservoir has a supply of toner, a magnetic developing cylinder, and a *doctor blade*. The toner particles are shaped like tiny pearls and are composed of acrylstyrene resin—a plastic-like substance. The center of the toner particles contain a ferrite (iron) core that enables it to hold an electrical charge and to be attracted to the magnetic developing cylinder.

The developing cylinder rotates in the toner reservoir through an external gear assembly connected to the motor in the laser printer. As the developing cylinder turns, it attracts a thick layer of toner particles with its magnetic core.

The doctor blade works like a butter knife that is set a fixed distance above the surface of the developing cylinder's entire length. The doctor blade spreads the toner that has been attracted to the cylinder to a uniform thickness. After the cylinder has the correct level of toner, it rotates close to the photosensitive drum that has an image in the form of an electrical charge. The toner is transferred to the charged area of the photosensitive drum corresponding to the image, and the excess toner is returned to the reservoir.

The Photosensitive Drum

The drum is composed of an aluminum tube covered with an organic photoconductive material that changes its electrical conductivity when struck by photons (light energy) from the laser. The photosensitive coating is given a strong negative charge by means of a nearby primary corona wire (see Chapter 1 for details), but it loses that charge in selected areas—corresponding to the printed page—when struck by the laser beam. The toner particles that have been given a negative charge by the developing cylinder stick to the EP drum where the negative charge has been dissipated and are repelled by areas that have retained the initial negative charge. When the paper is passed through the printer, it is given a positive charge that pulls the toner off the drum. During the final step, the plastic toner particles are melted into the paper in the fuser assembly and the paper is ejected.

The Cleaning Blade

The cleaning blade runs the length of the photosensitive drum and scrapes excess toner off the drum and into a *debris cavity*.

The Erasure Lamps

These lamps expose the entire drum surface, completely dissipating any remaining electrical charge so that the drum can be recharged by the primary corona wire and take on the next part of the page.

The Primary Corona Wire

This single strand of wire imparts a uniform negative charge on the photosensitive drum. This charge is dissipated when the drum is struck by the laser light.

Installing EP Cartridges

Toner cartridge installation is very easy. After you have done it once, you should be able to do it in less than a minute. The following two tips are for you to keep in mind:

1. When a cartridge has been in storage on one end, the toner might clump together. This causes uneven printing, with part of the page darker than the other. To avoid this, when you remove the cartridge from its aluminum foil sack, rock it several times at a 45 degree angle before inserting it into the machine (see Figure 6.2). This will redistribute the toner along the reservoir and eliminate the possibility of pages being printed unevenly.

2. The cartridge is shipped with a piece of protective tape that separates the photosensitive drum from the toner reservoir. The tape is connected to a plastic tab that serves as a handle for the tape removal operation. The tab protrudes from the side of the cartridge and must be bent back and forth until it separates from the tape guide. The tab should break free of the cartridge but remain attached to the plastic tape. When the tab is free, grasp it firmly and give one smooth, strong pull to remove the full length of the protective tape—about 16 inches (see Figure 6.3).

   When the tape breaks, you can still complete the removal operation by grabbing the remaining piece of tape with a pair of needle-nosed pliers. A medical hemostat (used to clamp blood vessels and often sold through small tool catalogs) is also very effective because of its long row of teeth and very tight grip.

   When the tape is not totally removed, the cartridge will not form an image on the portion of the drum that is obstructed. Return your cartridge to your dealer and exchange it for a fresh cartridge.

The Life of Toner

As you generate more copies, you will use up your supply of toner. The life of a cartridge depends on what you print. The greater the percentage of each page that you cover with toner, the fewer pages the toner cartridge will be able to print because the supply of the toner in the cartridge is finite. When you are printing double-spaced, Courier 10 pitch type on 8 1/2-by-11-inch pages—approximately 250 words per page—your cartridge will last longer than when you are using a smaller typeface, single-spaced, and printing heavy rules on each page. Before you begin to wonder if your toner cartridge is defective because it ran out sooner than you expected, review the kinds of documents you have been printing because the toner coverage will be heavier than you realized.

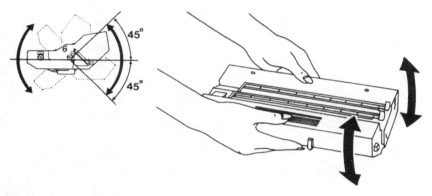

Figure 6.2. The cartridge rocking procedure.

Toner Level Indicators

The toner cartridges used in the LaserJet III and other Canon SX-based printers have a sensor in the reservoir that functions like an oil dip-stick and flashes the warning 16 TONER LOW on the printer's LCD display when the level drops to the point where only 100 double-spaced, 10-pitch pages could be printed. When your print job entails heavy coverage, the number of pages you have left could be significantly less.

Extending Cartridge Use

One way to forestall the inevitable end of an EP cartridge's useful life is to turn the print density down to a lighter setting. The print density regulates how much toner is applied to the drum. The greater the density, the faster the toner will be used up.

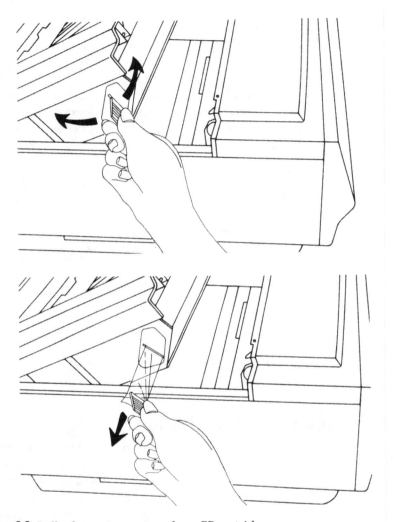

Figure 6.3. Pull tab to remove tape from EP cartridge.

On the LaserJet III printer, the density dial is made of bright green plastic and is located inside toward the front of the machine. The dial ranges from 1 to 9, and operates counterintuitively, with 1 being the darkest setting and 9 the lightest. The print density setting has a significant effect on the darkness of images laid down on the paper, and the extremes will have a marked effect on the rate that an EP cartridge consumes toner. (It also has an effect on the Resolution

Enhancement Technology, as explained in Chapter 3.) For normal printing, you can use the 5 setting. When you want lighter copies for draft printing, set the density closer to 9 and save the 5 setting for final output. Only set the density dial for 1 when you have a graphic image or rule that you want to print extremely dark.

Reviving the Cartridge

When your laser printer displays a low toner message, keep on printing until the image begins to fade on the page. Then, remove the toner cartridge and rock it at a 45 degree angle several times. This will redistribute any remaining toner that has clumped together and make the last bits sitting in the toner reservoir available to the imaging process. The rocking action may extend the life of the cartridge for another 100 pages, depending on the kind of material you are printing.

There will be a point, however, when you have run out of toner and the paper will begin to print unevenly. Eventually the paper will barely show any print, at that point the cartridge has expired and it is time to install a new one.

TIP

You should always have a second toner cartridge on hand. But if you don't, head for the office supply store or call your computer supply vendor when your printer indicates that the toner is low. Another reason for having a second toner cartridge on hand is the possibility of cartridge malfunction.

The Aging Cartridge

Many people believe that toner cartridges improve with age. Some even go to the extent of removing cartridges that are midway through their life cycle and saving them for special print jobs. The perceived improvement in darkness over time is really a degradation in print quality.

When the drum is new, each spot struck by the laser beam will be perfectly round. But from the first time the drum turns, the drum coating begins to break down—that is why Canon designed the drum to be part of the disposable EP cartridge—and the areas charged by the laser become slightly fuzzy. To the eye, the fuzziness appears to be heavier strokes so the overall image looks blacker and denser. However, the first page really is better than the last page produced by the cartridge. The graph shown in Figure 6.4 shows how the print quality degrades over time.

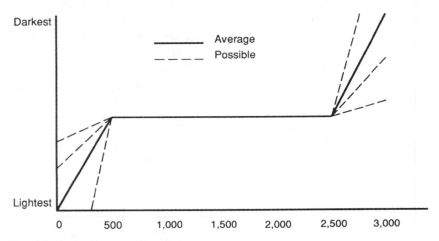

Figure 6.4. Print quality deterioration graph.

Storing Toner Cartridges

The following guidelines will help you store your EP cartridges properly and maximize their lifespan:

1. Do not open the aluminum foil packaging until you are ready to use the cartridge. Unopened EP cartridges will last two and a half years. Opened EP cartidges last six months.

2. Maintain the storage area between 32 degrees Fahrenheit and 95 degrees Fahrenheit.

3. Humidity should be normal.

4. Do not expose a cartridge to temperatures beyond 104 degrees Fahrenheit for more than two weeks.

5. Never leave a cartridge in a car on a hot summer day. The interior temperature can reach 140 degrees Fahrenheit or higher, which could fuse toner in place, rendering the cartridge useless.

6. When you bring a cold cartridge into a warm room and install it without letting it reach room temperature, condensation will immediately form on the toner and the drum when you pull the tape. This results in lumpy toner and poor print quality. When you store your toner cartridges in a separate room that is kept at a lower temperature, you can avoid this problem by enabling the cartridges to adjust to the temperature of the work area before installation.

Environmental Issues

The plastic resin toner used in the EP cartridges is nontoxic and poses no known health hazards to users. The biggest problem with toner is getting it out of your clothes or other fabrics. You can come in contact with toner from a cartridge that has been moved while inside a printer—the shutter through which the laser fires at the drum is still open; from a cartridge that has been refilled and has lost its sealing plug; or from the protective tape you removed when you first installed the cartridge—the tape usually has a slight trace of toner on it.

TIP

Do not use hot water to remove toner from your skin or fabrics. The hot water fuses the toner in place and makes it harder to remove. Use cold water and soap to clean toner spills.

Disposal

The growing environmental consciousness of the 1990s has made the disposal of toner cartridges a major concern for many of you. Each time you change a toner cartridge, you are removing the parts that are likely to break down. This enables the machines to print for tens of thousands of pages without problems. But what is good for the printer is not necessarily good for the environment. Every time you dispose of a toner cartridge, you are getting rid of a heavy plastic case that will sit for many years in a landfill. Although the contents of the case may be in good order, you are also wasting good amalgams of metal and plastic.

Some people have turned to toner refilling (see the following section) as a means of keeping toner cartridges out of landfills—and as a means of lowering the operating costs of their printers. In 1990, Hewlett-Packard began offering a recycling program. When your cartridge is used, call (800)752-0900 and request a LaserJet toner cartridge recycling kit. Hewlett-Packard will then send you an envelope with a plastic bag and a UPS call tag. Place the spent cartridge in the bag and insert it into the hard foam packing spacers included with the new cartridge. Place the cartridge and spacers in the box, affix the UPS call tag label and call UPS for a pickup—or take it to your shipping department. Hewlett-Packard pays for the transportation costs.

After the cartridge is returned to the Hewlett-Packard toner cartridge return center, all parts that are reusable are used in the manufacturing of new cartridges and the unusable parts are melted down and then incorporated into the manufacturing process. As an added incentive and show of environmental good faith, Hewlett-Packard donates fifty cents to the Nature Conservancy and fifty cents to the National Wildlife Federation for each cartridge it receives.

Toner Refilling

In the mid-1980s, a new cottage industry emerged: toner refilling. For half the price of a new cartridge, toner refillers would drill a hole in your old cartridge, add toner, and ship it back to you. Although some operations were able to maintain a high level of quality, many services sent back cartridges that eventually leaked, causing toner blackouts. Also, adding toner to a cartridge with a worn photosensitive drum or cleaning blades can cause the imaging to be extremely poor.

By the late 1980s, more sophisticated toner cartridge remanufacturers entered the scene. These operations disassemble the cartridges, replace worn parts, and maintain much higher quality control. They have even formed a trade group—American Cartridge Recycling Association, 1717 N. Bayshore Dr., Suite 2434, Miami, FL 33132, (305)539-0701.

Using a remanufactured cartridge will not void your warranty with Hewlett-Packard. But when a problem—such as a shorted circuit board—is traced to leakage from a remanufactured cartridge, you will be responsible for the damage.

CHAPTER

Selecting a Laser Printer

The selection of a laser printer used to be quite simple—when you needed the graphics power of PostScript, you chose an Apple LaserWriter, otherwise you selected the latest offering from Hewlett-Packard. Although they were based on the same Canon engine and had the same resolution and engine speed, the printer language, the number of included fonts, and the cost were different. At times, the LaserWriter alternative cost more than twice as much as the LaserJet alternative. Because the number of compatible printers and add-on enhancements has increased, the choice has become significantly more complex. The entry of such PC powerhouses as IBM and Compaq to the laser printer market has produced a truly competitive marketplace. The number of manufacturers now rank in the dozens and the number of models exceed 100. Even so the ultimate decision still comes down to price, performance and features.

Price

There has been a growing trend in the computer industry and the laser printer industry of lowering the prices for equal or better performance. No company or product has exemplified this trend more then Hewlett-Packard with its line of LaserJets. Each time Hewlett-Packard announced a major new model of one of its top-of-the-line products, the product included significant new features and was priced lower than the product it was replacing. This highly competitive approach to pricing has won Hewlett-Packard a loyal following and most of the market.

Early laser printers were restricted to use with high speed mainframe computers. The price tags were well over $100,000 and the printers required whole rooms for support. The introduction in 1983 of the first personal laser printer—the Hewlett-Packard LaserJet—opened a whole new horizon. Unfortunately, not many individuals could afford a LaserJet for personal use. Priced well over $4,000 and hard to find even at the suggested retail price, these printers set the base line for price and performance. The Hewlett-Packard printers were driven by the Printer Command Language (PCL) which became the standard mode for laser printers. The Apple LaserWriters that followed added significant performance and font features by including the PostScript command language and a sturdier internal processor, but at a higher cost. It is not unusual for the printer to cost more than the computer that was used with it.

The entry of IBM and Compaq, as well as the lower profile companies, has added competition to the market. IBM and Compaq ensured that their first products had dramatic performance features and were competitively priced. Other manufacturers compete on price, added features, or user's brand loyalty.

Performance

Most users look at the page per minute (ppm) figures of laser printers as the measure of performance without considering the key element of rendering speed, the actual measure used to determine how fast a printer can translate a print job. Although each laser printer has a theoretical maximum speed determined by the page throughput of the imaging engine, few meet that criterion except when printing multiple copies of the same page.

The difference between theoretical speeds and real speeds can be summed up in the term *rendering speed*. The printer's processor must translate the incoming print request into the individual dots on the page; this processing takes time. Different printers use different processors, printer languages, and amounts of memory to accomplish this critical task. Some printers and printer enhancements off-load the heavy processing to the PC's processor and memory. The theory behind this approach is that you are better off investing your money in a higher speed PC processor and additional PC memory that is shared with your printer than buying another processor and memory dedicated to your printer. You need to look beyond the engine speed to evaluate printers—two printers that are using the identical engine can have different performances. The causes for these differences lie in the choice of the printer's language and processor/memory combination. One of the key differences between PCL and PostScript is that PostScript is more powerful and more complicated. It requires more memory and a higher performance processor to render the same document as compared to PCL. When you present the same document to a machine capable of processing PCL and PostScript, it will usually take longer to process in PostScript mode than in PCL mode. However, it is possible to create documents that will perform better in PostScript than PCL on the same processor.

Processor and memory combinations have dramatic impact on rendering speeds. As with PCs, when you put in a faster processor and more memory, the printer will run faster. Another key factor is soft fonts. In a complex document, your software often needs to download one soft font for the headline at the top of a page and a second soft font for the body. When your printer does not have enough memory, it must discard the headline font before it can download the body font. When you reuse the headline font on that page or on the next page, your software will have to download it again—taking considerable time. However, when your printer has enough memory, it can retain both soft fonts for the duration of the print job. Both fonts can be downloaded only once with a considerable savings in processing time.

Features

The list of features available with the current laser printers is almost endless. When making a purchasing decision, it is critical for you to establish what features you need for your printer's tasks. For example, higher resolution is better, but at what cost or in exchange for losing what other features? When all you plan to print is correspondence, do you really need 600 or 800 dpi resolution? Can anyone really tell the difference? Look at the main features that you ought to consider before making a purchase. These features are not presented in any particular order. The feature that is most critical to your application may be found at the bottom of the list.

Speed

You need to be discriminating when you are looking at rated speeds. Ask to see true performance ratings, including rendering times for the type of material you will print compiled by an independent reviewer.

Languages

The question of PCL versus PostScript (see Chapters 13 and 14) used to be simple—when you wanted graphics, you chose PostScript; when you wanted speedy text only, you chose PCL. However, the introduction of scalable fonts and HP-GL/2 to PCL5 have made these issues become more blurred as PostScript and PCL move closer together. You need to check the compatibility with those around you. When you need to interface with Mac-based users or your print shop supports a direct file transfer for PostScript-based printing, then PostScript is the way to go. Otherwise you can save money by sticking to PCL. When you are undecided, pick a printer that starts with PCL and enables you to add PostScript later. If you plan to use PCL and PostScript, you need to choose a printer that can intelligently switch between these two languages.

Paper Handling

Xerox once touted its mission as being the creation of the automated and paper-free office. However, PCs and laser printers have increased the amount of paper in the office. Every printer should have at least two software selectable paper sources—one for plain white paper and a second for everything else—letterhead, colored stock, legal sized paper. If you frequently need to use legal paper, you will need a dedicated source. When you use first and second sheet letterhead, you will need a third paper tray, including one for plain paper.

Think in terms of your everyday needs. Everyone has a special case that will arise from time to time that will require manual intervention, but do you really need full-time automatic capability? Most printers enable you to manually feed a special sheet, pausing the printer for you.

You may want to consider a dedicated envelope feeder. However, they don't really work well. First, they require a uniform stock of feeder compatible envelopes. As pointed out in Chapter 4, the main cause of envelope feeder problems is incorrectly sized envelopes. Second, when you are planning to print 1,500 envelopes on your laser printer, you should expect the job to run approximately 3.125 hours minimum printing time at 8 p.m. When you use standard labels, the job takes only 6 minutes to print the same number of labels. However you still have to transfer the labels to the envelopes.

When you are selecting a network printer, the quantity of document output is the driving issue. When the printer has multiple trays, make sure that you can set the printer to switch to the second tray when the first tray is empty.

I/O Ports

When you are selecting a printer, make sure that it has the I/O port or ports that you currently need. In addition, select a printer that you can add an optional I/O port to, such as one of the high-speed ports or multiple-user shared ports offered by third-party developers. When you are on a network or are planning to move to one in the future, you need to make sure that you can purchase the appropriate interface card for your network. Network interface cards are not only faster, but reduce the overhead on the printer server.

Add-On Ability

Most of the printers on the market today offer a variety of add-on options. Some printers contain more optional slots, cartridges and interface ports than standard parts. Planning for the future is harder than evaluating your current needs, but when you are growing and you want to provide the maximum path for enhancements, be sure to look over the add-on options carefully.

➤ **I/O ports.** Which ports are included and which ones can be added? How many can be active simultaneously and can the printer intelligently switch between them? Can you add a network or other interface directly to the printer?

➤ **Memory.** How much memory is standard and how much can you add in the future? Do you need to buy only from the manufacturer or can you purchase from a third party?

➤ **Languages.** What languages are standard and what languages can you add? When you add a language, can the printer automatically switch between them? When you add a new language such as PostScript, do you need to also add more memory? How well integrated would the add-on language be with the printer's processor? Can the processor deal with the new language directly or must it interpret the new language into the native language? These considerations will impact the rendering speed of the add-on language.

➤ **Fonts.** You can never have too many fonts. What fonts or typeface families come installed with the printer? Are they scalable and can you apply special effects such as drop shadows or outlining? When they are cartridge or SIMM based fonts, are they faster than downloaded fonts?

Duty Cycle

Few users understand the concept of the duty cycle until their printer malfunctions. This is partly the fault of the construction of the original LaserJets and LaserWriters—they never died. They would last forever with a minimum of preventitive maintenance. However, as you place laser printers into network environments, you need to ask the length of the model's duty cycle. Although many of the wearable parts are meant to be replaced each time you change the EP cartridge, the rest of the printer suffers wear as well. Placing a printer that was designed for intermittent use in an environment that generates continuous use is a sure road to printer failure.

Resolution

More resolution is better for your printer than less. The problem is that there is a trade-off. The printer is more expensive or you are losing some other feature. For example, look at the impact of raising the resolution of a printer from 300 to 600 dpi—it quadruples the memory requirements of the printer. It also requires a faster processor to render four times as many dots as before in the same amount of time. You can add memory and processing speed at a higher cost or you leave something else out—the extra port, built-in PostScript, or two large paper trays. When going for higher resolution, be honest with yourself and ask when you truly need it, and what are you willing to give up in exchange.

Printer Review

The cost of a laser printer is another issue to consider. Laser printers come in various price ranges and are marked as street prices or list prices as appropriate. The prices discussed in this chapter were in effect when this book was written and they will give you some idea of what your options are. The discussion is limited to some of the major retailers in the laser printer market. The inclusion or exclusion of a particular manufacturer or brand should not be construed as an endorsement or rejection of a particular brand.

Printers under $1,000

At the low end of the market, with street prices near or even below $1,000, you will find the market-leading Hewlett-Packard LaserJet IIP and IIIP, featuring PCL 4 and 5, 4-ppm printing, and excellent quality. Similar models by Brother, Okidata, Panasonic, and others offer equivalent price and performance. For this price range, you will get slower performance for engine speed and rendering speeds, although they are fast enough for most low-volume text applications. The low-cost printers have a shorter duty cycle and are not intended for continuous use. When you run one of these printers continuously, it will die. The other major cost saving is the reduction of upgrade and enhancement options. You need to make sure that your selection can be upgraded to your anticipated requirements.

Printers from $1,000–$2,000

Moving up to the next tier, you enter the realm of the printers based on 8-10-ppm engines by the Canon SX engine, the Canon P-270 (used by Hewlett-Packard in the new LaserJet 4) or similar performance engines by Minolta, Brother, TEC, Ricoh, Ecosys, Lexmark (IBM), Samsung, Sharp, and others. At this tier, the market is again led by Hewlett-Packard with its LaserJet 4 with prices in the $1,500 to $1,700 range. At this price level, you can buy a slow PostScript printer, a slow high-resolution printer, or a higher-speed PCL-based printer. When $1,500 is your budget for a printer, you need to evaluate your needs to determine what feature is most important and what can be compromised.

When speed is the most important feature, you should look at the 10-ppm Fujitsu Print Partner 10. This PCL-based printer delivers true 10-ppm speeds for PCL text and reasonable graphics performance for just under $2,000. You can add PostScript for an additional $500. When PostScript capability is your top priority, you should consider the Apple Personal LaserWriter NTR that is based on the Canon SX engine and delivers a solid four ppm with reasonable graphic rendering times for about $2,000. When the resolution is critical, look at the LaserMaster WinPrinter 800 that delivers 800 dpi resolution and PostScript emulation for only $1,600. The WinPrinter's PostScript rendering speed is slower than that of the Personal LaserWriter NTR, but it delivers more than twice the resolution.

Printers from $2,000–$3,000

After you break the $2,000 barrier, your options expand. You can find excellent speed, resolution, and PostScript capability in a single package. All of the major manufacturers are battling for market share in this arena and that brings great benefits to the consumer. The top-of-the-line Hewlett-Packard LaserJet 4M—the same as the LaserJet 4 with the PostScript and memory options added—lists for just under $3,000 with street prices $500 below that. The LaserJet4 delivers 600 dpi, true PostScript Level 2, true 8-ppm processing speeds, excellent rendering speeds in both PCL and PostScript mode, and the craftsmanship you expect from Hewlett-Packard.

Close to the LaserJet 4M in price and performance is the Fujitsu Print Partner 10, with a PostScript option included. This printer delivers 300 dpi resolution at 10 ppm. This throughput advantage will only be true on simple documents because the Fujitsu lags behind the Hewlett-Packard 4M model in rendering speeds for complex documents.

Printers over $3,000

Above $3,000, you enter the realm of network printers that deliver speeds of more than 16 ppm, automatic language switching, and direct network interfaces. Because of the volume of activity on network printers, features that are important include larger and multiple paper trays, longer duty cycles, additional font memory, and high speeds in terms of higher engine speeds and higher rendering speeds. No one wants to wait in a network printer's queue behind a complex graphics design that has brought the 20 ppm printer to a halt as its underpowered processor rasterizes the image.

It is into this market that Compaq aimed its first laser printer products, the PageMarq 15 and 20. The PageMarq 15 runs at 15 ppm, holds up to 1,000 sheets of paper in two trays, delivers 800-by-400 resolution, and switches automatically between PostScript and PCL. The PageMarq 20 delivers 20 ppm, holds up to 1,500 sheets in three trays, and can be fitted with a hard disk to hold all of your soft fonts. Both use high speed RISC-based processors that deliver rendering speeds up to their engine speeds for even moderately complex documents. As with most printers in this league, they are offered with a variety of I/O options suitable for almost any situation. The only downside to the Compaq PageMarqs is their relatively high price. The PageMarq 15 lists at $3,999 and the PageMarq 20 lists at $5,499.

Hewlett-Packard's entry into the shared laser printer market, the venerable LaserJet IIISi, is a solid performer with an enviable track record. It lags behind the competition, such as the Compaqs, in a feature for feature comparison primarily due to the age of its design. It even lags behind the LaserJet 4 in all areas except engine speed, paper capacity, and duty cycle. When Hewlett-Packard deems fit to release the inevitable combination of the LaserJet 4's brains and the LaserJet IIISi's brawn with their customary price reduction, the competition will really heat up.

Other contenders for the network system printer include the Dataproducts LZR 1560 ($3,795 list), Toshiba PageLaser GX400 ($4,499 list) and the QMS-PS 1700 ($6,995 list). Each offers a unique combination of features in the 15-17-ppm market. Finally, for those who want speed, there is the Kentek K30D that has throughput speeds of up to 30 ppm and rendering speeds in PCL and PostScript that are close behind. When speed and duty cycle are your only concerns, then you shouldn't be put off by the $20,000 plus price tag. You should know that you could also buy four PageMarq 20s for almost the same investment, yielding a theoretical maximum speed of 80 ppm with the added advantage of distributed placement and redundancy should one or more fail. Obviously, your mix of work tasks will dictate the relative advantage of multiple printers versus one super fast one.

The Network and Its Problems

This chapter discusses how the structure and functions of a network relate to printing. You will see a variety of solutions for sharing printers and their common problems. You will also learn about some of the network-related problems that arise, and ways to combat them. But what is a network and what can it do for your printing?

Laser printers and networks have always been closely associated. The reason for creating networks was to enable the sharing of costly resources such as the original laser printers. By linking all of the computers in an office or company together by wire, fiber-optic cable, or radio waves, users can communicate with each other and share the big expensive laser printer down the hall. This arrangement not only justifies the high cost of a laser printer, but also introduces the company and its employees to the joys of high resolution, plain paper printing.

After being hooked on network-installed printers, users wanted more fonts, more features, more speed, and more access. If every user was satisfied with sharing a Courier 10, 8 1/2-by-11-inch plain paper printer, most of the printing problems encountered with network installation would go away. However, each user in each department wants to use a different font and paper configuration which can lead to many problems.

Down the Wire

Most users are introduced to networks when they arrive at the office one morning only to discover a new wire dangling in the spiderweb of cables found behind their desktop computer. In some cases, it may have been there for weeks but remained unnoticed. If you were to take the case off of your computer and look inside, you would find the new wire attached to a thin board inserted in an expansion slot in the back. One day a company technician shoves a disk into your computer, copies some files, changes your CONFIG.SYS and AUTOEXEC.BAT files, whispers your new network sign-in name and password to you, and welcomes you to the network.

After a few timid forays into the network, you become emboldened and spend an entire afternoon looking at all of the new software and hardware features that have become available. You redirect your word processor to access the laser printer and its new fonts. You experiment with sending junk e-mail to your fellow employees. In general you become hooked on the power and features of the new network. After a while, though, you become concerned because some of your print jobs seem to disappear into thin air. Others defy your most fervent efforts to format them exactly right. Eventually, you find yourself wanting to know exactly what is happening on that wire between your computer and your network printer.

Physical Ports and Logical Ports

The first step in understanding networks and printers is to understand the concepts of logical ports, physical ports, redirectors, and print queues. First let's study logical and physical ports. When you look at the back of your computer, you will notice a number of plugs or sockets. One is connected to your monitor, a second is connected to a local printer if you have one, and a third may be connected to a modem or mouse. The specific configuration is unimportant. The important concept is that these are the physical ports on your computer.

Information sent to one of these physical ports will be transmitted through the wire conected to the port and the device at the other end. At least one of these ports usually has 25 holes and is called a parallel port. It is often attached to a local printer. When you turn on your computer, the initial start-up program—called the System BIOS— assigns this physical port a logical name—usually LPT1. Depending on your personal setup, you may have one or more parallel ports assigned to LPT1 though LPT3.

Alongside the parallel port or ports is another port with 9 or 25 pins. This is called a serial port and is usually assigned the logical port named COM1. In most cases, serial ports are used to communicate with modems and mice, but they are sometimes connected to a local printer. Some inexpensive networks use the serial port as the network interface.

To sum up the preceding discussion, the physical port is a plug on the back of the computer and the logical port equals a name—such as LPT1— that is the plug.

When you install a software package such as a word processor or spreadsheet program or an operating environment such as Microsoft Windows, you are prompted to tell the program what resources are available on your system and where they are located. For example, WordPerfect asks you what printer you have and to which logical port it is attached. When you have a local printer such as an IBM ProPrinter, you say IBM ProPrinter is attached to LPT1. This tells WordPerfect to use the printer control language or the print driver for ProPrinters, and to send print requests to LPT1. The same process is repeated for each software package, because you need to tell what printer is being used and to which logical port it is attached. Some programs, especially less expensive software or shareware, set the logical port to LPT1 by default.

Redirectors

When you print on a network, the printer is no longer physically attached to one of the physical ports on your computer. The network software must intercept print jobs and redirect them to the network printer. The software that performs this task is conveniently called the Printer Redirector. It is loaded on your computer when you start up the network software and sits in memory looking at one or more logical ports. When your application sends a print job to one of the monitored logical ports, the redirector intercepts it and sends it to a network printer. Networks can be configured in an endless number of ways with numerous types of redirectors. You will look at a few specific configurations later, but now you will follow a WordPerfect print job as it moves down the wire.

Spoolers and Queues

If you have used a software program in an operating environment such as Windows, you may have already been introduced to the concept of print spoolers. In essence, these utilities enable you to quickly generate a print job and return to your application. The spooler temporarily stores the print job as a file on disk then feeds it to your printer at the speed with which it can print it. In this way the spooler disassociates the high speed application from the slower speed printer, allowing the application to be more responsive. Network print queues are just sophisticated, multi-user spoolers. They not only temporarily store print jobs on disk, but automatically sequence multiple print jobs sent by many users according to priority, First-In-First-Out, or another logic. They even enable administrative control to put some jobs on hold, move another to the top of the queue, or cancel a job that was generated in error. The ability to control a print queue is usually restricted to the system administrator.

Print queues are assigned to individual logical ports by the redirector at the time you sign onto the network. They can be assigned for the entire company, or they may be assigned for each individual user. Without going into too much detail about network configurations—which change for each network hardware, software, and user installation—most network operating systems enable a unique user profile that is stored along with your access name and password. When you sign onto the network, your personal profile is used to set the printer redirectors to specific printer queues assigned to you. From that point on during your network session, any print job sent to a redirected logical port will be intercepted and sent to the queue assigned to that port. By assigning different queues to different ports, you can access different printers on the network by selecting different logical ports in your software application. For example, when you are assigned access to two printers: a LaserJet IIISi high-speed system printer on logical port LPT1 and an Apple LaserWriter IINTX PostScript printer on logical port LPT2, you can select between them just by selecting LPT1 or LPT2 in your application. Because they use different printer control languages—PCL5 and PostScript—you have to ensure that you changed the print driver as well.

Let's follow a particular print job from your application to hard copy. Suppose that you are writing a memo in WordPerfect and want to print it on the network's LaserJet IIISi. Before you begin to write your memo, you must establish three key settings. All of these may have been set by your network administrator, but you should understand how they were made. First, you must tell WordPerfect the manu-facturer's name and model number of the printer you will be using. This ensures that the application uses the correct print driver. In the example, you are using a LaserJet IIISi. Simply select the Printer Selection option and choose LaserJet IIISi. If the printer driver for the LaserJet IIISi has not been installed on your system's copy of WordPerfect, you would have to install it first.

Second, you must determine which logical port has been redirected to the desired LaserJet IIISi. These assignments are fixed by company policy. For example, LPT1 = Local Printer, LPT2 = Departmental Printer and LPT3 = System Printer. When you need to make a change, you usually depend on your network administrator. Suppose that the desired printer is assigned to logical port LPT2 for your workstation. You must ensure that WordPerfect also assigns the selected printer to logical port LPT2. You need to choose the Printer Selection option and select Edit to change the printer installation to LPT2. Start your print job and watch it print on the LaserJet IIISi. If you have more than one

Hewlett-Packard LaserJet III on the network, you would be able to distinguish them by assigning them to different logical ports and then setting up each instance as a separate printer in WordPerfect. You use the same LaserJet III driver, but assign each to different logical ports.

Installation Considerations

Whenever two network engineers or administrators get together, they discuss protocols, hardware, software, and comparative topologies. Fortunately, you do not need to understand much more than has been discussed to get your laser printer to work for you. There are, however, a couple of more generalized issues that may concern you. For example, what is the best mix of laser printers for my installation? Should I also retain local dot-matrix printers? Do I need several small printers or one high-speed one? How many fonts are enough? How much memory should I install on each printer? Can I mix PCL and PostScript on the same network?

Unfortunately most of the answers to these and a thousand additional questions are the same—it depends on the circumstances. For example, the question of how many and what size laser printers to purchase is based not only on the number of users, but such issues as the physical distance between workstations, time-sensitivity, confidentiality of the documents, and special printing requirements—letterhead, large format, PostScript or other page description language, and so on.

Diversity is an asset as long as all of the printers have some minimum level of commonality. For example, it is great to provide PostScript capability to one printer on a network that is otherwise PCL based, but not when that means giving up PCL capability. You would be better off buying a PCL printer and adding the optional PostScript functions, thereby assuring a minimum PCL capability for all printers. However, if all of your printers are PostScript capable, this point is moot. Mix and match capabilities. One high-speed printer centrally located with several cheaper, slower printers dispersed around the office is better than two high-speed, centrally located printers. You will quickly learn to route quick jobs to the convenient local printer and longer jobs to the higher-speed printer.

Multiple Low Cost Laser Printers

As the cost of laser printers has come down, the need to use networks to share a single high-speed, expensive printer has been reduced as well. Now, many networks provide local laser printers for every two or three employees. The use of multiple smaller, less-expensive printers instead of one high-speed central printer has several additional beneficial effects.

First, the physical location of printers can be spread out so that they are closer to their users. Second, because printing correspondence is the most common use for such printers in an office situation, your time-critical letter won't get hung up behind a big report for the finance department. Third, because the printers are nearby, you can monitor them easily when printing reports. Finally, multiple low cost printers provide their own backup. On networks that depend on a single high-speed printer, the loss of that printer effectively shuts down the network. In the case of multiple low cost laser printers, you can simply redirect the job queue of the faulty printer to another printer.

Cheap Networks—Printer Sharing Devices

Rather than spend the thousands of dollars required for a full network system installation, you can reap the benefits of a network by adding an intelligent printer sharing device. While these devices do not provide e-mail or facilitate data sharing as a full network would, they do provide limited device sharing at a fraction of the cost. For example, you could share a laser printer between three or four users located near one another and the printer with a simple parallel port, four-way switch. However, beware of mechanical unbuffered switches because they may damage the printer; intelligent switches or buffered switches protect the printer from the electronic pulses associated with the mechanical switch. To set up more or widely separated users—parallel cables are generally limited to 10–15 feet in most environments—you can either use a serial switch box or purchase an intelligent printer sharing device with a high-speed interface and built-in spooling functions (see product reviews in Appendix C).

Direct Connect Network Cards

Many networks are now accepting direct connection printer network cards. These cards fit into the expansion port of the laser printer or attach to the serial or parallel port and connect directly to the network wiring without an intervening PC. The card contains the necessary processor and software to talk directly to the network and the interface to talk to the printer. The key advantage of these cards is that they are less expensive than purchasing a full blown PC to act as a remote printer server. In addition, they do not draw on the workstation resources of a PC that is serving as a workstation and a printer server. Finally, cards that use the option I/O port of the printer or are integrated into the printer design are much faster than a PC-based server or other cards that depend on the serial or parallel port for the interface to the printer. One caveat—because the card must contain hardware and software logic for talking to a specific network—is, by definition, network specific. You must ensure that you purchase a card that is hardware and software compatible with your network.

Impact of PJL and NPAP Print Job Control Languages

With the release of the LaserJet 4, Hewlett-Packard has introduced a new higher-level printer language called Printer Job Language or PJL (see Chapter 12). At the same time the Network Printing Alliance has promulgated its own standard for a job control protocol called, appropriately, the Network Printing Alliance Protocol or NPAP. In both cases, these languages/protocols enable the network and the printer to communicate about specific print jobs and the status of the printer. This enables the network and the printer to work more cooperatively. For example, without PJL or NPAP when the printer is out of paper, the queue simply backs up until someone notices that his or her job has not been printed. With PJL or NPAP, the printer can call for help by notifying the network that it is out of paper. After network software becomes PJL or NPAP cognizant, it will be able to forward such a message to someone responsible for filling the paper tray. Another use for PJL or NPAP is to automatically switch between different printer command or page description languages. Unfortunately without PJL or NPAP, it is easy to send a PostScript job to a printer configured for PCL with frustrating or comical results depending on your deadline.

Common Problems and Suggestions

The following discussion covers some common problems you will encounter and how to deal with them.

Print Job Collisions

The most common network printer problems fall under the title of job collision. Although most network operating systems do a good job of keeping one job from printing on top of another, minor problems continue to surface. The two most common problems are printing with the wrong font and printing on the wrong paper. These result from similar causes—a failure to set or reset the printer's environment before or after printing with a special font or paper. Although current production software applications that have been developed for network environments work well setting and resetting the default printer environment some older applications, and especially applications intended for single-user environments, often fail to properly avoid this problem. The solution to setting and resetting the default printer environment is to ensure that your software issues a printer reset before and after each print job. By issuing a reset before beginning a print job, you can be sure that your subsequent commands will act upon a standard starting environment. Likewise by issuing a reset at the end of the print job, you are just being polite to the print job following yours.

Because most current software provide these services automatically, why do you care? In most cases, you don't; but when your next print job comes out in landscape compressed on letterhead, at least you will know why. If it occurs frequently, either add a printer reset command (Esc E in PCL5) to the start of your print job or determine which application printed before yours and add a reset to the end of its print job.

Lost Print Jobs

How often have you started a print request and then waited forever for it to print and nothing happens? This is especially frustrating when the same software works 90 percent of the time but every once in a while goes off again—what happened?

Most *Lost Print Jobs* are misdirected print jobs. When your network has multiple printers and multiple print queues, it is quite probable that your lost job is sitting in the output bin of another printer. There are several potential causes for such misdirection. First, each network establishes certain default print queues for the system and for the individual user. In addition, each application can be set to a default printer. Finally, it is possible for you to set an individual printer selection for your use of a particular application. As you can imagine, the permutation and combinations of defaults and overrides are endless. Each network and even each application will use a different strategy for setting printer defaults. Although this does not pose a problem after the system is properly set up, it can result in confusion when one of the defaults is intentionally or accidently changed.

Here are some specific examples of how these defaults can become confused. WordPerfect requires that you set up print drivers for all possible printers and ports on the network system. In addition, the system administrator selects a default printer and logical port from among those installed to be used by all new users of WordPerfect. When you sign into WordPerfect, you create your own user profile. Initially, it is the same as the default profile, including the default printer and port. You can change your default printer or port selection in your individual profile, and WordPerfect will recall it each time you start up. WordPerfect stores your personal selections in a file identified with your sign-in name. The missing print job problem arises when you accidently misspell your sign-in name when you start up WordPerfect. Rather than report a sign-in error, WordPerfect creates a new profile for you under your *new* name, again copying the system defaults. If you had previously changed your default printer, it has now been reset to the system default in your *new* profile. When you go to print your document, it won't appear at your regular printer but will be redirected to the system default printer instead. Thus, simply misspelling a sign-in name can cause a print job to run amuck.

Another major cause of lost print jobs is a blocked queue. When the printer is halted due to a paper jam, lack of paper, or simply a missing page eject on the last page of a print job, the printer will wait until it is fixed, leaving the rest of the print requests to pile up in the queue. In some instances, all it takes is an accidental PrintScreen to block a queue. Because a PrintScreen is only 25 lines long, it does not fill a page, and therefore does not generate a page eject. Because the laser printer is a page printer and will wait for a full page before printing, it will sit with its Form Feed light on waiting for the rest of the page. Because the queue is waiting for the signal that the current job is finished before sending the next, it too is waiting. Meanwhile, all the new print requests are piling up on disk. When you must use PrintScreens, make sure you provide a method for generating the final page eject, by adding one to the print job trailer specification for the network or by providing a simple batch program for echoing a Form Feed to the printer—for example,ECHO _>LPT? where _ is ASCII 12, the Form Feed command, created by holding the ALT key while typing 12 on the numeric keypad. Some older versions of Lotus 1-2-3 and other software also failed to generate the final page eject required by laser printers, and so, they too need to be explicitly ejected to prevent them from blocking the queue.

Incompatible Printer Configuration Problems

Many networks include several laser printers located throughout the office. Often individual users have the option of selecting a high-speed laser printer located centrally or a smaller, slower printer located in their own department. Very often, print jobs that print perfectly on the central printer won't print correctly on the local printer. Why? There are several possibilities, but they all come down to the laser printers having different configurations. They either have different amounts of user accessible memory, different soft fonts downloaded, or they have different font cartridges/language add-ons inserted. The problem is that such differences are often hard to determine. You can check the two printers to see if they have the same cartridges installed, but how do you check memory without opening up the printer? Or, how do you determine which fonts are supported by each printer? Fortunately, there is an easy solution with most printers. For example, all of the Hewlett-Packard LaserJets provide two simple printouts that show both items. The printer self-test—accessed by pressing and holding the Test button on LaserJet IIIs and earlier models, or by selecting the Self-Test item from the Test menu on the LaserJet 4— shows how much memory is installed in the printer as well as other interesting items. The list and samples of available fonts can be generated by selecting the Type List from the Test menu on the LaserJet 4 or by pressing and releasing the Test button on previous models.

Printer Generates Pages of Command Codes

There are two common laser printer command or page description languages, PCL by Hewlett-Packard and PostScript by Adobe. As you might expect, they are incompatible. At one time you could distinguish between PostScript and PCL printers by manufacturer—when the label said Apple, it was PostScript—when the label said Hewlett-Packard , it was PCL. However, now there are many other manufacturers of laser printers that support PCL and PostScript on the same machine or can have PostScript capability added by inserting a card or cartridge. Even Hewlett-Packard has joined the PostScript bandwagon with the Hewlett-Packard LaserJet 4M, which has PCL and PostScript built-in. Getting back to the generating code problem, when you send PostScript commands to a PCL printer, the printer does not recognize them as commands and prints the command text as if it were your next report. Likewise, sending PCL codes to a PostScript printer will generate spurious printing, although much less prolific and much less intelligible—at best raw PCL codes look like a bad foreign spy novel.

There are several approaches to fixing the problem of sending the wrong codes. The first step is to determine which codes you need to send for the printer on which you intend to print. If you are sending the wrong codes, change your print driver (select the proper printer) in your application and try again.

When the printer supports both languages, the problem becomes more involved, because different printers use different systems for switching between the two languages. With some of the older cartridge-based, PostScript add-ons, you need to turn the printer off, remove the cartridge, and turn the printer back on to switch between PostScript and PCL, reversing the process to switch back again. Some intermediate-level printers and PostScript add-on products enable you to switch by pressing a special menu panel key combination. Current multiple language printers and add-on products are more intelligent about the whole process, enabling you—or your software—to tell the printer what language is coming with the next print job. The LaserJet 4 introduces the Printer Job Language (PJL) (see Chapter 12) to perform this function. Finally, many printers such as the LaserJet 4 can also perform their own analysis of the print job, by sensing the appropriate language and processing the request accordingly. They look at the incoming printer codes and pose the question—Does this make more sense if I read these as PCL codes or PostScript codes?—selecting the best option before processing the code.

Fixing the spurious printing will depend on how your printer selects the appropriate control language. If you can proceed, you print request with an explicit language selection command such as the PJL:

```
@PJL ENTER LANGUAGE = PCL
```

or

```
@PJL ENTER LANGUAGE = POSTSCRIPT
```

If you must perform a manual switch, you are better off funnelling all print jobs of a particular type into individual queues. This will enable you to explicitly switch between queues as you manually switch the printer's language mode.

Queue Management Problems

Most networks enable the system administrator to control jobs waiting within a queue and to switch printers from one queue to another. By mixing and matching queues to specific priorities and needs, you can develop a level of control appropriate to your needs. For example, when you have large jobs or jobs that require special setup, you can route them to a holding queue that is not normally directed to an active printer. Only after the selected printer is properly prepared or other demand is low (after hours) is the holding queue redirected to an active printer.

When a print job has been interrupted because of paper jams or other printer/queue-sensitive errors, most networks and printers are able to recover by themselves simply by reprinting the damaged or missing pages. On the other hand, if a job has executed in error, using the wrong font or printing on the wrong paper, all is not lost. Most networks enable a limited time to cancel and reprint a particular job, only deleting the print job from disk after the deletion delay period has expired. This time limit is controlled by the system software and your system administrator. When you experience repeated printer problems, you may want to set the print job deletion time to a high number—over 30 minutes. After you have resolved the problems and your printer queues are being processed correctly, you can reset the delete time to a shorter time—3 to 5 minutes.

Single Print Jobs That Are Split into Multiple Jobs

Most networks use a timing-based logic for determining when a particular print job is complete and ready to send on to the designated print queue. When a software application starts to print a particular job to the designated port, it proceeds smoothly until it is complete, at which time it stops transmitting. The network software looks for the end of continuous transmission to determine the end of the print job. The time that a particular network waits before determining that the end has arrived is set by the system administrator and generally ranges from 3 to 10 seconds. But what if your particular print request is full of stops and starts. For example suppose that you are printing a report that needs to search a large database. When it takes more than the established wait-time for the database software to find the next record, the network sees the delay as the end of the print job and spools the unfinished report off to the print queue. When the next record is found and printed, it is perceived as the beginning of the next print job. The best way to deal with this problem is to reset the printer time-out to a higher figure for those programs that experience such stops and starts. It is possible to set and reset the time-out setting from each workstation, (see Chapter 3 for information about resetting the time-out). Make sure you reset the time-out setting to the default when the problematic program or report is finished.

Home versus Office Printing

Many workers who have come to rely on computers at the office have also discovered that they can get a lot of office work done at home on their personal computer. The only problem is that they have a dot-matrix printer at home instead of the high-quality laser printer at the office. The documents that they have composed at home just don't print the same at the office as they appeared at home. The primary cause of this problem is that the home printer does not support the same fonts that are used on the laser printer at the office. When you set the print drivers for your software to the home printer, you are limited to the fonts and formats available on that printer. This problem is especially bad when you are working with desktop publishing programs with WYSIWYG displays. The document appears correctly formatted at home only to revert to garbage when printed at the office. The simplest solution to this dilemma is to install the same print drivers at home as you use at the office. You also need to install any soft fonts that you plan to use on both machines. Many software companies now enable you to install your software on your home and office computers so long as you never use both simultaneously. Make sure you check your licensing agreements to verify this feature. Because you don't really have a laser printer at home, you can not print the final copy there, but you can correctly format the document and then carry it by disk or transmit it by modem to your office for printing.

PART III

Problem Solving

The Laser Printer Troubleshooting Guide

When you select the right paper as described in Chapter 4 and take care of your printer on a routine basis as described in Chapter 5, chances are that you won't encounter a hardware problem for 100,000 copies. Nevertheless, there are certain conditions that you may encounter after the initial setup and in your day-to-day use of the machine. This chapter identifies the most common problems you will encounter. In each case you are provided with one or more checkpoints. The checkpoints start with the simplest remedies that you can do and work up to the point where you should call your manufacturer for assistance.

Printer Power Problems

If the lights do not glow when you flip the rocker switch to on, and no noise emanates from the printer, use the following checklist:

1. Make sure the printer is connected to a functioning wall outlet. Check the circuit breaker and/or try plugging another device such as a table lamp into the outlet to confirm that the outlet is working.

2. Is the printer plugged into a surge suppressor (which it should be) and, if the surge suppressor has an on/off switch, is the switch on? If the surge suppression circuit has tripped, have you reset it? Also, surge suppressors can wear out. As their protection devices perform their essential functions, they actually deteriorate. Eventually, a surge suppressor that is valiantly protecting your equipment in an environment with a high potential for electrical problems will give up the ghost. Try bypassing the surge protector to see if it has died to save your hardware. If it has, replace it because you clearly need its protection.

3. Is the power cord fully seated in the receptacle located at the back of the printer? As you move your printer or other equipment, you can slowly work the power cord loose. It may not fail immediately, or it may take several weeks to lose contact. When it does, you will have a dead printer on your hands.

4. When the printer still won't power up after you have completed steps one through three, call your dealer. The printer has an internal fuse that provides a last line of defense against circuit overloads. This fuse might be blown and it is not user-accessible.

Printer Output Problems

Three basic situations need to be addressed in regard to a seemingly *live* printer that refuses to print:

➤ A new printer has just been installed.

➤ A printer appears to have gone on strike after weeks or months of flawless operation.

➤ A printer prints from DOS but won't print from an application program.

Each of these situations is discussed below.

A Newly Installed Printer

1. Make sure the printer is on-line. The printer cannot accept characters from the computer unless it is on-line. Press the On-Line button. The light above the On-Line button should glow steadily.

2. Do a screen print. The acid test of whether your computer is successfully transmitting data to your printer is to do a screen print from DOS by simultaneously pressing the SHIFT and Print Screen keys. The screen print utility is one of the lowest level print commands, sending data directly from the computer's RAM memory to the printer via LPT1:. By using this utility as a test, you will eliminate most other potential computer problems from your test. When you can see something on the screen while in DOS—such as a directory listing—you should be able to print it with the screen print utility. When you cannot, the problem is one of the following: the printer, the connection to the computer, the port assignments on the computer, or a missing or incorrect mode command.

When data is going from the computer to the printer, the light above the Form Feed key will glow steadily. Because a screenful of data does not constitute a full page of data, and a LaserJet III printer will not begin printing until a full page of data is in its buffer, you will have to issue a manual eject. You can do this by pressing the On-Line button to take the printer off-line, and then pressing the Form Feed button. This will start the printing process and eject the page. Don't forget to put the printer back on-line!

When you can successfully carry out a screen print but cannot print from your application program, make sure that you have properly installed the program and have selected the right drivers for the laser printer. If there are no drivers for the make and model of your printer, you can generally use the driver for the LaserJet Series II for PCL-based printers, the Apple LaserWriter for PostScript printers, or select *Unlisted* or *Standard* printer during the installation procedure. To change fonts or use page formatting features, you will have to enter change commands manually as described in Chapter 14.

3. Do a self-test. As described in Chapter 3, most laser printers have a built-in self-test that checks key functions of the imaging system. When the printout from the self-test is successful, you can be assured that the imaging system is working properly.

4. Make sure the computer and printer have the same interface. When you are using a parallel cable, is your laser printer menu

set for parallel (see Chapter 3)? When you are in serial mode, make sure that the following commands are in your AUTOEXEC.BAT file:

```
MODE COM1:9600,N,8,1,P

MODE COM1: = LPT1:
```

When you are using COM2: or COM3:, substitute their names for COM1: in the example. When you are using a parallel interface, you can include the following optional MODE command:

```
MODE LPT1:,,P
```

WARNING

Make sure that the file MODE.COM is in your root directory. When it is located in another directory, make sure that the directory is included in the path in your AUTOEXEC.BAT file.

Cables

If the printer still doesn't do a screen print, try a different cable. Printer cables, especially serial printer cables, have many differences. Cables manufactured for use with one serial printer often will not work with others. Even cables complying with the same standard, such as RS-232, can be legitimately different. When you want to make your own cable or purchase one from a source other than your printer's manufacturer, make sure that the pin configurations correspond to the requirements specified in the user's manual. (See also the following discussion regarding crossed and straight-through serial printer cables.)

When a new cable does not solve the problem, you may have a defective port on your computer or laser printer. Either way, contact your dealer or local computer repair center for recommendations.

A Previously Installed Printer

1. Check what has changed. When a laser printer has been operating properly for a period of time and then suddenly does not

print, either a malfunction has occurred, or the printer's environment has been changed. In corporate settings, people from the data processing or MIS department are often responsible for setting up and maintaining microcomputers; a user is sometimes surprised when he or she walks into the office one morning and finds altered equipment. If that is how things work in your company, check for the following:

➤ Has someone added another printer or plotter and changed the port to which the laser printer is connected? If so, have your MODE commands and software also been changed? Correct them if necessary.

➤ Has a switch box been added? If so, make sure that you are actually selecting the LaserJet III printer when you turn the switch dial or press the switch button. Trace the cables if necessary.

➤ Also, when you are using a serial cable, make sure that the cable from the computer to the switch box is straight-through and the cable from the switch box to the printer is crossed. The serial cable for most laser printers has a special pin configuration. Pins 2 and 3 are crossed in the cable. That is, the signal entering the cable on pin 2 goes out on pin 3 and vice versa. This is a relatively common practice with computer cables, because pin 2 is designated for transmitting data and pin 3 is designated for receiving. Somewhere in the connection between the computer and the printer, the system needs to connect the computer's *mouth* with the printer's *ear*. This is usually done by crossing the wires in the connecting cable. When you don't use a crossed cable, your computer is, in effect, shouting into your printer's mouth and this causes a communications problem.

➤ When you add a switch box to an existing system, you will need two cables: one from the computer to the switch box and one from the box to the printer. There may be other cables attached to other computers and other printers as well, but concentrate on the two required for your connection. When both cables cross pins 2 and 3, they will undo each other and the desired cross-over will be lost. You must ensure that only one of the two cables is crossed while the other is straight-through—2 to 2 and 3 to 3. Because other printers connected to the switch box may not require a crossed cable, it is best for you to use the crossed cable between the switch box and the laser printer, and to use the straight-through cable between the computer and the box.

➤ To isolate the switchbox, try connecting your laser printer directly into your computer using the crossed pin cable. If the printer works correctly without the switchbox, either the cabling between the switchbox and computer is incorrect, or the switchbox is defective.

➤ Has your serial MODE command been deleted? If a new software package has been installed on your computer, a new AUTOEXEC.BAT file also might have been installed, overwriting your existing AUTOEXEC.BAT file. Because the old AUTOEXEC.BAT file contained information needed to run your laser printer as a serial printer, your computer will not know where to transmit print output.

➤ A related problem occurs when the *PATH* command in your AUTOEXEC.BAT file has been deleted or altered. The path command tells the computer, If you cannot find the file you are looking for here, search for it in directory X. For example, say your AUTOEXEC.BAT file has the following lines:

```
PATH=C:\DOS
MODE COM1:9600,N,8,1,P
```

➤ Also, say that your MODE command program (MODE.COM) resides in a directory called *DOS*. When the computer boots up in the C drive, it will look for the file called MODE.COM, so that it can output printer data serially through the port called COM1:. Even though MODE.COM is located elsewhere—in the directory called *DOS* rather than in the root—the system will know where to find it because of the PATH command. When the PATH command is accidentally or intentionally removed, however, the system will be unable to find MODE.COM and will display the following line:

```
Bad command or file name
```

➤ Consequently, the printer output will not be directed to COM1: and your printer will not print.

NOTE

Some application software packages contain their own printer re-direct command that allows you to specify the COM port used by your printer when you install the software. Although these programs do not require a MODE command, the command will not interfere with them and may be required by other applications.

➤ When you do need to alter your AUTOEXEC.BAT file (see Chapter 2 for modifying batch files), run it as *hot* to test it. Make sure that you are in the root directory—where the AUTOEXEC.BAT file must reside. Type the following and press Enter.

```
AUTOEXEC.
```

➤ This will run all of the commands from the AUTOEXEC.BAT file without rebooting the system, and will enable you to isolate problems specifically within the AUTOEXEC.BAT file. If the system responds with one of the following lines,when the MODE command line is executed from the AUTOEXEC.BAT file, reedit it according to the method described in Chapter 2 (misspellings, missing punctuation marks, or impossible parameters, such as COM42:, will cause such error messages).

```
Bad command or file name
Illegal device name
Invalid parameters
```

➤ Has new hardware been added or changed? Many different devices compete for the limited number of external interfaces on a PC. If you have added an internal modem or a mouse, they may be competing with your printer for one of the ports. Specifically, modems and mice generally use serial ports. Most come from the factory configured for COM1:. When you or a colleague have added such a device and changed your old COM1: to COM2: (intentionally or accidentally) you might be sending your print jobs down the phone line or through your mouses's tail. Check to see which port your printer is listening to and reset the MODE command in your AUTOEXEC.BAT accordingly.

2. Make sure the cables are fully plugged in and screwed down. If your laser printer has been moved recently, the cables might not have been fully plugged in and fastened with the seating bolts. When the cable is not plugged in all the way, your laser printer may not print. All cables should be bolted down to make sure they stay put.

3. Analyze the printer as if it were new. When the preceding steps, one and two, have been unsuccessful, run through steps one, two, and three of the troubleshooting procedure for new printers. If those fail, contact your dealer.

Cannot Print from Software, but Can Print from DOS

Check your software installation. Does your software support a LaserJet4 printer? If so, there's probably an installation process during which you can indicate the make and model of your printer. A common problem is that people who have been using a dot-matrix printer purchase a laser printer but forget to inform the software that they have changed printers. Reinstall the software or, if the software enables you to, just change the printer driver selection. When the hardware is correctly set up, you should be able to print.

Font Problems

The most exciting part of using a laser printer is using different fonts to convey different looks and feelings for various types of communications. Unfortunately, getting the printer to actually print a desired font can be tricky. The following suggestions should help you resolve problems when using cartridges or soft fonts.

Fonts on a Cartridge Don't Print

1. Enter the proper PCL codes or select the font with your software. Merely inserting a font cartridge into a cartridge socket will not cause the printer to change from the default Courier typeface. You must enter either a PCL code (see Chapters 14 and 15) or otherwise instruct your software to access the desired font. The latter usually requires a setup procedure during which you tell the software which cartridge you are using. If the software supports your font cartridge(s), it will also provide a means for inserting the font change in your print output.

2. Make sure the cartridges are fully inserted. When you first insert the cartridge, you'll feel a point where the cartridge seems to stop. That's only the point at which the contacts of the plug inside the cartridge have met the contacts of the printer. Keep pushing until you hear and feel a solid click. At that point, the cartridge will be properly seated.

NOTE

Be sure to take the printer off-line by pressing the On-Line button before inserting or removing a font cartridge; otherwise, you will get an FE CARTRIDGE error, indicating that the printer has detected a cartridge change while it was on-line. If that happens, there is no way to clear the error, and you must power the printer off. Wait five seconds, and then turn the printer on again. With the PostScript cartridge, turn the power off before inserting it. This is critical to avoid possible damage to the cartridge's electronic components.

3. Run a print fonts test. Initiate a font printout as described in Chapter 3. This will show all fonts of the cartridge(s) plugged into the printer. If the printout does not show the fonts on a cartridge, the cartridge may not be fully inserted, or the cartridge may be defective. The latter is very unlikely, however, as only a

very small percentage of cartridges have had to be replaced over the last five years. Moreover, a defective cartridge generally isn't totally dead; rather, it will have problems such as a missing or shifted dot above the letter "i" or characters that print askew. When you have a defective cartridge call your dealer.

Soft Fonts Won't Print

1. Install your software drivers for soft fonts. As with cartridge-based fonts, you must inform your printer that you are using soft fonts with your laser printer. If there are no printer drivers for the situation, you will have to load the soft fonts manually before you run your application (see the following discussion on downloading).

2. Download the fonts. Just copying a soft font to the directory where your application software resides won't enable you to access the fonts. Nor can you just copy a soft font directly to your printer using the DOS COPY command without first alerting the printer via the proper PCL command. Your application software must be able to recognize the presence of the soft font and provide a means for downloading and using it with your data.

   With WordPerfect 5.1, for example, you must inform the program about which fonts are available and where they are located. This is done by editing your printer definition(s). Select Shift-F7, Select Printer, and Edit. Select item #6 to indicate the location of the fonts (drive and directory), and item #4 to inform WordPerfect about the fonts you intend to use. Designate infrequently used fonts with a plus sign. This indicates that they are temporary fonts and will be downloaded (i.e., copied) as needed from your hard disk to your printer. Mark fonts that you will use frequently with an asterisk, indicating that they will be downloaded from the computer and stored in the printer. Such downloaded fonts are called permanent fonts because they remain in your printer's memory for as long as the printer is powered on. Once you make your selection, you must initialize the printer by pressing Shift-F7, option 7. This will copy the fonts marked with an asterisk from the font directory to the printer's memory, where they will be available for use during the current printing session.

NOTE

While the initialization process may take some time, it only needs to be performed once during a computing session. Once the fonts are downloaded, the actual printing process moves quite quickly. On the other hand, fonts marked with a plus sign will be downloaded each time they are needed, which may considerably slow down the printing process. When your software does not provide a way for automatically downloading the soft font from your computer disk to your printer, you must manually download the font or use a utility program, as described in Chapter 14.

3. Check the flashing green READY light. When a font appears to be downloaded, but is not coming up on the font print out, it may not have been transmitted from the computer in its entirety. If the READY light only flashed for a second or two, you probably don't have the whole font, indicating that the downloading was unsuccessful. Remember, the only sure proof you have that the font is in the printer is whether it prints out in the font test.

Paper Path Problems

Under the right circumstances, your laser printer will output thousands of pages without a single jam or multiple feed (more than one sheet of paper enters the printer, causing a jam). The most likely causes of jams and multiple feeds are described as follows.

Paper Jams or Misfeeds

1. Check to make sure the fuser roller shipping spacers have been removed if the machine is new. Your printer is shipped with a variety of packing materials that prevent delicate parts from getting damaged. Two green plastic spacers keep the fuser roller from rotating while the printer is in transit (refer to Chapter 2). If left in, they will block the paper path and cause the paper to jam. Remove the spacers and try again.

2. Make sure the paper tray isn't overloaded. The paper tray should never be filled above the white plastic retaining clips. Otherwise jams will result.

3. Use the right paper. Selecting the right paper is critical to the smooth operation of your laser printer, regardless of the model. The printer will run most smoothly with xerographic paper. With the exception of a few brands, cotton bond papers will give the worst image quality and cause the most jams. Also, paper that is under the minimum weight (16 pounds) or above the maximum (36 pounds) will likely crease or catch on the paper transport mechanisms, causing jams. Switch to a recommended stock, as discussed in Chapter 4.

4. Store your paper properly. Any paper can jam in the printer if it is too dry. The reason is that the lower the humidity, the greater the static electricity. Increased static electricity not only affects the image quality (see below) but can also cause two or more sheets of paper to stick together as the top sheet in the paper tray passes into the printer.

   Similarly, but for the opposite reason, high humidity can lead to poor imaging and jams. When paper contains a great deal of water, its ability to hold a uniform electrical charge decreases, and it is more likely to curl when it is instantly dried while passing through the 400 degrees Fahrenheit fuser assembly. The greater the curl, the greater the likelihood of jamming. This is especially true with the new Hewlett-Packard LaserJet 4.

   To minimize the effects of moisture, store your paper in a place that has average humidity. Also, reseal reams after you open them. In areas of extremely high or low humidity, do not leave the paper in the tray overnight. If the paper is stored in a different location from the printer, allow it to reach room temperature before using it. This is necessary to prevent condensation from forming on the paper.

5. Remove the top and bottom sheets from a ream. Always remove the top and bottom few sheets from a new ream of paper. These are the most likely sheets to have been creased from normal storage.

6. Don't fan the paper or envelopes as you put them into the tray. It seems natural to fan the paper before inserting it into the tray to loosen it up and keep the sheets from sticking together. The fact is, fanning the paper can generate an unwanted static charge and introduce air pockets that can cause sheets of paper to bulge slightly and misalign themselves while entering the registration stage of the paper path.

Paper Curls after Printing

Curling is usually a problem with high quality cotton bond. Since the paper is rich in cotton fibers, it absorbs more moisture than low fiber (xerographic bond) paper. As the cotton paper passes through the fusing assembly, it is subjected to high heat in the fusing assembly (400 degrees Fahrenheit) and curls in the same fashion as heated hair rollers curl hair.

The ultimate solution is to switch to a xerographic bond paper or one of the cotton bond papers recommended by the printer manufacturer. If, however, you have just ordered 50,000 sheets of your letterhead on fine cotton bond, you might try using a dehumidifier to reduce the moisture in the air. The tradeoff though, is that if the humidity drops low enough, static electricity will increase, and you may see a reduction in image quality and an increase in multiple paper feeds.

Paper Emerges from the Printer with Indentations

Let the paper sit for a few moments. The laser printers using the Canon SX engine have six plastic rollers located at the paper exit. When the paper emerges, it is spongy because of the heat treatment in the fuser assembly, and the rollers leave an indentation. This is more noticeable with high quality cotton bond papers than with xerographic papers, because the cotton bond papers are thicker and the roller indentations are deeper. The paper will normally fluff up and return to a smooth state once it cools down. Cotton bond papers may take slightly longer than xerographic bond papers because of their bulk.

Envelopes Jam in the Envelope Tray

1. Make sure the tray is not overloaded. The tray can accommodate up to 15 normal weight envelopes. If you cram in any more, jams will likely result because of this bulk.

2. Make sure the envelopes are in good condition, and the edges are crisp. Any paper fed into the printer should have good clean edges. With envelopes, the edge condition is critical. If the edges are even slightly bent or ragged, jams will occur. When an envelope jams, never try running it through the printer again. To ensure that the edge catches in the registration rollers, crease the front edge of the envelopes before you load them into the envelop tray.

3. Make sure the envelopes are aligned with the felt strip in the envelope tray. When the envelopes extend beyond the black felt strip and touch the plastic tray, jams will occur. The envelopes should be separated from the plastic tray by an eighth of an inch to ensure proper feeding.

Envelopes Have Excessive Curl

Open the rear exit door if available. When the rear door is open, the envelope will travel along a straight path (see Figure 9.1). This greatly reduces curling problems.

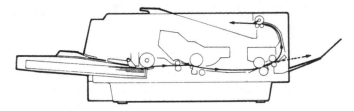

Figure 9.1. A straight paper path.

Envelopes or Odd-Sized Paper Won't Feed Manually

Make sure the envelope is inserted all the way into the feed slot. The manual paper feed mechanism pulls the envelope into the registration assembly. When the paper is not inserted far enough, it will not be grabbed by the rollers and fed into the printer.

Image Quality Problems

There are a variety of problems that can degrade the images that your laser printer produces, from streaking to poor definition or *dirty backgrounds*. Most imaging problems are caused by using the wrong kind of paper or by a buildup of cotton dust from cotton bond papers, which is a later-stage problem. The most common types of image quality problems are discussed in the following section.

Page Prints Blank

1. Make sure the toner cartridge is not empty. When a toner cartridge runs out of toner, and none can be shaken free by rocking it as described in Chapter 6, the images will gradually fade until nothing appears on the pages. The toner cartridge is the first problem area to check when the pages come up blank.

2. Check to see if the tape has been pulled out of the EP cartridge. As explained in Chapter 6, the EP cartridge is shipped with a piece of clear tape that separates the toner and the drum during shipping. When the tape is not removed, no toner can reach the drum and get transferred to the paper.

3. Make sure the transfer corona wire is clean and intact. When the transfer corona wire is obstructed or broken, no charge is administered to the paper and the paper will not be able to attract the negatively charged toner particles. Clean the wire with a cotton swab and try printing again. If the wire is broken, call a service representative because this is not a do-it-yourself fix.

4. Try another EP toner cartridge. The EP cartridge contains numerous moving and electrical parts. When any of these fail, the electrical image may never form on the drum. If a different cartridge operates correctly, return the defective one to your dealer.

5. Get authorized service. When tests 1 through 4 fail to produce an image, your printer has a drum, laser, or other serious problem that requires dealer service.

Page Has Gray Background

Switch papers or humidify the room. A gray cast is technically called *background* and is most likely to occur with cotton bond papers during a period of low humidity. With the drop in humidity, static electricity increases and causes toner to stick in inappropriate places on the drum and paper. Xerographic bond papers are less likely to be affected by the drop in humidity because they have a lower fiber content than cotton bond paper. Another alternative is to maintain the humidity of the room and storage areas at a normal level by means of a humidifier.

Page Has Smudged Band and Overprinted Area

Get authorized service. Paper is not properly advancing through your printer and the feed roller may need replacement. Call for service.

Page Prints Solid Black

1. Exchange your cartridge. When the primary corona wire in your EP cartridge is broken or defective, no charge will be applied to the drum. As a result, the toner will be attracted to all areas of the drum, instead of only those areas that have been discharged by the laser beam in a pattern corresponding to the page image.

2. Get authorized service. When a new cartridge still prints black, you probably have a hardware problem and should contact your dealer. A problem that the service representative would look for is with the laser beam controller. If the laser beam was on all the time, the entire drum would be discharged by the beam and attract toner producing a solid black page.

Page Has Horizontal Black Lines

1. Try another brand of paper. As explained in Chapter 4, the electrical properties vary from paper brand to brand, and can

vary for batches of the same brand purchased at different times. The problem may vanish when you use another stock.

2. Dealer Service. When the problem continues with all stocks, contact your dealer because the imaging assembly may need service. Note any errors displayed by the printer.

Black Stripe on the Right Side

Clean the primary corona wire. Use the brush supplied with your laser printer to clean the primary corona wire. (See Chapter 5.)

Black Pages with Horizontal White Stripes

Get authorized service. Most likely, the fiber-optic cable, the laser scanning assembly, or the laser controller is operating improperly. This requires a service call.

Parts of Page Have Faint Print

Change papers or dehumidify the room. An oblong area of faint print is called *drop out* and is caused by the use of cotton bonds during periods of high humidity. The humidity tends to get trapped in the cotton fibers, so that in some areas the toner won't properly absorb into the paper during the fusing process. Shift to a different paper stock, preferably xerographic bond that has no cotton fibers, or use a dehumidifier to drop humidity levels to normal in the printer and storage room.

Whole Page Prints Faint

1. Change the EP Cartridge. When a cartridge is empty, it does not simply cease printing. The last 50 or so pages will gradually fade out. A defective EP toner cartridge will also yield a faint image and should be returned to your dealer.

2. Get authorized service. When a fresh cartridge still produces a faint image, contact your dealer. The transfer corona may need to be replaced. Note any errors displayed by the printer.

Page Prints Slightly Faint

1. Check the density dial. If the dial was inadvertently changed to a lower density (toward 9), the page may be faint. Try turning it back toward 1 to increase the density.

2. Replace the EP cartridge. A defective toner cartridge can cause faint printing. Return the cartridge to your dealer for replacement.

3. Change paper. A defective batch of paper, or the wrong kind of paper, may be the culprit. When the paper cannot hold and maintain the proper charge, imaging will be faint.

4. Get authorized service. When a change in toner cartridges and paper fails to correct the problem, you may have a problem with the drum sensitivity control, the erase lamp assembly, or the laser itself. Contact your service representative.

Page Has Speckled Print

Speckled print results when the primary corona grid in the EP cartridge is defective, so that the charge across the photosensitive drum is uneven and attracts blotches of toner. The only solution is to change the defective EP cartridge. Contact your dealer for a replacement.

Page Has Vertical White Streaks

1. Clean the transfer corona wire. Any toner, cotton dust, or dirt stuck on the transfer corona wire can produce an uneven electric charge on the paper which will, in turn, pull the toner from the photosensitive drum unevenly. Cleaning the wire will restore a uniform charge across the paper (see Chapter 5 for instructions for cleaning the transfer corona wire).

2. Replace the EP Cartridge. When a toner cartridge is nearing the end of its printing life, the toner may not distribute evenly across the drum, leaving streaked areas. This can happen before the 16 Toner Low message is flashed on the LCD display.

3. Get authorized service. If the streaks persist with a new EP cartridge, contact your dealer for service. The mirror that bounces

the laser beam off the photosensitive drum may need cleaning. Note any errors displayed by the printer.

Page Has Vertical Dark Streaks

1. Make sure you are not using incompatible paper stock. Pre-printed and coated paper may contaminate the fusing mechanism. If a buildup of ink appears on the cleaning pad, this may be the problem. Choose paper stock according to the criteria listed in Chapter 4.

2. Clean the primary corona wire in the EP cartridge. If portions of the primary corona wire are coated with ink or contaminants from preprinted forms or paper coatings, streaking may occur. Clean the corona wire with the supplied brush according to Chapter 5.

3. Replace the EP cartridge. A defectively manufactured or refilled cartridge may contain contaminants. Try a new cartridge when the preceding troubleshooting tips fail.

Right-Hand Side of the Page Is Blank or Distorted

1. Repair or Replace the EP Cartridge. If the toner in the EP cartridge cannot reach the photosensitive drum uniformly, it will leave part of the page blank. First try rocking the cartridge back and forth at 45 degree angles to distribute the toner evenly as described in the installation procedures. If the blank portion persists and it is a new EP cartridge, you probably failed to remove the entire strip of tape separating the toner from the drum. If you can reach the remaining portion of tape with a pair of pliers, you may be able to correct the problem. If not, you will have to exchange the defective cartridge for a new one.

2. Get authorized service. When the problem continues with a new cartridge, contact your dealer for service. The mirror that bounces the laser off the drum may be improperly installed or knocked out of alignment. Note any errors displayed by the printer.

Page Has a "Suede" Print Pattern

Contact your Hewlett-Packard dealer for service. When the pages have a suede-like appearance, the laser may not be firing correctly, leaving randomly charged areas where the toner will be attracted. Diagnosis and correction of this problem requires a qualified technician. Note any error message that the printer displays.

Page Has Smeared or Blotchy Print

1. Check the fuser cleaning pad. When the cleaning pad is caked with toner, the fuser roller is not able to melt the toner into the paper uniformly. Use an ordinary hair comb to remove the toner from the pad. Remember that you should be replacing the cleaning pad each time you change the EP cartridge.

2. Try a different paper. As emphasized in Chapter 4, not all papers have the same electrical properties. Try another batch of paper or a different brand.

3. Get authorized service. If the smearing continues, contact your dealer. You may have a defective fuser assembly or the static teeth that discharge the paper after the toner has been transferred may be bent, leaving an uneven residual electric charge on the paper. The uneven charge will diffuse the toner particles producing a smeared image. Either situation requires professional service. Note any error messages that the printer may display.

Page Has Distorted Print

Contact your dealer for service. The paper path mechanism is not properly advancing the paper in sync with the rotating EP cartridge drum, or the laser assembly is not firing properly. Both require professional service. Note any error messages that your printer displays.

Printed Page out of Registration

1. Make sure you are using the right kind of paper. The surface of the paper is critical for proper paper handling. If it is too smooth, it may not feed properly into the printer and registration will be off.

2. Replace the paper tray. A defective paper tray may cause the paper to enter the printer improperly, causing registration problems.

3. Get authorized service. When the preceding steps do not cure the problem, the registration roller assembly, which guides the paper, may be worn or damaged. Contact your dealer for service.

Page Has Repetitive Marks

1. Clean all rollers. Dirt on any of the rollers in the printer can cause an aberration or *hickey* to appear regularly on a page. Use a slightly damp cloth to remove the dirt.

2. Change toner cartridges. A physical defect in the EP cartridge will also cause repetitive marks. Return the cartridge to your dealer.

3. Get authorized service. When the marks still appear, you may have a defective fuser roller. Contact your dealer for service.

Image on Page Is Skewed

1. Check the paper tray. If paper is placed cockeyed in the tray or the tray is not properly in the printer, the paper may not feed properly into the registration roller assembly.

2. Get authorized help when the paper tray and its contents are not the problem. You might have worn or defective registration roller assembly parts. Contact your dealer for service.

Print on Page Is Not Properly Aligned

Contact your dealer for service. The paper path gear mechanism or registration assembly may be out of adjustment. This requires a qualified technician to diagnose and correct. Note any errors displayed by the printer.

Wrong Size Image

Get authorized service. The tray size sensing switches may be malfunctioning so that the printer formats images for the wrong size paper. Call your dealer for service.

Characters and Graphic Images Have Unprinted Areas

1. Use the correct stock. If the coating on the paper is too smooth, toner won't uniformly stick to it, leaving gaps in the printing (see Chapter 4). Transparencies not designed for laser printing can also cause the same problem.

2. Get authorized service when the problem persists. Despite your use of the proper paper, your fuser mechanism may not be operating properly.

Envelopes Have Gray Streak Running Top to Bottom

1. Turn the density to maximum. Although it seems counter-intuitive, turning the print density dial to the maximum setting (#1) can clear certain streaking problems. Don't forget to turn the dial back to position #5 when the problem clears, or you will greatly shorten the life of your cartridge.

2. Change the EP Cartridge. When the problem does not clear after a few envelopes, change the EP cartridge. It may be defective.

Return Address on an Envelope Is Fuzzy

Move the address farther away from the edge. The flap on the envelope tends to trap air, which pushes the edge of the envelope slightly out of alignment with the imaging mechanism. The farther away from the edge that you can tolerate the return address being printed, the less chance of fuzzy printing.

Envelopes Are Blank

1. Check your font. The most common reason that people cannot print on envelopes is that they have not selected a landscape font. The easiest way to see whether you are printing in landscape font is to run a piece of 8 1/2-by-11-inch paper through the printer instead of an envelope. If the address appears somewhere on the page, but in portrait orientation, you know that the

address is being transmitted by the computer. Check your application software manual or write an appropriate PCL code (see Chapters 14 and 15) to access a landscape font.

2. Set appropriate top and left margins. Remember that an envelope will not be treated the same as a piece of paper in terms of the top margin; the 10th line will not even reach the top edge of a standard (#10) envelope. A top margin of 45 to 75 lines and a left margin of 65 columns will probably get the address near where you want it on a standard #10 envelope fed into your printer. You can adjust both settings for your letterhead and personal taste.

Front Menu Panel Problems

The front menu panel of most laser printers greatly simplifies the use of the printer. Nevertheless, some users experience the following difficulties when using the menu.

Menu Options Don't "Stick"

1. Redo your menu options and press the Enter Menu button. When you select menu options, such as number of copies and form length, you can either set them for the current printing session or include them as printer defaults (see Chapter 3). In the former case, the menu will revert to its previous entries when you turn off the printer and power it up again. In the latter case, the printer will default to the values you enter each time you turn on the computer, until you enter a new set of values. To enter values as defaults, you must first select them and then press the Enter Menu key, which will place an asterisk in the LCD display after the item. Only items with asterisks are stored as default values.

2. Reset the system. After changing a value on the menu panel (see Chapter 3 for instructions), you must cycle the menu back to the 00 Ready state and reset the printer by taking it off-line (which is done by pressing the On-Line button once), and then pressing down the Reset button until 07 RESET appears in the display. Release the Reset button, and the printer will return to on-line status.

3. Check the printing options in your software. Your software may override the format settings in the menu control panel (except those related to serial/parallel interface and internal font defaults). For example, if you selected Line Printer (compressed type) as the default via the menu panel, and your word processor is set for Courier 10-point type, the software will issue a PCL command that overrides the Line Printer selection, and your document will print in Courier 10.

Forms Length Option Does Not Change the Number of Lines Printed on a Page

Software overrides the defaults. The Forms Length option of the menu only sets the default number of lines per inch. This is the line spacing that will be used whenever the printer is reset from the control panel or is reset by your software. If your software specifies another line spacing and issues the correct PCL command, it will override the default value set on the control menu. (See Chapter 3 for a detailed discussion.)

Strange Sounds

The following strange sounds coming from your laser printer are more of an annoyance than a printing problem. However, if a printing problem accompanies the noises, contact your dealer.

A Grinding or Squealing Noise Coming from the Back of the Printer

Try another cartridge if print problems also occur. The EP toner cartridge contains a number of gears and mechanical assemblies, any of which can bind or stick. If no printing problems accompany the sounds, live with it. (If it really gets on your nerves, return it to your dealer for a replacement cartridge.) When no image appears at all, one of the *doctor blade*s (see Chapter 6) may be defective, so no toner sticks to the drum. In that case, you should return the cartridge to your dealer.

A Momentary "Whirling" Noise Every Half Hour

Ignore it. When the laser printer is on but has not been used for about 30 minutes, the printer's main motor will kick in and rotate the fuser roller. This *laser printer stretch* ensures that the fuser rollers don't become permanently deformed by sitting too long in one position while hot and under pressure.

Strange Odors

Unlike strange sounds, odors emanating from the laser printer mean that there is a problem. The following describes what to do when the air is foul after printing.

The Air Has a Slightly Pungent Smell After the Printer Has Been in Use

1. Change the ozone filter, provide better ventilation in the room, or move the printer to another location with more air movement. As explained in Chapter 5, your laser printer generates ozone. When you are working in a dusty environment, the ozone filter becomes clogged and rendered less effective.

2. Unusual odors may emanate from the printer after printing labels or preprinted forms. As described in Chapter 4, the glue used on labels and the inks used on preprinted forms must be able to withstand the high heat of the fuser assembly (400 degrees Fahrenheit). If not, various gases—some of which may be toxic—can be released into the air. In general, glues with an acrylic base are safe for use in your laser printer. (See Chapter 4 for information about specific labels that have been proven safe for use with a laser printer.) Check with the forms manufacturer regarding the ink used on preprinted paper. If you use custom-printed, self-adhesive mailing labels, ask your printing vendor about the heat tolerances of the stock.

10

Interpreting Laser Printer Status Indicators and Error Codes

Most laser printers provide extensive feedback about their internal status through error codes displayed on the front panel. The error code information is not only important in guiding you during your daily use of your printer, but can assist you when you seek technical support from the manufacturer or its dealer. This chapter discusses the codes for an Hewlett-Packard LaserJet III and 4, and explains what causes them to appear, and what you can do about the problem. It also indicates the codes that warrant an authorized service check. If you have a laser printer other than an Hewlett-Packard, your error codes may vary, but the concepts will remain the same. Codes 0 through 10, and 15, are really status indicators that describe the current disposition of the printer. Codes 11 through 81 represent actual error conditions.

Status Codes

Code: 00

Message: READY

Meaning: Printer can receive data.

Code: 02

Message: WARMING UP

Meaning: Fuser assembly heating to proper temperature.

Code: 04

Message: SELF-TEST

Meaning: Continuous printout self-test.

Code: 05

Message: SELF-TEST

Meaning: Nonprinting self-test—checks circuitry.

Code: 06

Message: PRINTING TEST or FONT PRINTOUT/TYPEFACE LIST

Meaning: Printing self-test, or printing a sample of all installed fonts.

Code: 07

Message: RESET

Meaning: Printer reset from the control panel.

Code: 08

Message: COLD RESET

Meaning: Printer cold reset—printer resets to factory defaults.

Code: 09

Message: MENU RESET

Meaning: Menu has been reset to factory defaults.

Code: 10

Message: RESET TO SAVE

Meaning: The user-default environment has been changed when data was in the page buffer. You must reset the printer in order to copy the user-default settings to the current environment. When you press Continue or On-Line, the current print job will compete with the old settings and the environment will be reset before the next print job. When you press Reset, the printer will be reset immediately, but the data in the print buffer will be lost.

Code: 15

Message: ENGINE TEST

Meaning: Test the Print button to see if it has been pushed. The printer will generate a continuous line pattern for checking the registration.

Error Codes

Code:	11
Message:	PAPER OUT
Explanation:	Paper tray is empty.
Action:	Refill tray and reinsert it. The printer will resume operation. If you return a different size paper tray, the printer will ask you to reinsert the original tray.

Code:	12
Message:	PRINTER OPEN
Explanation:	The top of the printer is not fully closed.
Action:	Press the top until you hear and feel a positive click. Note that the message may be displayed for a moment or two before it clears—there is no need to push again.

Code:	13
Message:	PAPER JAM
Explanation:	A piece of paper or envelope is caught somewhere along the paper path.
Action:	Press the rectangular button on top of the printer, and the cover will pop open. Swing the back part of the cover upwards.
	Remove all paper by carefully pulling it forward until it clears the machine. Push the cover back down.

NOTE

If the jam occurred because of a manual feed and you can retrieve the paper or envelope by pulling it straight out, you still must open and close the cover to reset the printer and resume operation.

Code: 14

Message: NO EP CART

Explanation: You are attempting to run the printer without a toner cartridge.

Action: Install an EP toner cartridge according to the instructions supplied with the cartridge and your printer manual.

Code: 16

Message: TONER LOW

Explanation: The toner supply in your EP cartridge is nearly exhausted, and may be empty in 50 to 100 pages.

Action: Make sure you have another toner cartridge on hand.

Code: 20

Message: ERROR

Explanation: You do not have enough memory in your printer to handle the soft fonts, data, and graphic images transmitted by the computer.

Action: Press the Continue button to print out whatever information the LaserJet can hold in its memory. The remainder of the image will be printed on the next page. To accommodate the memory requirements, do one of the following:

1. Simplify the print job by removing fonts or graphic elements from the page, or reduce the resolution of a graphic element. When you are using soft fonts, you can free up more memory by reducing the number of permanently stored soft fonts (See Chapter 11).

2. Increase the amount of printer memory.

Code: 21

Message: ERROR

Explanation: The page you are trying to print is too complex for the printer's microprocessor—too many small characters close together, cursor positions, rules, or graphic elements. The problem occurs because the printer must translate the information into 1's and 0's that designate dots and white spaces. If there is too much information, the printer's formatter, which carries out the translations at a speed determined by the complexity of the image, cannot keep up with the imaging system, which must run at a constant speed. Therefore, the printer registers the error. This limitation is not a matter that can be solved by adding more memory, but is inherent in the printer's design.

Action: With the LaserJet Series II, III, and compatibles, press the Continue button to eject the page with whatever data the printer was able to format up to the point of the error. You will lose some of the pages. To eliminate the error, simplify the page design by increasing the type size and loosening up the spacing, or by removing extraneous graphic elements such as lines or boxes. If you are printing graphic images for desktop publishing, you can separate the images from their texts, print them individually, then manually paste them together or double-print a single sheet.

The LaserJet 4 uses advanced logic to try to work around this problem by first reducing the resolution of the page, then by reducing page protection and finally by compressing the data. The printer will display the 021 error message. If you have set the Clr Warn setting to On (the default) the printer will wait until you press the Continue button before proceeding with its attempt to print the page. If you have set Clr Warn to Job, the printer will attempt to print the page on its own and will clear the warning message at the end of the print job. See Chapter 3.

Code:	22
Message:	ERROR
Explanation:	The computer and printer are not *handshaking* properly; that is, they are not informing each other when they are ready to transmit and receive data. When you are using the parallel port, the probable cause is a loose cable. When you are using the serial port, the probable cause is an incorrect Pacing setting.
Action:	Press continue to clear the warning. Check your cables and menu settings.

Code: 40

Message: ERROR

Explanation: This is a communications error and that will occur in two situations: when the printer is turned on before the computer is turned on, or when the computer is turned off before the printer is turned off. It will also occur if the printer is set for a different baud rate than the computer when using a serial interface (See Chapter 2 for more information.)

Action: If the printer was simply turned on prior to the computer or the computer was turned off and on (e.g. to reset or "cold boot"), simply press the Continue button and the error will clear.

If the error occurred during actual operation, check to make sure the printer and computer have the same baud rate setting. Serial interfaces can generally be run most efficiently (highest speed without errors) at 9,600 Baud.

Code: 41 - LaserJet III

Message: ERROR

Explanation: A temporary problem has occurred with the laser beam detector. The beam detector is used to sense the scanning laser beam in order to establish the timing of data transmission to the laser. If the printer fails to sense the laser when it expects to, it will automatically try to recover and issue an error 41 message. If the printer can't find the beam and resynchronize within two seconds, it will issue an error 51 message.

Action: Press Continue to clear the error message. The LaserJet will print out the entire page again. If the error persists, you may have a dirty or misaligned laser detect mirror. Contact your dealer for service.

Code: 41.x - LaserJet 4

Message: ERROR

Explanation: The paper in the cassette tray does not match the tray setting. This usually occurs when the paper size knob on the optional 500 sheet tray is set to the wrong paper size for the trays contents.

Action: Reset the paper size knob to the correct paper size.

Code: 42, 43

Message: ERROR

Explanation: Occurs when an option board is not communicating properly with the printer.

Action: Turn the printer off and unplug it. Check to make sure that the option board is properly seated. Restart the printer. If the problem persists, contact the manufacturer of the option board.

Code: 50, 57 or 58

Message: ERROR

Explanation: The printer has detected an internal problem such as the fuser assembly overheating.

Action: Turn off the LaserJet for 10 minutes, then turn it back on. If the problem persists, get professional service.

Code: 51

Message: ERROR

Explanation: The temporary problem with the beam detector (Code 41) did not clear within two seconds, and is now defined as a malfunction. This usually results from a failure of the beam detection system, which uses a small mirror to reflect the scanning laser beam through a fiber-optic cable to the detector. The mirror is located at the left edge of the beam scan, so the reflection indicates that the beam is at the beginning of the scan line. This in turn indicates that the laser is ready for a line of image data to be sent. If the mirror is dirty, misaligned or broken, the laser beam can not be detected and the printer's timing circuit reports an error.

Another possible cause of mechanical failure has to do with the printer's shutter mechanism. The laser assembly has a shutter that prevents the beam from escaping when the printer is open. The EP cartridge has a small plastic protrusion that is used to open the laser assembly shutter when the cover is closed. If the protrusion is broken, the shutter won't open and the beam will not be detected.

Action: Try replacing the EP cartridge. If the problem persists, arrange for service.

Code: 52

Message: ERROR

Explanation: The motor that spins the scanning mirror and produces the characteristic sound that accompanies the printing process has failed.

Action: Arrange for service.

Code:	55
Message:	ERROR
Explanation:	The circuit board controlling the communication interface with the computer, and the board controlling the operation of the printer are having difficulty communicating between themselves. Either one of the two boards has failed, or the cable between them is loose or broken.
Action:	These are not user serviceable parts, so call your dealer for assistance.

Code:	53.xy.zz - LaserJet 4
Message:	ERROR
Explanation:	The printer has detected an error with an add-on SIMM module. The xy and zz numbers will indicate which module and the detected problem. (See the user's manual for the printer or module.)
Action:	Try removing and reinserting the problem module. If the error persists, contact the manufacturer of the add-in module.

Code:	61
Message:	SERVICE
Explanation:	The printer has an internal memory error.
Action:	Arrange for service.

Code:	62,x
Message:	SERVICE
Explanation:	The printer has detected an error in the font data stored in its internal ROM memory (x=0), an add-in module (x=1-4) or font cartridge (x=5).
Action:	If x>0, try removing and reinserting the problem module or cartridge. If x=0 or the problem persists, arrange for service.

Code:	63
Message:	SERVICE
Explanation:	The printer has detected a problem with one or more of its RAM memory chips. This problem may be transient, resulting from static discharge or passing electronic interference. Alternatively, it might be a permanent problem, resulting from a damaged memory chip.
Action:	1. Turn the printer off and then on again. This may clear any temporary *glitches* in the electronics. If the printer still displays the error code or it occurs repeatedly, arrange for service.
	2. If you have an additional memory card, turn off the printer and make sure the card is properly seated. Turn the printer on again.
	3. If the problem persists, turn the printer off and remove the memory card. Turn the printer back on. If you no longer have a 63 error code, you have isolated the problem to the memory card and should contact the memory card dealer to repair or replace the card.

Code: 64

Message: SERVICE

Explanation: An error was detected in the area of memory
                used for the scan buffer.

Action: Arrange for service.

Code: 65

Message: SERVICE

Explanation: An error was detected in the circuit that controls
                the printer's memory.

Action: Arrange for service.

Code: 67

Message: SERVICE

Explanation: This is a miscellaneous hardware error and may
                be the result of a poorly seated font cartridge.

Action: Turn the printer off, remove and reinsert the
                font cartridge, then turn the printer back on.
                If the problem persists, arrange for service.

Code: 68

Message: ERROR

Explanation: If ERROR is displayed, the printer has detected an
                error in the RAM used to store menu setup
                information.

Action: Run the printer self-test to print a listing of all of
                the setup parameters and compare them to the
                settings displayed on the menu. If the param-
                eters differ, try reentering them via the menu
                control panel (see Chapter 3). If this error
                persists, arrange for service.

Code: 68

Message: SERVICE

Explanation: If SERVICE is displayed, the nonvolatile RAM used to store the menu setting is full and must be replaced.

Action: Arrange for service.

Code: 69

Message: SERVICE

Explanation: An error has occurred between the communications interface and the expansion interface.

Action: Turn the printer off and on again. If the error persists, arrange for service.

Code: 70 - 71

Message: SERVICE

Explanation: A firmware problem has occurred

Action: Arrange for service.

Code: 72

Message: SERVICE

Explanation: A font cartridge problem has occurred, possibly from inserting and then removing a cartridge too quickly. It can also indicate a defective font cartridge or hardware problem in the printer.

Action: Turn off the printer, then turn it back on again. If that does not clear the message, arrange for service.

Code: 79

Message: SERVICE

Explanation: A hardware problem has occurred.

Action: Turn the printer off and on again. If that does not clear the message, arrange for service.

Code: 80

Message: SERVICE

Explanation: There is a problem with the optional I/O port.

Action: Turn the printer off and on again. If that does not clear the message, arrange for service.

Code: 81

Message: SERVICE

Explanation: The printer has detected an unspecified problem.

Action: Turn the printer off and on again. If that does not clear the message, arrange for service.

IV
PART

Advanced Topics

Understanding Type Fonts

One of the most exciting features of laser printers is their ability to print a variety of type styles on the same page. This gives you the opportunity to create aesthetically pleasing and professional-looking pages for reports, newsletters, brochures, and all of your other publications. Compare the document in Figure 11.1a prepared by using a single type style with the one shown in Figure 11.1b that mixes several complimentary fonts. Notice how the page in Figure 11.1b is much easier to read than the one shown in Figure 11.1a; the different type styles and *weights* each convey a different graphic message and level of importance.

Although you might not have a need or want to create such sophisticated pages, you will find that even basic documents can be made more attractive and more effective for communicating information with some simple typographic enhancements. This chapter gives you the information you need to access fonts for your laser printer and to use them in a manner that produces the most pleasing and graphically sound results.

Figure 11.1. (a) A page printed with a single font (Courier). **(b)** A page printed with several proportional fonts.

What Is a Font?

A font is a set of characters, including letters, numbers, and special symbols—such as the pound and number sign (#), the dollar sign ($), the copyright sign (©), and the legal paragraph sign (¶). Hewlett-Packard defines fonts according to eight criteria in the PCL 5 specification listed in the following sections.

Spacing

Spacing refers to the amount of space allocated to each character. Fonts can be fixed or proportional. Fixed or monospaced means that each character is assigned the same amount of space. Proportional means that the space assigned to different characters varies, depending on the shape of the characters, giving a smoother look and texture. Proportional spacing is a major feature that gives professionally printed material its *typeset* appearance. (See Figure 11.2 for a comparison.)

```
This sentence is printed
in Courier 10, a fixed
pitch font.
```

This sentence is printed in Times
Roman, a proportional font.

Figure 11.2. Comparison of fixed fonts with proportional type.

Pitch

Pitch is the number of characters per inch (cpi). This is only relevant to monospaced fonts; with proportionally spaced fonts, the number of characters per inch will vary with the combinations of the characters being printed.

Point Size

Point size is the vertical height of the character. Font height is measured in terms of descenders and ascenders. If you imagine a lowercase "p," the round part or body sits on the baseline. The downward stroke that extends beneath the baseline is the descender. In contrast, the upward stroke of a lowercase "b" is called the ascender. The vertical height of a font is measured from the bottom of the lowest descender to top of the highest ascender in points. One point equals approximately 1/72 of an inch. (See Figures 11.3 and 11.4.)

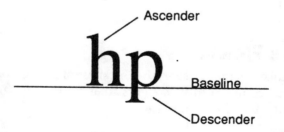

Figure 11.3. Ascender and descender.

This is 14 point type.

This is 18 point type.

This is 24 point type.

This is 30 point type.

Figure 11.4. Various point sizes, 14–30.

Orientation

Orientation is the alignment of the print across the face of the paper—either portrait, vertical printing on an 8 1/2-by-11-inch sheet of paper, or landscape, horizontal printing on an 11-by-8 1/2-inch sheet.

Style

Style can be upright—sometimes called Roman—or slanting—italic. Figure 11.5 shows the difference in the two styles.

This is Roman (upright) type.

This is Italic (slanted) type.

Figure 11.5. Roman versus italic styles.

Stroke Weight

Stroke weight measures the thickness of a stroke or character. The most common stroke weights are light, regular—also called medium—and bold. (See Figure 11.6.)

This is Helvetica 14 point medium weight type.

This is Helvetica 14 point bold weight type.

Figure 11.6. Comparison of stroke weights.

Typeface

Typeface is the artistic design of characters, such as Avante Garde, Helvetica, Courier, Gothic, Times Roman, and Zapf. (See Figure 11.7.)

Helvetica Bold
Bookman Medium
Zapf Chancery Bold
Palatino Medium

Figure 11.7. Comparison of various typefaces.

Symbol Set

The symbol set describes which letters, numbers, and special characters are contained in the font. Specialized symbol sets—such as legal, international, and mathematical—contain unique characters appropriate for the use described by their name. (See Figure 11.8 for samples.)

®	Registered
©	Copyright
°	Degree
§	Section
¶	Paragraph
†	Footnote
™	Trademark

Figure 11.8. Samples of special symbols from different fonts.

Some symbol sets contain a larger numbers of characters. For example, the ASCII symbol set contains 128 characters including control codes while the Roman-8 symbol set contains 94 additional special characters. Because a greater number of characters requires more memory for downloaded soft fonts, you should generally choose the smallest symbol set that contains all the characters you need.

The preceding criteria define unique fonts or sets of characters. A group of fonts, related by the typeface criteria, composes a font family. For example, the Courier font family available on the Hewlett-Packard font cartridge "C" (#92286C) contains the individual fonts shown in table 11.1.

TABLE 11.1. FONTS FOUND ON HP COURIER FONT CARTRIDGE

Spacing	Pitch	Point	Style	Weight	Orientation
Fixed	10	12	Roman	Medium	Portrait
Fixed	10	12	Roman	Bold	Portrait
Fixed	10	12	Italic	Medium	Portrait

Some font cartridges offer more than one font family. For example, the Hewlett-Packard cartridge "F" provides one Helvetica style font, four members of the Times Roman style family, and a special compressed font called Line Printer; cartridge "Q" offers two gothic fonts and two courier fonts. The combinations are based on type compatibility and demands of a particular user application; for example, legal work would have requirements different from those for tax work.

The new scalable cartridges from Hewlett-Packard also offer a variety of fonts. For example, the scalable cartridge called Distinctive Documents I and Compelling Publications I (see Figure 11.9) offers CG Century Schoolbook, ITC Souvenir, Univers Condensed, Antique Olive, CG Palacio, Stymie, and ITC Zapf Dingbats (symbols and icons). Brilliant Presentations I and Compelling Publications II (see Figure 11.10) contains a number of elegant typefaces—ITC Benguiat, ITC Bookman, Shannnon, CG Bodoni, Garamond Antiqua, CG Omega, Cooper Black, and Revue Light. Each font is scalable from 0.25 to 999.75 points and is available in a variety of stroke weights and slant angles.

NOTE

The names given to a particular font family may vary between software and font designers. This is because certain names, such as Helvetica or ITC Zapf Chancery, have been trademarked by a particular typographic design company (Helvetica is a trademark of Linotype while ITC Zapf Chancery is a registered trademark of International Typeface Corporation). Many designs that appear identical will be given different names to avoid infringing these trademarks. For example, a Helvetica-like typeface may be given the name Swiss by some software packages while a Times Roman-like font might be called Dutch.

Types of Fonts

Fonts must be stored in the memory of the printer before they can be used to print the characters on a particular page. Fonts can be stored in temporary internal RAM, in permanent internal ROM, or in interchangeable external ROM cartridges. ROM—meaning *read-only memory*—in this case refers to chips containing information that the printer can read and use, but cannot change.

The Bit-Mapping Concept

Regardless of the storage location, the printer designers must select one of two techniques for storing the information describing each character of the font. The first is to store individual bit-mapped images of each character in the font. A bit-mapped image is a string of binary code—zeros and ones—with ones representing the dots required to form a character or graphic element, and zeros representing white space around the characters or graphic elements. (See Figure 11.11 for an illustration of the bit-mapping concept.) The Hewlett-Packard LaserJet printers have used the bit-mapping technique to store font information.

Antique Olive
ABCDEFGHIJKLMNOPQRSTUVWXYZ
abcdefghijklmnopqrstuvwxyz
1234567890 = [];',!@#$%^&*()_+{}:"<
Antique Olive Bold
Antique Olive Italic
Antique Olive Compact

CG Century Schoolbook
ABCDEFGHIJKLMNOPQRSTUVWXYZ
abcdefghijklmnopqrstuvwxyz
1234567890-=[];',./!@#$%^&*()_+{}:"<
CG Century Schoolbook Bold
CG Century Schoolbook Italic
CG Century Schoolbook Bold Italic

CG Palacio
ABCDEFGHIJKLMNOPQRSTUVWXYZ
abcdefghijklmnopqrstuvwxyz
1234567890-=[];',./!@#$%^&*()_+{}:"<>?
CG Palacio Bold
CG Palacio Italic
CG Palacio Bold Italic

ITC Souvenir Light
ABCDEFGHIJKLMNOPQRSTUVWXYZ
abcdefghijklmnopqrstuvwxyz
1234567890-=[];',.!@#$%^&*()_+{}:"<>
ITC Souvenir Demi
ITC Souvenir Light Italic
ITC Souvenir Demi Italic

Stymie Medium
ABCDEFGHIJKLMNOPQRSTUVWXYZ
abcdefghijklmnopqrstuvwxyz
1234567890-=[];',.!@#$%^&*()_+{}:"<>?
Stymie Bold
Stymie Medium Italic
Stymie Bold Italic

Univers Medium Condensed
ABCDEFGHIJKLMNOPQRSTUVWXYZ
abcdefghijklmnopqrstuvwxyz
1234567890-=[];',./!@#$%^&*()_+{}:"<>?
Univers Bold Condensed
Univers Medium Condensed Italic
Univers Bold Condensed Italic

ITC Zapf Dingbats

Figure 11.9. Type samples from Distinctive Documents I and Compelling Publications I.

The second approach is to store a mathematical model describing the outline of each character in a font family. The model is then used to create the specific font required—point size, stroke weight, and so on—at the time the page is composed. This is the technique used by Post-Script and DDL laser printers, and the PCL scalable fonts available on the LaserJet III and 4.

When the bit-mapped technique is used, the printer must store a complete set of bit-mapped images for each point size, stroke weight, and style for each font used on a page. The primary advantage of the bit-mapped technique is that it does not require a special microprocessor to create the character images each time they are needed, as in the case of PostScript or DDL printers. As a result, bit-mapped printers are less expensive than PostScript or DDL laser printers.

ITC Benguiat Book
ABCDEFGHIJKLMNOPQRSTUVWXYZ
abcdefghijklmnopqrstuvwxyz
1234567890- =[];',.!@#$%^&*()_+{}:"<>
ITC Benguiat Bold
ITC Benguiat Book Italic
ITC Benguiat Bold Italic

Garamond Antiqua
ABCDEFGHIJKLMNOPQRSTUVWXYZ
abcdefghijklmnopqrstuvwxyz
1234567890-=[];',./!@#$%^&*()_+{}:"<>
Garamond Halbfett
Garamond Kursiv
Garamond Kursiv Halbfett

CG Bodoni Book
ABCDEFGHIJKLMNOPQRSTUVWXYZ
abcdefghijklmnopqrstuvwxyz
1234567890-=[];',./!@#$%^&*()_+{}:"<>
CG Bodoni Bold
CG Bodoni Book Italic
CG Bodoni Bold Italic

CG Omega
ABCDEFGHIJKLMNOPQRSTUVWXYZ
abcdefghijklmnopqrstuvwxyz
1234567890- = [];',./!@#$%^&*()_+{}:"<>
CG Omega Bold
CG Omega Italic
CG Omega Bold Italic

ITC Bookman Light
ABCDEFGHIJKLMNOPQRSTUVWXYZ
abcdefghijklmnopqrstuvwxyz
1234567890-=[];',./!@#$%^&*()_+{}:"<>
ITC Bookman Demi
ITC Bookman Light Italic
ITC Bookman Demi Italic

Revue Light
ABCDEFGHIJKLMNOPQRSTUVWXYZ
abcdefghijklmnopqrstuvwxyz
1234567890- =[];'.!@#$%^&*()_+{}:"<>

Shannon Book
ABCDEFGHIJKLMNOPQRSTUVWXYZ
abcdefghijklmnopqrstuvwxyz
1234567890-=[];',./!@#$%^&*()_+{}:"<>
Shannon Bold
Shannon Oblique
Shannon Extrabold

Cooper Black
ABCDEFGHIJKLMNOPQRSTUVWX
abcdefghijklmnopqrstuvwxyz
1234567890- =[];',.!@#$%^&*()_+{}:"<

Figure 11.10. Type samples from Brilliant Presentations I and Compelling Publications II.

A second advantage of the bit-mapping approach is the speed with which the characters can be printed. Because the bit-mapped patterns are already in the printer's memory, the printer need only lay them out in the correct position on the page—Hewlett-Packard accomplishes this with its printer command language, PCL. However, bit-mapped image sets can become extremely large for the bigger point sizes, requiring considerable memory. For example, 8-point Helvetica requires 16K, and 72-point Helvetica requires 731K.

Dot Row	Bit Map
01	00000000 11111100 00001111 1100000
02	00000111 11111111 00011111 1110000
03	00001111 11111111 10011111 1100000
04	00111111 11010111 11011110 0000000
05	00111110 00000001 11111110 0000000
06	01111100 00000000 01111110 0000000
07	01111000 00000000 01111110 0000000
08	11110000 00000000 00111110 0000000
09	11110000 00000000 00111110 0000000
10	11110000 00000000 00011110 0000000
11	11110000 00000000 00011110 0000000
12	11110000 00000000 00011110 0000000
13	11110000 00000000 00011110 0000000
14	11110000 00000000 00111110 0000000
15	01111000 00000000 00111110 0000000
16	01111000 00000000 01111110 0000000
17	01111100 00000000 11111110 0000000
18	00111110 00000001 11111110 0000000
19	00011111 11010111 11011110 0000000
20	00001111 11111111 10011110 0000000
21	00000111 11111111 00011110 0000000
22	00000000 10101000 00011110 0000000
23	00000000 00000000 00011110 0000000
24	00000000 00000000 00011110 0000000
25	00000000 00000000 00011110 0000000
26	00000000 00000000 00111110 0000000
27	00000000 00000000 00111100 0000000
28	00000000 00000000 01111100 0000000
29	00000000 00000001 11111000 0000000
30	00000001 11111111 11110000 0000000
31	00000011 11111111 11100000 0000000
32	00000001 11111111 10000000 0000000

Figure 11.11. The bit-mapping concept. Ones correspond to white areas; zeros correspond to dark areas.

The Scalable Font Concept

Printers using scalable fonts such as PostScript printers and the new LaserJets supporting PCL 5 only need to store a character's outline once and can use it to create any of the differing point sizes, weights, or styles as needed. This permits scalable font printers to store many families of fonts in a small amount of memory and create an almost unlimited number of point, weight, and style combinations. One limitation of the scalable font creation technique is that it requires a microprocessor to create the character images as they are needed. You can use a separate microprocessor on an adaptor board that is plugged into an expansion slot in your computer. This technique is used by many PostScript add-on systems for LaserJet printers. An alternative scalable font approach is for you to embed the font outlines into a ROM chip in a plug-in cartridge and use the printer's microprocessor to create the fonts on the fly. You can use this technique for the PCL 5 scalable font cartridges and the PostScript add-on cartridges supplied by Hewlett-Packard and various third-party vendors.

Another approach you can use to bring the PostScript page description language and its font outlines to LaserJet printers is a software PostScript emulator that translates the PostScript commands generated by the software application into PCL commands.

The dedicated board approach is fast but expensive; the software emulator approach is inexpensive but slow; and the cartridge approach is a compromise. The choice depends on your budget and printing needs.

PostScript versus PCL 5 Scalable Fonts

One of the key questions raised by the introduction of the LaserJet III and expanded by the LaserJet 4 and PCL 5's scalable type fonts is how they compare to PostScript and its scalable type faces. The correct answer depends on your application. PostScript add-ons provide the complete PostScript page description language in addition to the scalable font features. This is easy for you to use and is compatibile with many different software packages that support PostScript printers. It also provides compatibility with all PostScript soft fonts available from many different vendors. The PostScript cartridges and software emulators for the LaserJet III and the built-in PostScript capability of the Hewlett-Packard LaserJet 4M provide good implementations of the PostScript language and deliver all of the features of PostScript including the basic 35 typefaces. Their major liabilities are the additional cost, and, in the case of the add-on cartridges, relatively slow performance.

The built-in scalable font capability of the LaserJet III and 4 provides an alternative. The font generator is built into PCL 5 and therefore operates quickly by scaling the fonts. The PCL 5 approach to scalable fonts is to maintain compatibility with previous releases of PCL. To accomplish this, PCL 5 detects the call for a scaled font and creates it by scaling the font outline and storing the resulting bit-mapped image in the printer's RAM memory in the same fashion as a temporary, downloaded, bit-mapped soft font is stored. The printer can then access the scaled font at the same speed as it would a RAM- or ROM-based font. The scaled font will remain in the printer's memory until the space it occupies is needed by another scaled or downloaded font. When a given scaled font is already in memory, it will be used; when it has been replaced, the printer must regenerate it.

This technique is extremely fast as long as you are not constantly changing between scaled fonts. The basic LaserJet III comes with two built-in scalable fonts—Univers and CG Times. The LaserJet 4 expands this list to 45 built-in font faces, meeting all but the most demanding design requirements. You can add additional font families either with cartridges or soft fonts supplied on disks. This simpler approach can save you money when you have limited font requirements. It also allows you to add more fonts when needed.

Font Sources

As mentioned above, the font information can be stored in one of three different storage locations: permanent internal ROM, interchangeable, external ROM-based cartridges, or temporary internal RAM. Internal ROM contains the resident fonts of the printer. These are the fonts that are "burned" onto chips inside the printer, so they are always available when the power is turned on.

Interchangeable Font Cartridges

With the introduction of its original LaserJet, Hewlett-Packard also introduced the concept of interchangeable font cartridges. The cartridges contain ROM chips that hold the actual bit-mapping information—the dot patterns—for several different fonts. Because the font cartridges are interchangeable, you can select the ones most appropriate for you. At the time of this writing, Hewlett-Packard had developed numerous different font cartridges including new scalable font cartridges for use with the PCL 5 compatible printers such as the LaserJet III. Third-party developers offer a variety of cartridges with high-quality bit-mapped and scalable fonts.

Soft Fonts

Your laser printer's memory can store fonts transmitted from your computer before the actual print job is set. These fonts are called soft fonts because they are stored on computer files and need to be down-loaded—transferred from disk to the printer's memory. A variety of soft fonts are now available from Hewlett-Packard as well as a number of font makers, such as Bitstream, Inc. of Cambridge, Massachusetts, that licenses its fonts to many hardware and software manufacturers. With Bit-stream and other fonts, you have a full range of typefaces at your disposal for creating a wide range of professional documents.

A soft font is a software file that contains the bit-mapped image of the characters. They are distributed in one of two ways: as a finished font with a specific typeface, point size, weight, and style, or as a font family outline together with a software program that can create a specific font from the outline. Although this font creation process may be time-consuming, it enables you to create the specific fonts you need from a single compressed source file for that family or a font whose disk file is too large to fit on a single floppy diskette— 72-point Helvetica requires 731K.

Bit-mapped soft fonts are appealing in concept for their deatil and low cost, but have some drawbacks for everyday use. First, each dot requires 1 bit of memory with 8 bits making up a byte. A single character can require thousands of bits. For example, an average 24-point character requires a 75-by-75-bit box of data for a total of 2,875 bits, or approximately 354 bytes for just one character. A complete Times Roman 24-point bold font requires about 87,000 bytes. As the point size increases, so does the storage requirement. Times Roman 30-point bold needs 130,000 bytes of disk space, 60 points requires 510,000 bytes, and 72 points requires 731,000 bytes. These figures quadruple when you move up to 600 dpi.

To carry out sophisticated desktop publishing activities with multiple typefaces, you need to dedicate 10 megabytes or more of hard disk storage for storing soft fonts. Furthermore, the fonts require a similar increase in the amount of printer memory required for storage after downloading, reducing the amount of printer memory available for complex documents. Because the files are large, they can take a considerable amount of time to download to the printer each time they are used. A complex page with multiple fonts may require 15 minutes or more just to transfer the fonts from the computer to the printer. Note that a parallel interface will be faster than a serial one for downloading soft fonts.

With the addition of scalable soft fonts with PCL 5, many of these space and transmission problems are solved. The scalable soft font is stored on disk, like a bit-mapped soft font. But instead of storing the complete bit map for each potential dimension, you need to only store and transmit the font's outline. After it is downloaded, the scalable soft font can be scaled to whatever size is required by PCL 5 as needed.

Whether you decide to use bit-mapped or scalable soft fonts, you must decide which process you want to use to download the fonts from your computer to your printer. Several downloading options are available, depending on your application. First you must determine if the software you are using contains its own integrated soft font downloader that automatically transfers soft fonts to the printer as needed. If it does, your use of soft fonts will be simplified. If it does not, the job of downloading falls on your shoulders.

Integrated Downloaders

Many of the newer software packages, especially those involved in advanced text and graphics printing—such as Ventura, PageMaker, WordPerfect, and Microsoft Word—contain their own soft font downloader. To use the internal downloaders in these programs, you need to indicate which soft fonts are available, and the drive and directory where they are located. The software will detect the need to download a particular soft font whenever it is called. For example, suppose that you are using Times Roman 12 point as the standard font for a Page-Maker document and decide to use Times Roman 24 point for the headlines. PageMaker would first look at its record of installed soft fonts—that you created during the installation procedure—to determine when the font is available and where it is located. It will further check whether it had already downloaded the font earlier on the page. If not, PageMaker would initiate the process automatically. When the font is already in the printer's memory from a previous downloading request, it is used immediately.

In most cases this procedure is easy, but in others you must also supply the software package with detailed character spacing information tables—character width tables or printer font metric tables. These tables, stored as disk files, tell the software package the exact width of each character. The software requires this information to determine word length so that it can properly wrap or hyphenate lines of continuous text. Fortunately, most packages that require font width or metric tables provide pregenerated tables or the ability to generate this information by scanning the soft font file at the time of installation.

Manual Downloading

When your software does not support soft fonts, you can still use them with your various application programs, although you will have to do more of the work. You can manually download fonts by issuing special PCL printer language commands from your computer prior to starting an application. Alternatively, you can use a software utility—such as Hewlett-Packard's Type Director—that downloads scalable typeface files from your computer to your LaserJet III or 4, and scales them from 0.25 to 999.75 points in 0.25 point increments. It also manages and downloads your bit-mapped fonts. Many other downloaders are available from third-party vendors.

How Software Uses Manually Downloaded Fonts

After you have downloaded soft fonts, some application programs, such as WordPerfect 5.1, can handle them intelligently—that is, properly space the characters. Other programs, such as 1-2-3 without WYSIWYG or dBASE III Plus, blindly use soft fonts as if they were standard fixed pitch. What's the difference? With WordPerfect 5.1, you can specify the point and pitch setting for a given font that has been downloaded to the printer and WordPerfect will properly space and wrap text according to the font specifications.

Permanent and Temporary Fonts

When manually downloading soft fonts, you can specify them as permanent or temporary. Permanent fonts are stored in the printer's memory for the entire session, until the printer is either turned off or the font is specifically deleted via software. Temporary fonts are stored only for the time they are needed—for example, creating a headline—and are deleted when the printer is reset from the control panel or via software. Temporary fonts can also be overwritten by other temporary fonts or graphics as if new fonts are needed on the page. When a font is downloaded, it can overwrite a previously downloaded temporary font, clearing the necessary space in the printer's memory. If the temporary font that has been overwritten is required again at a later time, it will have to be downloaded again.

The LaserJet III and 4 can handle a virtually unlimited number of downloaded fonts simultaneously—the theoretical limit is 32,769 fonts. As mentioned earlier, however, fonts of different sizes, using different symbol sets, will require varying amounts of printer memory.

Depending on the amount of memory available in your laser printer and the size of fonts you are using, you may be able to download some or all of the fonts at any one time. You will have to develop the most efficient strategy for your particular memory configuration that will download fonts permanently or temporarily. The situation becomes more complex when the printer is shared among several users in a local area network (LAN) because one user's soft fonts may overwrite another user's. You will have to develop a coordinated strategy among all of the users for downloading temporary and permanent soft fonts, and for assigning font ID numbers.

Permanent fonts are recommended when the font is used frequently during the session, and if it is not very large. Large fonts, such as those used for 60-point headlines, should not be downloaded permanently, because they are used infrequently and require a considerable amount of printer memory that could be used for other temporary soft fonts or graphics.

Selecting among Downloaded Soft Fonts

After a soft font is downloaded, you can specify its use in a document in one of three ways. First, if it was downloaded as a permanent soft font on a LaserJet III printer, it can be specified as the default font via the control panel menu. To do so, you need to enter the font ID number that was assigned by the printer when the font was down-loaded. Note that this number will probably be different from the font ID number that you or your software assigned during the downloading process. The only way to determine the internal ID number assigned by the printer is to print the font test after you have downloaded the font in question. See Chapter 3 for a discussion of the LaserJet III control menu.

Second, you can select a downloaded soft font by transmitting its software-assigned ID number through the following PCL printer language command, where # represents the ID number that you assigned to it when you installed the font earlier with a downloader.

```
Ec(#X
```

You can also issue a command via BASIC or another language (see Chapter 14), or you can issue a printer command from within many application software packages. To select a particular soft font by the ID number in dBASE III Plus for example, you would issue the command, where "??" is dBASE's command to transmit a string to the printer without moving the paper, and the pound sign (#) is the soft font ID number in its ASCII decimal code. See Appendix B for an ASCII table that will enable you to translate Arabic numbers into decimal code.

```
?? "027 0400 # 088"
```

From within Lotus, the following command would select a soft font where "||" is 1-2-3's in-line printer control command.

```
||027 0400 # 088\
```

Third, you can select any available font—resident, cartridge-based, or soft font—by specifying its eight parameters—spacing, pitch, point size, style, orientation, face, stroke weight, and typeface—via a PCL printer language command embedded in your software. For example, if you had downloaded Helvetica 30 point, bold, upright, portrait, you could translate that information into the following PCL string:

```
Ec(8UEc(s1p30v0s5b12T
```

See Chapter 14 for details of the PCL printer language.

As in the previous description, you can issue this command in application packages by transmitting its ASCII decimal code directly to the printer. For example, you convert the string into ASCII decimal code by looking up each character in an ASCII conversion table. This yields the following decimal code that can be used with dBASE or Lotus, in the previous example, for inserting an ID code command.

```
027 040 056 085 027 040 115 049 112

051 048 118 048 115

053 098 049 050 084
```

In the next chapter you will see numerous examples that will enable you to download any font in your typographic storehouse.

Crash Course in Typography

It is far beyond the scope of this book to offer a complete discussion of typography and design. Nevertheless, with the knowledge of how to download soft fonts, you have a powerful tool at your disposal and should use it properly. In fact, you have the typesetting and page composition capabilities that 10 years ago would have cost $100,000 or more.

Given this power, it is important for you to adhere to some of the rules of graphic design regarding the use of type. Type is more than just a collection of strokes; it is a means of communicating a message. The right choice of type will convey your message forcefully and with the greatest impact; the wrong choice may leave the viewer or reader cold.

The following list of rules for selecting and using type is by no means exhaustive, but it will get you started in the right direction.

1. Select the most readable typefaces for body text. For blocks of texts in brochures, newsletters, books, and other documents meant to be studied, the most readable fonts have serif typefaces. Serifs are the small horizontal lines attached to the vertical strokes on characters (see Figure 11.12a). They make the text more readable because they keep the eye flowing from character

to character. Sans serif typefaces lack the horizontal strokes and are more suitable for headlines and subheads than for blocks of text (see Figure 11.12b for sans serif samples).

> When I was a boy of fourteen, my father was so ignorant I could hardly stand to have the old man around. But when I got to be twenty-one, I was astonished at how much the old man had learned in seven years
>
> - Mark Twain

Times Roman is a serif type font.

(a)

> When I was a boy of fourteen, my father was so ignorant I could hardly stand to have the old man around. But when I got to be twenty-one, I was astonished at how much the old man had learned in seven years
>
> - Mark Twain

Helvetica Narrow is a sans serif type font.

(b)

Figure 11.12. (a) Samples of serif type. **(b)** Samples of sans serif type.

2. Use a medium weight for blocks of text. While bold and italic can be used to add emphasis, they are not well suited to long blocks of text. Use the regular or medium weight for best readability. Figure 11.13 enables you to see the difference in readability of various weights.

3. Use a contrasting face for captions, subheads, and other elements of the page that must stand out. If you have used a medium weight serif typeface for the body copy, a bold or italic weight might make subheads, callouts—extracted quotes or phrases from the text—or captions stand out better. You can also shift to a sans serif typeface, provided it is compatible with the body text.

When I was a boy of fourteen, my father was so ignorant I could hardly stand to have the old man around. But when I got to be twenty-one, I was astonished at how much the old man had learned in seven years

- Mark Twain

When I was a boy of fourteen, my father was so ignorant I could hardly stand to have the old man around. But when I got to be twenty-one, I was astonished at how much the old man had learned in seven years   - Mark Twain

Figure 11.13. Comparison of a paragraph set in italic, medium weight, with a paragraph set in Roman, bold weight.

4. Do not make the spacing between the lines of text too tight. The spacing between text lines is referred to as leading. The normal amount of leading is computed by taking the point size of the type and adding one point for small point sized typeface or 20 percent for larger ones. If the typeface is 10 points, then a leading of 11 points—in the parlance of graphic designers, "10 on 11" or "10/11"—would give you maximum readability (see Figure 11.14).

Leading is important with smaller point sizes—eight points and below—where the readability markedly drops as the amount of space between lines decreases.

NOTE

Captions sometimes look better when set slightly tighter, without the extra point of leading. For example, 9/9 type might be perfectly legible and work better as a contrast to the body text. Experiment for yourself.

When I was a boy of fourteen, my father was so ignorant
I could hardly stand to have the old man around. But
when I got to be twenty-one, I was astonished at how
much the old man had learned in seven years

- Mark Twain

When I was a boy of fourteen, my father was so ignorant
I could hardly stand to have the old man around. But
when I got to be twenty-one, I was astonished at how
much the old man had learned in seven years

- Mark Twain

Figure 11.14. Comparison of a paragraph set with 10/11 leading (top), and
a paragraph set with 8/7 leading (bottom).

5. Exercise extreme caution when combining typefaces. Unless
   you've had some experience with graphic design the best advice
   for mixing typefaces is don't. Typefaces, especially those with
   serifs, can clash like uncomplimentary colors. Figure 11.15
   shows the "Rambo" approach to design, demonstrating the worst
   possible outcome of throwing all your laser firepower at the
   printed page. The fact is, most font families provide enough
   variation between the various stroke weights, styles, and sizes to
   provide a visually pleasing and lively piece that gets the message
   across (see Figure 11.16).

One exception is the use of a sans serif face for headlines and subheads. For this purpose, you could use a typeface like Helvetica. Use
Helvetica bold for a headline, and various weights and styles of
Helvetica for subheads (see Figure 11.17). Helvetica can also be excellent for captions. There are few *rights* and *wrongs* in graphic design,
although certain tested ideas, such as those listed above, will maximize
your chances of successfully communicating your message. Above all,
experiment and see what works and what does not work best for you.

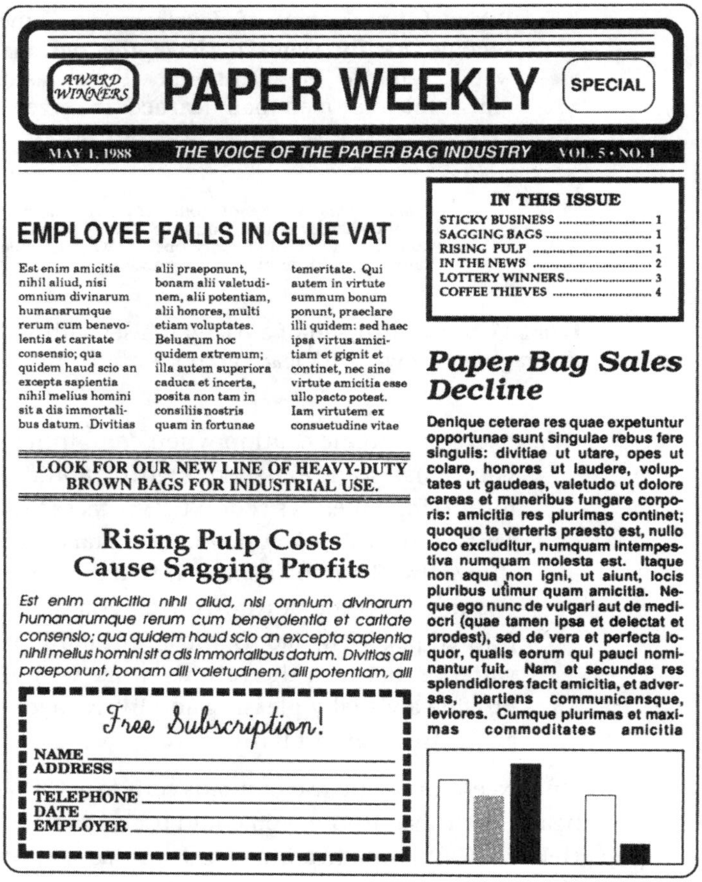

Figure 11.15. "Rambo" approach to typography.

July 1988 / Volume 7 / Number 7

Community News
Keeping People in Touch

Homeowners Agreement

Est enim amicitia nihil aliud, nisi omnium divinarum humanarumque rerum cum benevolentia et caritate consensio; qua quidem haud scio an excepta sapientia nihil melius homini sit a dis immortalibus datum. Divitias alii praeponunt, bonam alii valetudinem, alii potentiam, alii honores, multi etiam voluptates. Beluarum hoc quidem extremum; illa autem superiora caduca et incerta, posita non tam in consiliis

nostris quam in fortunae temeritate. Qui autem in virtute summum bonum ponunt, praeclare illi quidem: sed haec ipsa virtus amicitiam et gignit et continet, nec sine virtute amicitia esse ullo pacto potest.

Iam virtutem ex consuetudine vitae sermonisque nostri interpretemur, nec eam, ut quidam docti, verborum magnificentia metiamur; virosque bonos eos qui habentur numeremus.

Rent Control Update

Principio qui potest esse vita vitalis, ut ait,quae non in amici mutua benevolentia conquiescit. Quid dulcius, quam habere quicum omnia audeas sic loqui ut tecum. Qui esset tantus frustus in prosperis rebus, nisi haberes qui illis aeque ac tu ipse qauderet.

Adversas vero ferre difficile esset sine eo, qui ikllas gravius etiam quam tu ferret. Denique ceterae res quae expetuntur opportunae sunt singulae rebus fere singulis: divitiae ut utare, opes ut colare, honores ut laudere, voluptates ut gaudeas, valetudo ut dolore careas et muneribus fungare

corporis: amicitia res plurimas continet; quoquo te verteris praesto est, nullo loco excluditur, nunquam intempestiva numquam molesta est. Itaque non aqua non igni, ut aiunt, locis pluribus utimur quam amicitia. Neque ego nunc de vulgari aut de mediocri (quae tamen ipsa et delectat et prodest), sed de vera et perfecta loquor, qualis eorum qui pauci nominantur fuit. Nam et secundas res splendidiores facit amicitia, et adversas, partiens communicansque, leviores. Cumque plurimas et maximas commoditates amicitia contineat, tum illa nimirum praestat omnibus.

Condominium Maintenance

Verum enim amicum qui intuetur, tamquam exemplar aliquod intuetur sui. Quocirca et absentes adsunt et egentes abundant et imbecilli valent et, quod difficilius dictu est, mortui vivunt: tantus eos honos, memoria, desiderium prosequitur amicorum; ex quo illorum beat mors videtur, horum vita laudabilis quae ferunt ex doctum.

Id si minus intellegitur, quanta vis amicitiae concordiaeque sit ex

dissensionibus atque discordiis perspici potest. Quae enim domus tam stabilis, quae tam firma civitas est, quae non odiis et discidiis funditus possit everti. Ex quo quantum boni sit in amicitia iudicari potest.

Agrigentinum quidem doctum quemdam virum carminibus vaticinatum ferunt, quae in rerum natura totoque numdo constarent quaeque moverentur, ea contrahere amicitiam.

Figure 11.16. Example of a document with one typeface in a variety of styles.

Urban Renewal

A Report on Prospects for the Twenty-First Century

Nisi aedificaverit domum, in vanum laboraverunt qui aedificant eam. Nisi custodierit civitatem, frustra vigilat qui custodit eam. Vanum est vobis ante lucem surgere: surgite postquam sederitis, qui manducatis panem doloris. Cum dederit dilectis suis somnum: ecce haereditas filii: merces, fructus ventris. Sicut sagittae in many potentis: ita filii excussorum. Beatus vir qui implevit desiderium suum ex pisis: non confundetus cum loquetur inimicis suis in porta. Sicut erat in principio et nunc et semper, et in saecula saeculorum.

Where Do We Stand

Audi caelum, verba mea, plena desiderio et perfusa gaudio. Dic, quaeso, mihi: quae est ista, quae consurgens ut aurora rutilat ut beneficam? Dic nam esta pulchra ut luna electa, ut sol replet laetitia terras, caelos. Maria virgo illa dulcis, praedicata de propheta porta orientalis.

Nigra sum, sed formosa, filiae. Ideo dilexit me rex et introduxit me in cubiculum suum et dixit mihi. Surge, amica mea, et veni. Iam hiems transiit, imber abiit et recessit, flores apparuerunt in terra nostra. Tempus putationis advenit.

Illa sacra et felix porta, per quam mors fuit expulsa, introduxit autem vitam. Quae semper tutum est medium inter homines et

deum, pro culpis remedium. Omnes hanc ergo sequamur qua cum gratia mereamur vitam aeternam. Consequamur. Praestet nobis deus, pater hoc et filius et mater praestet nobis. Pater hoc et filius et mater cuius nomen invocamus dulce miseris solamen. Dum esset rex in accubitu suo, nardus mea dedit odorem suavitatis.

A Full Agenda

Quoniam confortavit seras portarum tuarum, benedixit filiis tuis in te. Qui posuit fines tuos pacem,et adipe frumenti satiat te. Qui emittit eloquium suum terrae; velociter currit sermo eius. Qui dat nivem sicut lanam, nebulam sicut cinerem spargit. Mittit crystallum suam sicut buccellas; ante faciem frigoris eius quis sustinebit? Emittet verbum suum, et liquefaciet ea; flabit spiritus eius, et fluent aquae. Qui annuntiat verbum suum Jacob, justitias et iudicia sua Israel. Non fecit taliter omni nationi, et iudicia sua non manifestavit eis.

Et exultavit spiritus meus in salutari meo. Quia respexit humilitatem ancillae suae, ecce enim ex hoc beatem me dicent omnes generationes. Quia respexit humilitatem ancillae suae, ecce enim ex hoc beatem me dicent omnes generationes. Quia fecit mihi magna qui potens est; et sanctum nomen eius. Et misericordi timentibus eum.

Paradoxes Persist

Fecit potentiam in brachio suo, dispersit superbos mente cordis sui. Desposuit potentes de sede, et exaltavit humiles. Esurientes implevit bonis, et divites dimisit inanes. Suscepit Israel perum suum recordatus misericordiae suae. Sicut locutus est ad patres nostros, et semini eius in saecula.

Nisi aedificaverit domum, in vanum laboraverunt qui aedificant eam. Nisi custodierit civitatem, frustra vigilat qui custodit eam. Vanum est vobis ante lucem surgere: surgite postquam sederitis, qui manducatis panem doloris. Cum dederit dilectis suis somnum: ecce haereditas filii: merces, fructus ventris. Sicut sagittae in many potentis: ita filii excussorum. Beatus vir qui implevit desiderium suum ex pisis: non confundetus cum loquetur inimicis suis in porta et in saecula saeculorum.

Prospects for the Future

Audi caelum, verba mea, plena desiderio et perfusa gaudio. Dic, quaeso, mihi: quae est ista, quae consurgens ut aurora rutilat ut beneficam? Dic nam esta pulchra ut luna electa, ut sol replet laetitia terras, caelos. Maria virgo illa dulcis, praedicata de propheta porta orientalis.

Nigra sum, sed formosa, filiae. Ideo dilexit me rex et introduxit

Figure 11.17. Example of a document using Helvetica heads and serif face body text.

Printer Job Language (PJL)

The increased use of laser printers on networks has made it more important for you to tell the printer exactly how to process a particular print job. Furthermore, because printers are often placed in remote locations and shared between many users, it has become necessary for the printer to be able to notify users about problems that need attention. With the introduction of the LaserJet 4, Hewlett-Packard has added a new layer of printer control commands called Printer Job Language—PJL. It is easier to think of PJL as a higher level command language than PCL or PostScript.

The PJL Concept and Purpose

PJL's primary function is to switch between PCL and PostScript on printers that support both languages. It is important for you to note that PJL is not supported by all the Hewlett-Packard LaserJet Printers. At the time of publication, PJL is recognized and properly handled only by the LaserJet IIISi and LaserJet 4. Sending PJL commands to a printer that does not support PJL can cause unpredictable results, especially in a network environment. Sending an incorrect PJL command to any printer can cause significant problems on a network, so do not use PJL unless you are certain that you know what you are doing.

PJL commands are used by application developers and not by individuals in an office environment. Unless you are developing your own applications, you probably will never see or use a PJL command. However, you will still benefit from knowing about the PJL command structure and how it can affect your printing experience.

As printing has become more sophisticated with multiple printer languages (PCL and PostScript) multiple users, multiple paper types, and sources, and remotely located printers, explicit job separation and control become more important. As described in Chapter 8 on network printing, many of the problems encountered by network users are related to the improper separation of print jobs.

You can avoid these problems by the proper use of PJL. In the case of the inherited settings, a Universal Exit Command resets the printer to its default state at the beginning and the end of each print job. In the case of the incorrect printer language, a language selection command could explicitly precede each print job. Alternatively, the printer could be reset to select a language at the end of the current job just in case the next job fails to select its own language. Finally, the absence of the terminal page eject could be remedied by supplying each print job—as determined by the timeout setting of the network—with a command that ejects the incomplete page when the printing is completed.

Look at a few specific PJL commands and how they work. PJL commands—with the exception of the Universal Exit Language (UEL) —, appear as easy-to-read English text commands. The basic syntax is:

```
@PJL ENTER LANGUAGE = POSTSCRIPT <CR><LF>
```

The @PJL is the PJL command prefix that identifies the text before the terminal <LF> line feed character as a PJL command. The specific command—ENTER LANGUAGE =—and its value—POSTSCRIPT—will vary according to the type of command. Some commands require a value, others do not. The <CR> carriage return is optional, but the <LF> line feed is required to indicate the end of the command.

The Universal Exit Language (UEL) command is special and uses the following unique structure:

```
<ESC>%-12345X
```

This command is recognized by PostScript and PCL as the end of the current job, passing the control back to PJL. The UEL command begins and ends all PJL print jobs. The UEL placed at the beginning of the print job must be followed immediately by an @PJL command, or the printer will be reset to its default printer language and environment. Look at two following examples of a PJL command sequence, the first is a PCL print job and the second is a PostScript print job:

Example 1. A PCL print job example.

```
<ESC>%-12345X@PJL  <CR><LF>

@PJL JOB NAME = "Peter's Report" <CR><LF>

@PJL ENTER LANGUAGE = PCL <CR><LF>

<ESC>E ... PCL report ... <ESC>E<ESC>%-12345X@PJL <CR><LF>

@PJL EOJ NAME = "End of Peter's Report" <CR><LF>

<ESC>%-12345X
```

Example 2. A PostScript print job example.

```
<ESC>%-12345X@PJL  <CR><LF>

@PJL JOB NAME = "Alice's Letter" <CR><LF>

@PJL ENTER LANGUAGE = POSTSCRIPT <CR><LF>

%!PS-ADOBE ... PostScript ... ^D<ESC>%-12345X@PJL <CR><LF>

@PJL EOJ NAME = "End of Alice's Letter" <CR><LF>

<ESC>%-12345X
```

In both examples, note that the command appears on the first line, and the UEL is followed by a PJL command prefix that sets the printer into PJL command mode. The next PJL command establishes the job name followed by the language selection. After selecting the language—PostScript or PCL—the next command initializes that language processor and is followed by the text of the report or letter. The contents of the letter or report are followed in turn by a language-specific termination and the UEL command that resets the language to the printer's default. The terminal end of the job command and a final UEL command complete the PJL command sequence. Note that the repeated language resets and UEL commands may appear redundant, and in many cases they are. But, by following this structure, you can be certain of properly starting and ending the enclosed print job regardless of the initial environment.

Additional PJL commands utilize the new bidirectional port of the LaserJet 4, enabling the printer to respond to specific inquiries or to provide continuous status feedback by setting its Unsolicited Status message feature to On. This latter feature is of particular interest to developers of network and printer control programs, enabling them to report to the user the status of the printer and specific print. The Windows Printing System created by Microsoft for its Windows operating environment, and the latest release of PrintCache by LaserTools, use the bidirectional communication feature of PJL. These products are described in detail in the product reviews found in Appendix C.

In summary, both products present the user with work-in-process status information, displaying not only what page is currently printing, but the estimates of the length of time until the print job is completed. The programs also give automatic notification of situations that require user intervention—low toner, out of paper, or paper jam problems. They also provide performance enhancements through the use of the high speed transmission, and, in the case of the Windows Printing System, reduced processing requirements.

13

PostScript

As anyone who has struggled with the installation of a new printer, monitor, or other hardware add-on to their PC will attest, the versatility of the IBM PC or compatible is often its worst enemy. You are able to attach virtually any printer or monitor with the proper connector, to a PC; and that is one of the appeals of the PC over its more closed-system rival, the Macintosh. However, you need to tell the computer and the peripheral how to talk to one another.

From their introduction, laser printers faced the same challenge. To print a document, the computer had to know how to place each character, image, or dot. If you changed the printer or the computer to a different device, you often had to completely reinstall your software or at least the appropriate drivers.

Concept of PostScript-Device Independence

In 1985, two innovators at a startup company called Adobe Systems, John Warnock and Charles Geschke developed a new concept called PostScript. They decided to create a new communications layer between the computer and the printer that was defined universally and independently of any device setting. Under the Adobe system, each computer was required to specify its print needs in terms of this standard language, and each printer had to be able to translate these commands into the specific placement of dots on the paper. As anyone who has followed the development of Adobe Systems PostScript can attest, the concept was a success.

In many ways, PostScript is best understood as a programming language. In this capacity, it has become the standard protocol of the non-PCL laser printer world. As its creators intended, PostScript has remained machine-independent. Any computer or other device capable of generating a PostScript print job can expect that job to be printable in the same appearance by any printer with a PostScript interpreter. This includes the widely recognized PostScript-based Apple LaserWriters, the PostScript-knowledgable high resolution typesetters, the plug-in PostScript emulators that can be added to LaserJet compatible PCL printers, and any PostScript-capable laser printers. The only significant difference in appearance should be the inherent resolution of the device used to print the job.

PostScript opened new opportunities in the typesetting field. Users can create draft documents printed at 300 dpi on the PostScript laser printer in the office or studio. When the same file was sent by modem or disk to a PostScript typesetter, users could be assured that the high resolution output of the typesetter would have the same typefaces and layout as the draft on the printer. PostScript became a hit with the corporate art and design departments. Suddenly desktop publishing was a reality. The feature of device independence enables a PostScript-equipped printer to communicate with a Macintosh as easily as a PC when each is equipped with a PostScript printer driver.

The second feature that endears PostScript to the artistic community is the inclusion of 35 scalable typefaces in the base interpreter. This expanded the opportunities for PostScript-equipped designers. No longer were they limited to Courier 10-pitch or Times Roman 12-point type. Add to this PostScript's faces and its ability to scale, rotate, and skew each font, and it is easy to see why the designers were impressed.

Page Description Language

PostScript is called a page description language because it literally tells the printer how to lay out the page. The instructions can be displayed in uncompiled ASCII text and can be read by a text editor—for example, DOS's EDIT program. The language consists of a series of instructions that tell the printer to move to such and such a position and draw a line, square, curve, or circle. The key to PostScript is that by limiting itself to vector images based on geometric formulas, it becomes scale independent. The instructions are the same whether the image is printing at 300 dpi on a laser printer, or 2,400 dpi on a photo-typesetter. The printing device decides how to draw the requested shape at the device's highest resolution.

The process of translating the vector instruction into individual dots is called *rasterization*. The command processor of the printer receives each of the PostScript commands, translates it into the individual dots on the page, stores that image in the printer's memory, and passes the bit-mapped image to the print engine one line at a time. In the case of typefaces, the vector instructions for creating each face is stored in the processor's ROM memory, or downloaded to the processor's RAM memory as a soft font. Instead of storing the bit-mapped image of each letter as PCL does, PostScript stores mathematical instructions for drawing the outlines of the character along with further details called hints for enlarging or scaling the outline. It is the responsibility of the processor to generate the dot pattern of each character on the fly. Because the printer knows how to create each letter mathematically, it can easily manipulate that process by rotating, stretching, or skewing a letter. This ability to artistically alter the character set of a PostScript font is particularly useful to artists and designers.

Cost of PostScript

PostScript's flexibility and power come at a price. PostScript-based printers cost $500 or more than the PCL-based printers. The added costs of a PostScript printer are determined by three factors. First, is the license fee paid to Adobe Systems by the printer manufacturer for the right to use the PostScript language and interpreter. The Adobe fee is not that outrageous. Second, translating the printer's vector-based instructions requires more horse power than converting bit-mapped images for a PCL-based printer. PostScript printers must perform their own rasterization of each character and image. The processing requires power, time, and lots of memory. To match rendering times to throughput capabilities of the printers, PostScript printers need more horse power than the PCL devices which adds to the real cost differences between the printers. PostScript-based printers have additional memory requirements because they need to store a complete rasterized image of the entire page before starting the printing process. Although memory prices have fallen recently, the several megabytes of additional memory required by PostScript add to a printer's difference in cost.

Price versus Performance

Some PostScript add-ons for PCL printers avoid the need for a special rasterizing processor by translating the PostScript commands into the native PCL commands already understood by the printer. Alternatively, they use the PC's own processor to create fully bit-mapped images that are transmitted to the laser printer engine, bypassing the printer's processor. Finally, some add-ons include their own processor and memory that link to the printers engine. In each case, the trade-off is price versus performance. When printing some moderately complex pages, it is not uncommon for different PostScript printers or add-ons to take radically different amounts of time. For example, a plug-in cartridge that translates the PostScript command to PCL and to a bit-mapped image might take over 20 minutes to render a page that a dedicated PostScript processor could deliver in seconds.

PostScript versus PCL

In the beginning, it was easy to decide between PostScript and PCL. If you wanted to print just letters or reports in a limited number of fonts and sizes, PCL was fast and cheap. When you wanted any artistic freedom in the number of fonts or the ability to manipulate them, you had to go to PostScript. This is no longer true. The addition of scalable fonts to PCL 5 and the inclusion of 45 TrueType and Intellifonts in the base system of the Laserjet 4 eliminates many of the differences. Further, the addition of PCL emulation to many of the high-end typesetters has reduced the device-independent advantages of PostScript documents. More importantly, however, the premium charged by Adobe for PostScript compatibility has dropped, bringing the cost of

PCL and PostScript within reach for more people. The introduction of PJL (see Chapter 12), intelligent autosensing, and language switching has eliminated the problems of a mixed system. Therefore, if you can afford both systems, you may find it worthwhile. If cost is a major concern, try working with just a PCL-printer that has a well-integrated PostScript upgrade option. When you already have a PCL-based printer, make sure you compare rasterizing times when looking at a PostScript add-on.

14

Using PCL 5: A Primer

Every printer must respond to a set of codes from the computer to put characters in the right place, set margins, and set the pitch. LaserJet printers are no exception; to create a page, the computer must instruct the printer about what to do with each dot. With the LaserJet family and compatibles, the codes comprise more than just a laundry list of numbers; rather, they are used in the printer command language (PCL). Hewlett-Packard wrote the printer command language for its laser printer line, and that has been emulated by a variety of laser printer manufacturers. The LaserJet III and 4 printers use the latest version of PCL, called PCL 5. This version of PCL contains all of the features of previous versions and adds many new commands and functions.

The major new features of the LaserJet III and 4 printers—resolution enhancement and scalable fonts, and 600 dpi printing in the case of the LaserJet 4—are transparent to the user, because there are no PCL 5 commands that directly access or control them. To access a scalable font, you specify the desired font and size as with previous releases of PCL. PCL 5 determines which font to use, scaling and rotating it as necessary.

Some new features of the LaserJet III and 4, however, do make use of new PCL 5 commands. For example, the ability to print in multiple directions on a single page requires a new Print Direction command. The ability to access the Hewlett-Packard GL/2 plotter command language also requires a new set of mode changing commands.

PCL 5 has grammatical rules and a vocabulary. The rules determine which *sentences* are valid, and the vocabulary conveys the meaning of the sentences. The grammar of PCL 5 is also generative. This means that from a small set of rules, you can generate many valid sentences, each of which instructs the printer to perform a different function, such as selecting fonts or altering the number of lines per page. By understanding the basic grammatical rules, you can combine *words* (command codes) from PCL 5's vocabulary and instruct your printer to carry out any desired action.

Why Learn PCL 5?

Many software programs support the LaserJet III, 4, or compatibles, meaning that after you install the applications, they know which PCL 5 printer language commands to issue to carry out various actions. The knowledge about your LaserJet—or any laser printer—is contained in a special file called a printer driver. Drivers for LaserJet III, 4, or compatible printers contain PCL 5 codes; drivers for Epson printers contain the command codes designed for Epsons. When a software program has drivers for a LaserJet III, 4, or compatible printers, after you have gone through the program's installation routine, you can print the most sophisticated page without ever entering a single PCL 5 printer language command code yourself.

Why bother to learn a new language if the software takes care of it for you? If you only plan on using software that has LaserJet III printer drivers, or you never plan on using any other font but the default Courier 10 pitch that resides in the printer, you really don't need to bother. But if you plan to use your laser printer with a software package that does not explicitly support it and you want to alter the output, you will have to learn how to read and write PCL 5 printer language commands.

Even if you don't plan on writing your own PCL 5 commands, you should browse through this chapter. Any time you don't understand why a piece of hardware or software is performing an action, you are at the mercy of the equipment and will be less likely to help yourself when unusual situations arise. Without a cursory understanding of PCL 5, your laser printer will be a black box.

This chapter is designed to open the lid. It provides an explanation of the grammatical rules of the language, giving plenty of practical examples. Chapter 15 provides an in-depth explanation of each command code. The two chapters thus constitute a tutorial and easy-to-use reference guide for creating your own PCL 5 printer language command library.

An Overview of PCL Printer Language: Grammar

When Hewlett-Packard introduced its original LaserJet printer, it had to decide whether to copy one of the existing printer languages: the language of Diablo printers—long regarded as the standard for thimble or daisy-wheel printers—or the language designed for IBM/Epson printers—the standard for dot-matrix printers. Unfortunately, neither the Diablo nor the IBM/Epson language was adequate for the complex task of controlling a 300-dot-per-inch page printer. So Hewlett-Packard started from scratch and created the PCL printer language that is suited to the demands of its LaserJet printers. PCL 5 represents the furthest stages in the evolution of the printer command language.

Although PCL 5 differs from other printer command languages in structure and complexity, it shares many features with its predecessors. For example, PCL 5 printer language instructions are sometimes called *escape sequences*, because they all start with the ASCII Escape character. The Escape character or code is the unprintable character assigned to the ESC key by some software. Because it is unprintable, it is often represented by its decimal ASCII number 027. If you have used printer commands before to control programs such as Lotus 1-2-3, you will recognize the ASCII Escape character. For example, in 1-2-3 you enter \027 015 through the \Print Printer Options Setup command to set an IBM/Epson dot-matrix printer into the compressed print mode.

The Nature of the PCL 5 Printer Language

The Printer Command Language is a type of computer programming language. Unlike most other computer languages such as Basic, Fortran or C, however, PCL is relatively limited. You use PCL to issue individual directive commands, such as *do this* and then *do that*. There is no provision for decision making; therefore, the printer understands the intent of your command and executes it immediately, or it fails to understand your intent and ignores your command altogether.

Most PCL printer language commands are also *state change* in nature, which means that they change the current operating state or values of the printer. For example, when the printer is prepared to print a page with a 1-inch left margin, "1-inch" would be considered the current value or state for the left margin. The printer would continue to print endlessly with a 1-inch left margin until you issue the correct command for another left margin value, say, 2 inches. "2 inches" would then become the new current value. The printer will continue to print 2-inch margins until you change it again or issue a reset command.

When you reset the printer by turning it off or by pressing the reset button on the control panel, it will return to its default configuration with each of the key values returned to its initial state—the LaserJet III and 4 have a default left margin of about 1/4 inch. The default configuration is set by permanent software contained in the logic of the printer, or, in the case of the LaserJet III or 4, it can be set by the user from the control panel at the time of setup. (See Chapter 3 for a complete discussion of the LaserJet 4 control panel menu system.)

Another way to look at a PCL printer is that it uses a printer configuration or environment consisting of many different parameters—page length, left margin, and font—each of which is assigned a value. Each parameter is set to its default value at the time of printer startup or reset. Each parameter will remain fixed until it is set to another value by the user or the user's software.

Components of a PCL 5
Printer Language Command

As with all programming languages, PCL 5 has a command vocabulary and a specific grammar for its use. The combination of vocabulary and grammar enables you to create PCL 5 printer language commands for specific purposes. In addition, it permits the creation of new and unique complex commands from the proper combination of simple commands. Although this opens the door for a virtually unlimited number of commands to be built with the PCL 5 printer language, most people find that they repeatedly use the same group of relatively simple commands. The complex ones are more commonly used by graphics and other application software when they communicate directly with your printer.

As previously mentioned, PCL printer language commands are sometimes called escape sequences or escape commands because they all start with the Escape character Ec—ASCII value 027. This character is used to tell the printer that the characters following the Escape character represent a PCL 5 command. The printer reads the PCL commands and, rather than trying to print them, splits them from the character and graphic data via a process called parsing (see Chapter 1). After they split off from the characters and graphic elements, the PCL 5 printer language commands are executed immediately when they affect the entire page—a paper size command—or are executed in their proper sequence when their actions occur in the middle of a page—a font change command.

PCL Printer Language Grammar

The leading Escape character is followed by a sequence of one or more characters, including upper- and lowercase letters, numbers, and special characters such as parentheses ( ) or ampersands (&). Escape sequences takes the following general form:

```
Ec X y # Z data
```

An explanation of each character is as follows.

Ec = Escape character. The introductory Escape character indicates that a printer command follows.

X = Parameterized character. Indicates variable data that the printer will have to interpret, rather than follow a fixed command. For example, when setting the page length, you will have to supply the number of lines on the page as a parameter. In contrast, when you issue a printer reset command, no parameter is required. The *parameterized character*—Hewlett-Packard's term—

alerts the printer that a parameter requiring special interpretation follows. The parameterized character will be one of the special ASCII characters within the range 33–47—"!" through "/." (See ASCII table B.1 in Appendix B.) Parameterized characters are only used when the command requires that a parametric value be supplied with the command and interpreted by the printer. Therefore, some commands will contain a parameterized character and others will not.

y = Group character. Tells the printer what type of command is being sent. This character is the primary means of distinguishing between the various types of printer commands. For example, all font selection commands contain the group selector "(," all of the page format commands use the group selector "&," and all of the raster (bit-mapped) graphics commands begin with an "*." The Group character is required for all PCL printer language commands. Group characters fall within the range of ASCII characters "'" (apostrophe) through "~" (tilde)—decimal 39–126.

 # = Value field. Some commands require special numerical data. These are called *parameterized commands* and are always preceded by the parameterized character described above. Positioning commands, for example, must indicate exactly how many spaces to move the cursor. Similarly, font selection commands require numerical data to select between various options such as symbol sets, styles, and typefaces. The value field may contain integers or decimal values and may be preceded by a "+" or "5" sign to indicate relative changes from the current value of the parameter—for example, to move the cursor 4 lines down from the current line, you would use +4 in the value field of the command.

Z = Terminating character. An upper- or lowercase ASCII letter corresponding to the parameter to which the preceding value field applies. When the character is lowercase, it indicates that the command continues. When it is uppercase, it concludes the Escape sequence.

data. Certain commands are used to precede data to which they apply. For example, graphics data is preceded by a command indicating how much data follows. The number of data bytes would be defined by the value in the value field.

NOTE

When you are reading or writing PCL 5 commands, it is very important for you to distinguish between several similar characters, as well as upper- and lowercase representation of alphabetic characters. One of the most common group characters is the lowercase "L," "l." This must be carefully differentiated from the number 1 that is also very common in PCL printer language commands. Likewise, you must differentiate between the uppercase letter "O" and zero "0." Also, PCL 5 uses the case of the terminating character of a command to indicate whether the command is finished (uppercase) or continues (lowercase).

The Structure of PCL Printer Language Commands

Three key concepts underlie PCL 5. First, a command starts with the Escape character Ec to announce that it is a command. Second, the command must tell the printer which instruction it represents. This is communicated in one or two characters—parameterized and group characters—following the Escape character. The range of characters assigned to parameterized characters and group characters overlap in the range ASCII numbers 39–47. This means that some characters can be used individually to represent a command from a parameterized group, and others will require two characters to convey this information.

For example, the following command is used to select the Roman-8 symbol set. The "(" character is used as the group indicator to specify font selection. It is also used to show that the command is parameterized. In this case, the value 8 is assigned to the parameter U.

Ec(8U

In contrast, to set the page length you would use the following command where the letter "l" (lowercase "L") indicates a page formatting command but does not indicate that the command will be parameterized. The lowercase "L" (*l*) is italicized in this book to help differentiate it from the number 1. It is preceded by the & character to indicate that it will be a parameterized page command. The value 60 is assigned to the parameter P for 60 lines per page in normal portrait orientation.

```
Ec&l60P
```

The third key concept is that the parameters for a particular variable precede the variable to which it is assigned. This is particularly important to understand before we start combining commands into more complex commands later in this chapter. Notice, for example, how the value 60 precedes the parameter P in the above example.

Creating PCL Printer Language Commands

The following discussion lists several examples of the PCL 5 printer language in action.

Single Commands

The following example is the easiest and the most important:

```
EcE
```

This is the PCL printer reset command. It causes the printer to return to its startup defaults for all variables. In general, it is a good idea to precede any series of PCL printer language commands with a printer reset to ensure that the commands that follow will be acting in the intended environment. This is important, because most printer commands remain in effect until they are specifically changed to something else.

For example, when the printer has been set for landscape orientation and you try to issue a font selection command for a portrait-based font without first switching to portrait orientation, the printer continues to remain in landscape. When the EcE command precedes your selection, all variables are reset to known default values and you can be sure that your commands will be executed as expected. With any LaserJet you can reset the defaults by turning the printer off and then on again. With the LaserJet III, 4, and compatible printers, you can restore the printer to its defaults by pressing and holding the Continue button.

When your setup requires more than one command, DO NOT reset the printer before EACH command, because this will undo the effect of prior commands that you have intentionally issued. Therefore, reset the printer only once before the entire series of commands.

Commands with Variables—Parameterized Commands.

Many commands require that you supply variable information for one or more parameters. For example, when setting the page length or margins, you must specify the number of rows or columns to use. The number specified is called a parameter or parametric value, and commands that use them are parameterized commands.

For example, suppose that you want to change the left margin to one inch. The command involves setting a parameter, the left margin, and using a parameterized character as part of the command. The following is the command structure:

```
Ec&a#L
```

Each component of the command means:

Ec   the Escape code that precedes all printer commands.

&a   indicates that you want to change a page format parameter.

will be replaced by the desired setting in column numbers.

L   indicates that it is the left margin parameter you need to change. The uppercase L indicates the end of the command.

To set the left margin to one inch, you need to replace the # character with a value determined by the number of characters per inch (cpi) of your font. If you are using a 12 cpi font, then the value for one inch will be 12. If you are using a 10 cpi font, the value would be 10. For illustration sake, say that the font is 12 cpi, so the command to set the left margin to one inch would be as follows:

Ec&a12L

In the same fashion, to set the top margin to three inches, you would issue the following command:

Ec&l18E

Each component of the command means the following:

&l = formatting command

18 = three inches with six lines per inch

E = top margin

To set the vertical line spacing to eight lines per inch, the command would be as follows:

Ec&l8D

Each component of the command means the following:

&l = formatting command

8 = eight lines per inch

D = vertical spacing

To select a soft font that has been downloaded and assigned ID #3 (more on this later), you would use the following command:

Ec(3X

Each component of the command means the following:

(= font command

3 = font ID #3

X = select font by ID number

As you can see, even parameterized commands are quite straightforward. They consist of a parameterized group identifier, the parametric value, and the character representing the parameter to be set.

Combining Commands

Most of the complexity of PCL printer language commands comes from the process of combining like commands into a single long command that can appear unfathomable at first glance. For example, the command for selecting 10-point, proportional, Times Roman, bold, upright, portrait type font with the Roman-8 symbol set could be expressed as follows:

```
Ec&l0OEc(8UEc(s1p10v0s3b5T
```

This consists of three separate commands that have been strung together, each starting with the Escape character. They are combined because all three are required to ensure that the desired font is selected. These could just as easily be shown and entered separately as follows:

```
Ec&l0O
Ec(8U
Ec(s1p10v0s3b5T
```

The first command sets the paper orientation to portrait. The parameterized group characters &l indicate that the command will be setting a format parameter. The parameter to be set is O, for orientation. In this command, the O parameter is set to the value of 0, that means portrait orientation. The alternative would be to set it to 1, that would change the orientation to landscape.

The second command selects the symbol set to be used. The single parameterized group character "(" indicates that this will be a command setting a font parameter, in this case the symbol set. The 8U combination, calls for the Roman-8 symbol set. The Roman-8 symbol set is comprised of the USASCII and Roman Extension symbol sets. (See Chapter 9 for more information about symbol sets.)

The third command in the series selects the specific font. It also introduces a new concept—combining like commands from the same group into a single command. To save space in memory and time in transmission, and to reduce the number of key strokes required to enter a command, Hewlett Packard enables commands from the same group to share the same Escape and group character as parts of a continuous single command.

The following rules are for combining commands:

1. They must have exactly the same group character(s).

2. You must shift all terminating characters to lowercase except the very last one, which must be uppercase. The lowercase terminating characters indicate that the command continues, and the final uppercase character indicates that the command does finally end.

3. You should always combine commands in the order that you want them executed from left to right.

Once again, you can break down the third command into simpler individual commands. The command is as follows:

```
Ec(s1p10v0s3b5T
```

It could have been written as follows:

```
Ec(s1P    Ec(s10V    Ec(s0S    Ec(s3B    Ec(s5T
```

Each of the terminating characters has been shifted to uppercase to indicate that each command stands on its own and terminates before the next one begins. Also note that you would have to enter the opening code Ec(s five times instead of once.

Each component of the larger command means the following:

Ec(s1P	indicates that the font will be proportional
Ec(s10V	calls for 10-point type size
Ec(s0S	specifies upright style
Ec(s3B	indicates a bold stroke weight
Ec(s5T	calls for Times Roman typeface

The following is recapping the meaning of the meaning of the command:

```
Ec&l0O  (Part1)     Ec(8U  (Part2)    Ec(s1p10v0s3b5T (Part 3)
```

The following list describes the font you need to use:

Portrait	(Part 1)
Roman-8	(Part 2)
Proportional	(Part 3)

10 Point	(Part 3)
Upright	(Part 3)
Bold	(Part 3)
Times Roman	(Part 3)

Because the font is one of the internal scalable fonts, it is selected and remains in effect until another font is selected or the printer is reset.

The PCL Page

Before you begin to create PCL printer language commands, you must understand how PCL treats a page. You have often heard the LaserJet called a page printer because it will not begin to print a page until it has all of the data it needs for the job. This enables the printer to compose the page from type and graphics commands that refer to positions all over the page in any order, and still print the actual page out one scan line at a time from top to bottom.

In contrast, a daisy wheel or dot-matrix printer must receive its printing instructions in strict printing order from the top left to the bottom right. The laser printer receives the combination of PCL 5 commands and text or graphic data in the order it is transmitted and stores it in a part of memory called the Page Intermediate (see Chapter 1). The data is placed in its proper logical position within the Page Intermediate. PCL 5 positions text and graphics according to their coordinates with-in the Logical Page. You can think of The Logical Page as the printer's equivalent of your computer's monitor screen. The current print loca-tion is called the cursor position. The printer does not have a cursor nor can you see the Logical Page, but the analogy helps you to visualize the positioning logic used by PCL 5.

Logical Page, Physical Page, Printable Area, Text Area

The best way to understand the Logical Page is to look at its relation-ship to the Physical Page, as shown in Figure 14.1. Due to physical limitations, laser printers are unable to print all the way to the edges of the paper—the Physical Page. This creates an absolute margin of about 1/6 of an inch on the sides of the paper and 1/5 of an inch at the top and bottom. The area within these absolute margins is called the Printable Area. By setting the proper margins, you can print a character or graphic anywhere in the Printable Area, hence, its name. Any character that falls entirely or partially outside the Printable Area will not be printed. Graphics will terminate at the edge of the Printable Area.

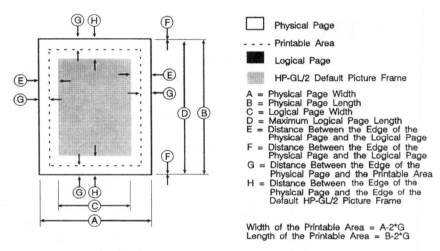

Figure 14.1. The relationship of Logical Page to Physical Page in portrait orientation.

The Logical Page is defined as running from the top of the Physical Page to the bottom of the Physical Page, but contained within the left and right edges of the Printable Area. Note that the Logical Page is somewhat relative. It is limited by the Printable Area as defined by the left and right boundaries, but it uses the top and bottom edges of the Physical Page for its top and bottom boundaries, although the printer cannot really print all the way to the top or bottom edges.

Furthermore, when you change the orientation, the Logical Page also changes. It will still be limited to the area bounded by the top and bottom edges of the Physical Page and the left and right boundaries of the Printable Area, even though these boundaries correspond to the opposite edges of the paper—long edge is top and bottom; short edge is left and right. (See Figure 14.2.) To further complicate matters, the top edge of the Logical Page can be moved down from the top edge of the Physical Page by setting the Top Margin. This means that the top left-hand corner of the Logical Page is set at the intersection of the left boundary of the Printable Area and the position of the Top Margin. This intersection is assigned the cursor position (0,0). All other positions on the Logical Page are referenced by their position relative to this single point. Although this may seem like a complicated method for defining a starting position, it does simplify all of the other commands, because they will be relative to the upper left corner of the Logical Page.

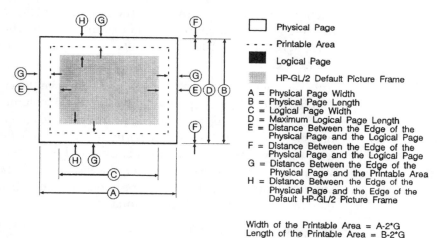

Width of the Printable Area = A-2*G
Length of the Printable Area = B-2*G

Figure 14.2. The relationship between Logical Page and Physical Page in landscape orientation.

Now that the concept of the Logical Page with the upper left corner defined as position (0,0) is established, you can position any character or graphic by moving the cursor to the desired position and instructing the printer to print the desired character. For example, to print the character T at a position two inches over and three inches down from the zero point, you instruct the printer to move the cursor over two inches and then down three inches. Finally, you instruct the printer to print the character.

This would be easy, except that the laser pritner does not think in terms of inches. It uses a measurement system based on setting two key parameters—the Horizontal Motion Index (HMI) and the Vertical Motion Index (VMI). These correspond to the width of a column used for a single character in a fixed pitch type, such as Courier 10, and the height of a single line of text—really the difference between the bottoms of two adjacent lines.

The HMI and VMI can be set in many different fashions and in many different units of measures. The values for the HMI and the VMI are actually stored in the printer in units of 1/3,600th of an inch. You can set the value of the VMI and HMI directly by specifying them in fractions of an inch. For the VMI, the PCL printer language uses the fractional measurement of 1/48th of an inch; for the HMI, PCL uses 1/120th of an inch. The VMI can also be set by specifying the number of lines per inch.

After setting the HMI and the VMI, you can move the cursor anywhere on the Logical Page by specifying the number of columns and rows to move. This technique is appropriate for cursor movement with fixed pitch type, and it moves the cursor in much the same fashion as that used to move the print head for a daisy wheel or dot-matrix printer. With the LaserJet printers, however, the VMI and the HMI can vary to accommodate different sizes of type and can be modified to accommodate the variable pitch of proportional type.

Margins—left, right, and top—Page Length, and Text Length are set in terms of the number of columns or rows that they represent. Because the physical size of a row or column will vary with different settings of the HMI or VMI, so will the physical position of margins and page lengths set with different HMI or VMI settings in place.

For example, suppose that you set a right margin of 60 columns with two different HMI settings. First, the HMI is set for 10-Point Prestige Elite type—12 characters per inch. This would set the HMI to 10/120th or 1/12th of an inch. This HMI is then the width of each column so a right margin setting of 60 columns would place the margin 60-by-1/12th inch or five inches from the left edge of the Logical Page. When you use a larger type, say 12-Point Courier—10 characters per inch—this sets the HMI to 12/120th or 1/10th of an inch. A right margin setting of 60 columns is placed at 60-by-1/10th of an inch, or six inches from the left edge of the Logical Page.

This makes intuitive sense as well as mathematical sense. 60 columns of a larger font should create a longer line of text than 60 columns of a smaller font. Therefore, you can see that the VMI and the HMI are appropriate units of measure for text printing.

However, HMI and VMI are not appropriate for graphic images, because graphics are seldom drawn in such discrete fractions of an inch. PCL uses two measurement units for graphics positioning—dots and decipoints. Dots are the smallest printable unit and equal to 1/300th of an inch. Remember that LaserJet printers can print 300 discrete dots per inch; the smallest printable unit is one such dot. Resolution Enhancement enables the printer to vary the size and relative position of a dot, but it still can print only 300 dots per inch.

The second unit of measurement is called a decipoint and corresponds to 1/10th (deci) of a point. A point is the typographic unit of measurement used to describe the size of type and corresponds to 1/72nd of an inch or 1/12th of a pica—there are six picas to an inch and 1/12-by-1/6 = 1/72. A measure of 1/10th of a point will therefore correspond to 1/720th of an inch. Although the LaserJet engine cannot print with a resolution of 720 dots per inch—the dots and the memory requirements are too big—it can position a particular dot to the nearest 1/720th of an inch.

Sending PCL Printer Language Commands to the Printer

Now that you have learned how to create and position a PCL printer language command, the next step in controlling the LaserJet is to transmit the command from the computer to the printer. Although the printer commands and the computer share the use of the Escape character, you cannot press the Esc key on the keyboard followed by the command. The computer will react to the pressing of the Esc key in its own way depending on the operating system and software you are using.

Instead of using the Esc key, you must tell the computer to send the escape character to the printer. You can do this from within your software by writing a special program in BASIC or some other programming language.

BASIC is an easy to use programming language that is supplied with all PC-DOS and most MS-DOS operating systems. You will use it to demonstrate the process of transmitting commands to the printer. Depending on your version of DOS, you should have access to BASIC, BASICA, QBASIC, or MS-BASIC. Because BASIC is the lowest common denominator of all the versions, it will be used in the examples. You can substitute any other language for BASIC as you choose.

If you are not familiar with BASIC, you should refer to the manual supplied with your computer or operating system software. Alternatively, you can refer to any of the many books on the subject available in your local bookstore or library.

The essential BASIC command instructing your computer to transmit data to the printer is LPRINT. This command transmits the characters following it on same the line. The characters to be transmitted must be contained in quotes as in "ABC" or "&l18E." You will again, however, run into the problem of determining how to tell BASIC to transmit the Escape character. Fortunately, BASIC provides a simple technique. You can describe any ASCII character by its decimal representation by using the following command, where XXX is the decimal ASCII number of the character (use the ASCII table in Appendix B to convert from characters to ASCII decimal values).

```
CHR$(XXX)
```

As mentioned earlier, the Escape character has the ASCII value 027. So you can transmit the Escape character as follows:

```
LPRINT CHR$(027)
```

The Line contains the command (LPRINT) and the object of that command (CHR$(027)). You can place more than one object of the LPRINT command on a single line with a single LPRINT command, by separating the objects with a semicolon (;). Therefore, to transmit the printer reset command, EcE, you would use the following BASIC command:

```
LPRINT CHR$(027);"E";
```

The Escape code must begin each line and a semicolon must end each line except the last line in a given program. The terminal semicolon suppresses the automatic carriage return and line feed sent by BASIC at the end of each line. To transmit the font selection command

(Ec&l00Ecc(8UEc(s1p10v0s3b5T) described earlier, you could use the following command that takes the three components of the font change command and sends them sequentially to the printer.

```
LPRINT CHR$(027);"&l00";
LPRINT CHR$(027);"(8U";
LPRINT CHR$(027);"(s1p10v0s3b5T")
```

Now you can try a BASIC program that does not depend on you having a particular font available. This will enable you to enter the command as listed here, test the results, and see for yourself how easy it is to send PCL printer language commands to your LaserJet. You will transmit the command described earlier to set the left margin to one inch, that will give you sufficient space to hole punch your documents. The following steps explain that process.

1. Start BASIC by typing the following from your DOS prompt (C: for hard disk users; A: for floppy disk users).

   ```
   BASIC
   ```

   When you are using an IBM clone, you may have to insert the diskette containing the BASIC interpreter (program), BASIC.COM, in drive A. You will be presented with a blank screen with a headline across the top, a listing of the function keys across the bottom, and a cursor located in the upperleft-hand corner underneath the BASIC prompt, "ok."

2. Carefully type the following command

   ```
   LPRINT CHR$(027);"&a12L"
   ```

   Make sure that the spacing and use of upper- and lowercase letters is absolutely correct. Press Enter at the end of the line. If you need to, you can retype it or use the BASIC editing commands. (See your BASIC manual.)

3. After you are sure that you have typed the command correctly, press the RUN key (F2) on the IBM PC, or type the command RUN on a separate line and press Enter. The program will transmit the command to the printer. The Form Feed light will be illuminated, indicating that the command was received by and is stored in the printer's memory, and will await the rest of the page data before printing.

4. Before you exit BASIC, you should save the PCL command program that you have just created for future use. This is done by entering the following BASIC command where file name is an appropriate file name of up to eight characters.

```
SAVE"filename
```

A shortcut for entering the word SAVE is to press the F4 key. BASIC will add the .BAS extension. For your 1-inch margin example, you might save it as MARGIN1 by entering the following:

```
SAVE"MARGIN1
```

The file will be stored on the default drive as MARGIN1.BAS. Now you can execute the program by loading it by name and running it.

5. Confirm that you have actually changed the margin by switching back to DOS. Type the following and press Enter.

```
SYSTEM
```

At the DOS prompt, type DIR and press Enter to list the current directory. With the screen still full of data, press and hold the Shift key and press the PRTSC key. This will cause the current screen to be printed. If your BASIC command was properly entered, you should see a perfect 1-inch left margin; if not, your file listings will be printed out with the laser printer's default quarter inch margin.

NOTE

The print screen utility only prints 25 lines of data. Because the laser printer waits for a full page before printing, you will have to eject the page manually by pressing the On-Line button and then pressing the Form Feed button. Press the On-Line button to return the printer to the Ready state. Alternatively, you could send the PCL page eject command—Ec&l0H. The BASIC program would be as follows:

LPRINT CHR$(27);"&l0H"

Batch Files and BASIC

Because BASIC is always available to IBM PC users—the program is actually stored on ROM chips in the computer—it is the language most easily used for quick setup PCL commands. The only problem with BASIC is that it has to be loaded, executed, and unloaded each time you want to issue the command. To facilitate this process, we recommend creating a batch file that will execute each BASIC program you write for your printer. Batch files are short programs written with DOS commands and are used primarily to start other programs such as the previous BASIC program. Batch programs can load and run a named BASIC program. The BASIC program can then be modified to unload itself.

Before creating a batch file to run the MARGIN1.BAS program you previously wrote for setting the left margin to 1 inch, you need to make one minor adjustment to MARGIN.BAS. The adjustment enables the batch file to return to DOS when it is done. The following steps accomplish this purpose.

1. Start BASIC by typing the following command and pressing Enter at the DOS prompt.

   ```
   BASIC
   ```

2. Load MARGIN1.BAS by typing the following command and press Enter.

   ```
   LOAD"MARGIN1
   ```

3. Add another line by typing the following command and press Enter.

   ```
   999 SYSTEM
   ```

   This will add the command to return to DOS at the end of the program. You can use whatever number you want to precede SYSTEM, as long as it is the highest numbered line of your program.

4. Save the new version by typing the following command and press Enter.

   ```
   SAVE"MARGIN1
   ```

5. Exit BASIC by typing the following command and press Enter.

```
SYSTEM
```

Now, you are ready to create the batch file for running MARGIN1. In this example, you will use the DOS COPY CON command, that creates the batch program file by copying the data entered from the keyboard (CON = Console = Keyboard) directly to a disk file. You could also use the EDIT editor or your favorite word processor in ASCII mode to create the batch file. However, for these tasks, the COPY CON command is the quickest and easiest. Start the process of creating a batch file by typing the following and pressing Enter.

```
COPY CON MARGIN1.BAT
```

Note the use of the special .BAT extension. You need to enter the text of the file carefully. If you make an error, you will have to start again. Type the following and press Ctrl-F6.

```
BASIC MARGIN1
```

This causes the character ^Z to appear at the end of the file. Press Enter and the system displays the following:

```
1 File Copied
```

That's all there is to creating a batch file.

You are now ready to test your new Batch file/BASIC program combination. Type the following and press Enter at the DOS prompt.

```
MARGIN1
```

The Batch file will start BASIC and execute the MARGIN1.BAS program that will return control to DOS and leave you back at the DOS prompt. You need to make sure that your program worked using the directory printing test previously described. By using MARGIN1.BAS and MARGIN1.BAT as models, you can create Batch/BASIC program combinations for all of your PCL printer language command needs.

Issuing PCL Printer Language Commands from Application Software

Most major word processing, database, and spreadsheet programs provide a method for transmitting printer codes directly to the printer.

When your software does not support direct transmission of printer control commands, you can usually transmit the necessary commands via BASIC before starting the application. You should be aware, however, that some applications send a printer reset upon start up. This will undo whatever PCL printer language codes you have transmitted through BASIC. In some cases, you can avoid the printer reset of these recalcitrant programs by turning your printer off-line when the application is loading and turning it back on-line when the reset command has been transmitted into oblivion.

You can also use one of the many RAM-resident laser printer utilities that specifically support PCL printer language commands or enable you to issue your own PCL commands after you have started your application.

Raster Graphics

PCL has the ability to transmit graphic images to the printer as strings of data that represent the image to be printed as series of zeros and ones. These are called raster or bit-mapped images. As the laser beam is scanned across the image, it is pulsed on and off, corresponding to the dots that make up the image. The instruction to pulse the laser on for a dot is a "1," and "0" represents the white areas of the image. Figure 14.3 shows how an arrow would be represented as a raster graphic.

To send a raster graphic image to the printer you must perform several steps. First, you must tell the printer where to start the image. Second, you must tell the printer what resolution the data will represent. The printer always prints with 300 dpi resolution, but you can send data that is lower in resolution and the printer will translate it to a 300 dpi representation. The image will appear coarser because each dot of data sent to the printer is printed as a fixed pattern of 300 dpi dots set according to the resolution. (See Figure 14.4.) For example, a 150 dpi resolution image uses a pattern of one dot printed in every four dots and a 75 dpi resolution image uses a pattern of one dot printed in every 16 dots. The chief advantage of using lower resolution images is that they require less user memory. For example, a 2-by-3-inch image at 75 dpi resolution requires 34,200 bits of user memory, but the same image at 300 dpi would require 540,000 bits of memory.

Dot Row	Binary Representation			
	Byte 1	Byte 2	Byte 3	Byte 4
1	00000000	00000000	10000000	00000000
2	00000000	00000000	11000000	00000000
3	00000000	00000000	11100000	00000000
4	00000000	00000000	11110000	00000000
5	00000000	00000000	11111000	00000000
6	00000000	00000000	11111100	00000000
7	00000000	00000000	11111110	00000000
8	00000000	00000000	11111111	00000000
9	00000000	00000000	11111111	10000000
10	11111111	11111111	11111111	11000000
11	11111111	11111111	11111111	11100000
12	11111111	11111111	11111111	11110000
13	11111111	11111111	11111111	11111000
14	11111111	11111111	11111111	11111100
15	11111111	11111111	11111111	11111110
16	11111111	11111111	11111111	11111111
17	11111111	11111111	11111111	11111111
18	11111111	11111111	11111111	11111110
19	11111111	11111111	11111111	11111100
20	11111111	11111111	11111111	11111000
21	11111111	11111111	11111111	11110000
22	11111111	11111111	11111111	11100000
23	11111111	11111111	11111111	11000000
24	00000000	00000000	11111111	10000000
25	00000000	00000000	11111111	00000000
26	00000000	00000000	11111110	00000000
27	00000000	00000000	11111100	00000000
28	00000000	00000000	11111000	00000000
29	00000000	00000000	11110000	00000000
30	00000000	00000000	11100000	00000000
31	00000000	00000000	11000000	00000000
32	00000000	00000000	10000000	00000000

Figure 14.3. Raster or bit-mapped image of an arrow.

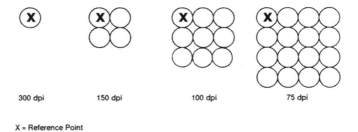

300 dpi   150 dpi   100 dpi   75 dpi

X = Reference Point

Figure 14.4. Dot pattern for each data point at various resolutions.

The third step in the process of sending a raster graphic image is to define the left margin as the current position or as the left edge of the logical page. In most cases, you want to position the cursor in the appropriate location for the upper left corner of the image, and define the left margin of the image as the current location. The fourth step is to send the actual data. As with all raster data, the command preceding each line of the data contains information describing how many bytes of data will be following. Although the image is most easily seen in terms of binary data, the command is sent by using the decimal equivalent of the data. For example, the binary byte 00000000 would be represented as 0, while the string 10000000 would be 128 and the string 11111111 would be 255. The final step is to indicate the end of the raster data.

For example, to send the arrow image contained in Figure 14.3, you would use the following series of commands:

Ec*p300x400Y	Positions the cursor coordinated at 300,400 on the page.
Ec*t75R	Sets the resolution to 75 dpi.
Ec*r1A	Sets the left graphics margin at the current position; i.e., 300 dots from the left edge of the page as set in step 1 above.
Ec*b4W001280	The first line of the raster data. The number 4 in the command indicates that four bytes of data (in decimal form) will follow for the first row of the image. The digit 0 represents the binary string 0000000, and the decimal number 128 represents the binary 10000000. The complete data for the image are shown in Figure 14.5.
Ec*rB	Indicates the end of the raster data. The completed image as it would be printed is shown in Figure 14.6.

Although this seems complicated, it is handled by your software. When you install software with the correct driver for use with your laser printer, you are telling the software how to transmit graphic data to the printer. Thereafter, the software will generate the necessary command strings to transmit its images to the printer. The only time that you might need to send graphics data to the printer manually would be if you wanted to create a unique logo for your company or product. This image could be inserted whenever and wherever you wanted by using the preceding procedure.

Dot Row	byte 1	byte 2	byte 3	byte 4	Decimal Equivalent*
1	00000000	00000000	10000000	00000000	E_C*b4W[0, 0, 128, 0]
2	00000000	00000000	11000000	00000000	E_C*b4W[0, 0, 192, 0]
3	00000000	00000000	11100000	00000000	E_C*b4W[0, 0, 224, 0]
4	00000000	00000000	11110000	00000000	E_C*b4W[0, 0, 240, 0]
5	00000000	00000000	11111000	00000000	E_C*b4W[0, 0, 248, 0]
6	00000000	00000000	11111100	00000000	E_C*b4W[0, 0, 252, 0]
7	00000000	00000000	11111110	00000000	E_C*b4W[0, 0, 254, 0]
8	00000000	00000000	11111111	00000000	E_C*b4W[0, 0, 255, 0]
9	00000000	00000000	11111111	10000000	E_C*b4W[0, 0, 255, 128]
10	11111111	11111111	11111111	11000000	E_C*b4W[255, 255, 255, 192]
11	11111111	11111111	11111111	11100000	E_C*b4W[255, 255, 255, 224]
12	11111111	11111111	11111111	11110000	E_C*b4W[255, 255, 255, 240]
13	11111111	11111111	11111111	11111000	E_C*b4W[255, 255, 255, 248]
14	11111111	11111111	11111111	11111100	E_C*b4W[255, 255, 255, 252]
15	11111111	11111111	11111111	11111110	E_C*b4W[255, 255, 255, 254]
16	11111111	11111111	11111111	11111111	E_C*b4W[255, 255, 255, 255]
17	11111111	11111111	11111111	11111111	E_C*b4W[255, 255, 255, 255]
18	11111111	11111111	11111111	11111110	E_C*b4W[255, 255, 255, 254]
19	11111111	11111111	11111111	11111100	E_C*b4W[255, 255, 255, 252]
20	11111111	11111111	11111111	11111000	E_C*b4W[255, 255, 255, 248]
21	11111111	11111111	11111111	11110000	E_C*b4W[255, 255, 255, 240]
22	11111111	11111111	11111111	11100000	E_C*b4W[255, 255, 255, 224]
23	11111111	11111111	11111111	11000000	E_C*b4W[255, 255, 255, 192]
24	00000000	00000000	11111111	10000000	E_C*b4W[0, 0, 255, 128]
25	00000000	00000000	11111111	00000000	E_C*b4W[0, 0, 255, 0]
26	00000000	00000000	11111110	00000000	E_C*b4W[0, 0, 254, 0]
27	00000000	00000000	11111100	00000000	E_C*b4W[0, 0, 252, 0]
28	00000000	00000000	11111000	00000000	E_C*b4W[0, 0, 248, 0]
29	00000000	00000000	11110000	00000000	E_C*b4W[0, 0, 240, 0]
30	00000000	00000000	11100000	00000000	E_C*b4W[0, 0, 224, 0]
31	00000000	00000000	11000000	00000000	E_C*b4W[0, 0, 192, 0]
32	00000000	00000000	10000000	00000000	E_C*b4W[0, 0, 128, 0]

Raster Image   Raster Data Commands

Figure 14.5. Raster data for arrow. The brackets and commas are not part of the raster data command; they are used only to delineate the data.

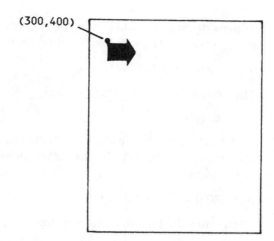

Figure 14.6. Printed image of an arrow.

Rectangular Fill Graphics

In addition to printing raster graphics, the PCL-based laser printer has the ability to generate and print rectangular lines and boxes with a shaded or patterned fill. To generate a shaded box or line, you must first position the cursor in the upper left corner of the space by using one of the positioning commands, then specify the size of the element and the type of filling, and finally issue a print command.

To position the cursor in the upper left corner of the box or line, you can use any of the positioning commands. For example, you could specify the position by its PCL coordinates in dots. To position the element starting at location 300,400, you issue the following command:

```
Ec*p300x400Y
```

To describe a rectangular graphic element such as a rule or box, you must define its shape and size by setting its horizontal and vertical dimensions relative to the current cursor position. To set a horizontal dimension of four inches in terms of decipoints (1/720 of an inch), you first calculate the following total number of decipoints:

4" x 720 dpi = 2,880 decipoints

Then enter the following command:

```
Ec*c2880H
```

To set a vertical dimension of three inches in terms of decipoints (1/720 of an inch), you first calculate the total number of decipoints as the following:

3" x 720 dpi = 2,160 decipoints

Then enter the following command:

```
Ec*c2160V
```

You can also specify the size in terms of dots as follows:

4" x 300 dpi = 1,200 dots

3" x 300 dpi = 900 dots

The same 4-by-3-inch box could be specified with the following commands:

```
Ec*c1200A
Ec*c900B
```

The next step involves setting the fill pattern or shading. The shading is set as a percentage from 1 to 100. One of eight specific shadings will be assigned based on the value specified as shown in Figure 14.7.

The fill patterns are assigned by selecting a number from 1 to 6 corresponding to the patterns shown in Figure 14.8.

You will notice that the fill pattern numbers and the possible percentage numbers overlap. The specific option is resolved when you specify the type of fill to be used in the final Area Fill command. To select a fill pattern of vertical lines (pattern #2), you use the following command:

```
Ec*c2G
```

To select a fill shading of 25 percent, you use the following command:

```
Ec*c25G
```

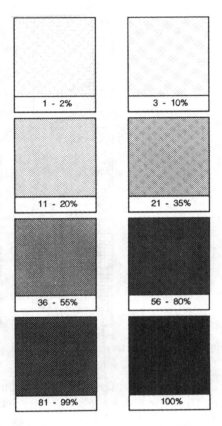

Figure 14.7. Shading patterns.

The final step is for you to instruct the printer to begin the drawing process with either solid, shaded, or patterned fill. The Area Fill command—Ec*c#P—is used to initiate the actual drawing process after the size and the fill have been defined. When the solid fill (#0) is selected, no shading or fill pattern needs to have been defined. If you select patterned fill (#3), you must have specified a fill pattern from 1 to 6. If you select a shaded fill, you must have specified a shading density from 1 to 100.

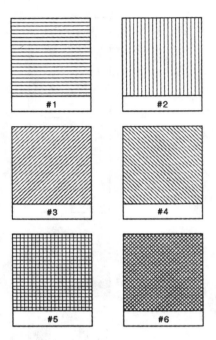

Figure 14.8. Fill patterns.

To draw a 4-by-5-inch box with #5 fill pattern at the position 700, 900, you issue the following sequence of commands:

`Ec*p700x900Y`	Positions the cursor
`Ec*c1200A`	Sets the width
`Ec*c1500B`	Sets the height
`Ec*c6G`	Selects fill pattern #6
`Ec*3P`	Starts drawing with a fill pattern

The shaded or patterned rectangles can be placed anywhere on the printable area of the page and are not affected by margin or perforation skip settings. They are also printed at the printer's maximum resolution (300–600 dpi) regardless of the resolution setting it used for raster graphics.

Soft Font Creation

Although some users will find it easier to purchase soft fonts from Hewlett-Packard or one of the many font designers, others may want to create special fonts or characters. With the PCL printer language, it is possible to create and download individual characters or even complete fonts. You can create bit-mapped or scalable fonts. The discussion will only cover the process of creating a bit-mapped font, because the process for scalable fonts is more complex and beyond the scope of this book.

The process of creating a soft font requires several steps. The first takes place before you turn your computer on and involves designing the individual characters on a 300 dpi grid. (See Figure 14.9.) The individual characters must be of the same general size and are drawn within a rectangular cell that must be the same size for all characters in the font. The cell size defines the size of the printed characters and is specified in the number of dots at 300 dots per inch.

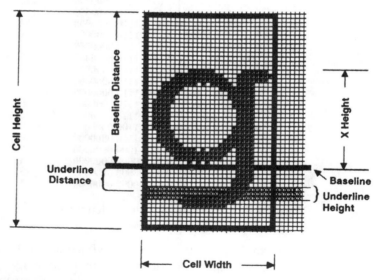

Figure 14.9. A character cell.

After drawing each character in its cell, the image must be translated into its raster or bit-mapped representation of ones and zeros. Figure 14.10 shows how the letter "g" is first converted to a bit map, and then to its decimal equivalent.

Dot Row	Bit Map	Decimal Equivalent			
01	00000000 11111100 00001111 1100000	0	252	15	192
02	00000111 11111111 00011111 1110000	7	255	31	224
03	00001111 11111111 10011111 1100000	15	225	159	192
04	00111111 11010111 11011110 0000000	63	219	224	0
05	00111110 00000001 11111110 0000000	62	1	254	0
06	01111100 00000000 01111110 0000000	124	0	126	0
07	01111000 00000000 01111110 0000000	120	0	126	0
08	11110000 00000000 00111110 0000000	240	0	62	0
09	11110000 00000000 00111110 0000000	240	0	62	0
10	11110000 00000000 00011110 0000000	240	0	30	0
11	11110000 00000000 00011110 0000000	240	0	30	0
12	11110000 00000000 00011110 0000000	240	0	30	0
13	11110000 00000000 00011110 0000000	240	0	30	0
14	11110000 00000000 00111110 0000000	240	0	62	0
15	01111000 00000000 00111110 0000000	120	0	62	0
16	01111000 00000000 01111110 0000000	120	0	126	0
17	01111100 00000000 11111110 0000000	124	0	254	0
18	00111110 00000001 11111110 0000000	62	1	254	0
19	00011111 11010111 11011110 0000000	31	219	222	0
20	00001111 11111111 10011110 0000000	15	255	158	0
21	00000111 11111111 00011110 0000000	7	255	30	0
22	00000000 10101000 00011110 0000000	0	172	30	0
23	00000000 00000000 00011110 0000000	0	0	30	0
24	00000000 00000000 00011110 0000000	0	0	30	0
25	00000000 00000000 00011110 0000000	0	0	30	0
26	00000000 00000000 00111110 0000000	0	0	62	0
27	00000000 00000000 00111100 0000000	0	0	60	0
28	00000000 00000000 01111100 0000000	0	0	124	0
29	00000000 00000001 11111000 0000000	0	1	248	0
30	00000001 11111111 11110000 0000000	1	255	240	0
31	00000011 11111111 11100000 0000000	3	255	224	0
32	00000001 11111111 10000000 0000000	1	255	128	0

Figure 14.10. A bit-mapped image of letter "g."

After you have created all of your characters and translated them to the decimal equivalent of their bit-mapped image, you are ready to create and download the font. The next step involves describing the font to the printer so it knows various parameters. The font description is called the Font Descriptor and you must declare it before downloading the font. The font descriptor will be used to select the font by its characteristics. In addition, you need to assign the font a unique font ID number, so it can be manipulated by number. The font descriptor for bit-mapped fonts consists of 64 bytes of data in the format described in Figure 14.11. Each of the elements of the font descriptor are required, although some elements are reserved for future use and should be set to zero. The others must fall within specific ranges, described as follows:

Byte	15 - MSB 8	7 LSB - 0
0	Font descriptor Size	
2	Reserved	Font Type
4	Reserved	
6	Baseline Distance	
8	Cell Width	
10	Cell Height	
12	Orientation	Spacing
14	Symbol Set	
16	Pitch (Default HMI)	
18	Height	
20	xHeight	
22	Width Type	Style
24	Stroke Weight	Typeface
26	Reserved	Serif Style
28	Reserved	
30	Underline Distance	Underline Height
32	Text Height	
34	Text Width	
36	Reserved	
38	Reserved	
40	Pitch Extended	Height Extended
42	Reserved	
44	Reserved	
46	Reserved	
48-63	Font Name	

Figure 14.11. Bit-mapped font descriptor format.

Font Descriptor

> **Size.** Declares the size of the font descriptor in bytes. Should be set to 64 for bit-mapped fonts.

> **Descriptor Format.** Specifies the following font type:

> 0 Bit-mapped

> 10 Scalable

> **Font Type.** Specifies one of the three following font types:

> 0 A seven-bit font with ASCII decimal values 32 to 127 printable.

> 1 An eight-bit font with ASCII decimal values 32 to 127 and 160 to 255 printable.

> 2 PC-8 font with all characters printable except ASCII decimal values 0, 7–15, and 27.

> **Style MSB.** Describes the font style in combination with Style LSB to make up the style word. The style word is created using the following formula where the values for posture, width, and structure are shown in tables 14.1, 14.2, and 14.3, respectively.

Word = Posture + (4 × Width) + (32 × Structure)

TABLE 14.1. VALUES FOR POSTURE

Value	Posture
0	Upright
1	Italic
2	Alternate Italic
3	Reserved

TABLE 14.2. VALUES FOR WIDTH

Value	Width
0	Normal
1	Condensed
2	Compressed

Value	Width
3	Extra Compressed
4	Ultra Compressed
5	Reserved
6	Extended or Expanded
7	Extra Extended

TABLE 14.3. VALUES FOR STRUCTURE

Value	Structure
0	Solid
1	Outline
2	Inline
3	Contour
4	Solid with shadow
5	Outline with shadow
6	Inline with shadow
7	Contour with shadow
8–11	Patterned
12–15	Patterned with shadow
16	Inverse
17	Inverse in open border
18–31	Reserved

➤ **Baseline Distance**. The measure from the top of the character cell to the imaginary line running along the bottom of each character (excluding the decenders of some characters). The legal values are zero to one dot less than the cell height.

➤ **Cell Width**. The width of the character cell used to declare the size of the characters of the font. The value must lie between 1 and 65,535.

➤ **Cell Height**. The height of the character cell used to declare the size of the characters of the font. The value must lie between 1 and 65,535.

➤ **Orientation.** Declares the orientation of the following fonts:

    0 Portrait

    1 Landscape

    2 Reverse portrait

    3 Reverse landscape

➤ **Spacing.** Either fixed spacing (zero) or proportional spacing (one).

➤ **Symbol Set.** This declares the symbol set that will be used for the font. The actual number must lie between 0 and 2,047 with 0 to 1,023 reserved for use by Hewlett-Packard and 1,02472,047 available for independent font developers. The value of the symbol set is determined by a complex formula based on its PCL escape sequence value field and terminal character and is determined by multiplying the value field by 32, adding the ASCII decimal value of the terminal character and subtracting 64. The common symbol sets and their values are listed in table 14.4.

TABLE 14.4. SYMBOL SET VALUES

Symbol Set Name	PCL Value Field	PCL Termination Character	Symbol Set Value
HP Math-7	0	A	1
HP Line Draw	0	B	2
ISO 60: Norwegian Version 1	0	D	4
ISO 61: Norwegian Version 2	1	D	36
HP Roman Extensions	0	E	5
ISO 4: United Kingdom	1	E	37
ISO 25: French	0	F	6
ISO 69: French	1	F	38
HP German	0	G	7
ISO 21: German	1	G	39
HP Greek-8	8	G	263
ISO 15: Italian	0	I	9
ISO 14: JIS ASCII	0	K	11
ISO 57: Chinese	2	K	75
Technical-7	1	M	45
HP Math-8	8	M	269

Symbol Set Name	PCL Value Field	PCL Termination Character	Symbol Set Value
ISO 100: ECMA-94 (Latin 1)	0	O	14
OCR A	0	O	15
OCR B	1	O	47
ISO 11: Swedish	0	S	19
HP Spanish	1	S	51
ISO 17: Spanish	2	S	83
ISO 10: Spanish	3	S	115
ISO 16: Portuguese	4	S	147
ISO 84: Portuguese	5	S	179
ISO 85: Spanish	6	S	211
ISO 6: ASCII	0	U	21
HP Legal	1	U	53
ISO 2: Intl Reference Version	2	U	85
OEM-1	7	U	245
HP Roman-8	8	U	277
PC-8	10	U	341
PC-8 (D/N)	11	U	373
HP Pi Font	15	U	501

➤ **Pitch**. Specifies the pitch of the font in units equal to 1/4th of a dot—1,200 per inch. The pitch defines the default Horizontal Motion Index (HMI) for the font and can be set to any value between 0 and 16,800.

➤ **Height**. Specifies the height of the font in units equal to 1/4th of a dot—1,200 per inch. The height defines the default Vertical Motion Index (VMI) for the font and can be set to any value between 0 and 10,922. When converted to points—1/72nd of an inch—this is the common measure of the size of a font.

➤ **xHeight**. Specifies the body height of the characters as measured by the height of the lowercase letter "x." This is entered in units equal to 1/4 dot —1,200 per inch.

➤ **Width Type**. Used to describe the general proportional width of the characters from condensed to expanded. This is not used by the LaserJet III printer.

➤ **Style LSB**. Describes the font style in combination with Style MSB. See Style MSB.

➤ **Stroke Weight**. Specifies the thickness of the strokes used to form the characters of the font. The weight can vary from -7 to 7, with -7 representing the thinnest strokes and 7 representing the boldest. The most commonly used values are -3 for light weight, 0 for medium, and 3 for bold.

➤ **Typeface Family**. Specifies one of the predefined typefaces. Hewlett-Packard assigns specific values to its own and third-party faces. The list is dynamic and additional values will be specified in the future. See the current Technical Reference manual for a complete list.

➤ **Serif Style**. Specifies one of the predefined serif styles, from sans serif square to script broken letter and many others. See the current Technical Reference manual for a complete list.

➤ **Underline Distance**. Specifies the distance from the baseline of the font to the position for underlining the characters. The distance is measured to the top line of the dots of the underline and is measured in dots. Positive values will place the underline above the baseline, while negative values will place the underline below the baseline.

➤ **Underline Height**. Describes the vertical thickness of the underline stroke in dots. The LaserJet always uses three dot thick underlines and ignores this field.

➤ **Text Height**. Specifies the interline spacing of the font in units of 1/4 of a dot. This field is ignored by the LaserJet III printer.

➤ **Text Width**. Specifies the average horizontal width of a lowercase character in the font. This field is ignored by the LaserJet III printer.

➤ **First Code**. Specifies the code character of the first printable character. This field is ignored by the LaserJet III printer.

➤ **Last Code**. Specifies the last code in the font.

➤ **Pitch Extended**. This field is used as an addition to the pitch field and fine tunes the pitch. It is measured in 1,024ths of a single dot, giving it extreme precision. The final font pitch is equal to the sum of the pitch and the pitch extended fields.

➤ **Height Extended**. This field is used as an addition to the height field and is used to fine tune the font height. This field is measured in 1,024ths of a single dot, giving it extreme precision. The final font height is equal to the sum of the height and the height extended fields.

➤ **Cap Height**. The distance from the top of an unaccented capital letter to the baseline. This is ignored for bit-mapped fonts.

➤ **Font Number**. A unique number combining the vendors assigned identification number and their unique font number. This field is ignored for bit-mapped fonts.

➤ **Font Name**. A 16-character name that can be used by some software to show what fonts are available to be used. This name is also displayed by the LaserJet III printer in its Font Sample Printout.

To send a font descriptor for a font about to be downloaded, you would first declare the font ID number with the following command, where # is the font ID number.

```
Ec*c#D
```

Then you would send the actual 64-byte font descriptor with the following command, where the data is the 64 bytes of the font descriptor.

```
Ec)s64W data
```

For example, to download the font descriptor for a Courier 10 pitch portrait font—upright, medium, 12 point, HP Roman-8—with the ID number 3, you use the following command, where the data of the font descriptor appears in table 14.5.

```
Ec*c3D
```

```
Ec)s64W data
```

TABLE 14.5. FONT DESCRIPTOR

Field Name	Value	Description
Font descriptor size	64	
Reserved	0	
Font type	1	8 bit
Reserved	0	
Baseline distance	35	
Cell width	30	
Cell height	50	
Orientation	0	Portrait
Spacing	0	Fixed pitch
Symbol set (8U)	277	(8×32 + (85-64))
Pitch	120	30 dots
Height	200	50 dots
x Height	92	23 dots
Width type	0	Normal
Style	0	Upright
Stroke weight	0	Medium
Typeface	3	Courier
Reserved	0	
Serif style	2	Serif line
Reserved	0	
Underline distance	-5	
Underline height	3	
Text height	200	50 dots
Text width	120	30 dots
Reserved	0	
Reserved	0	
Pitch extended	0	
Height extended	0	
Reserved	0	
Reserved	0	
Reserved	0	
Font name	Courier10	

Now you are ready to transmit the actual character data. The first step is to tell the printer which character is to be sent. This is accomplished by assigning each character a character code. This code is generally the ASCII decimal value assigned to that character, although the specific code assigned is up to you. The command to assign a character code is the following, where # is the code to be assigned.

Ec*c#E

The next step is to describe the individual character in much the same fashion that you described the font in general above. This is done by sending a Character Descriptor command followed by the data of the descriptor and finally the bit-mapped data of the character itself. The character descriptor consists of specific fields as shown in Figure 14.12. Like the font descriptor, each field has defined meanings and designated ranges of allowable values.

Byte	15 - MSB	8	7	LSB - 0
0	Format		Continuation	
2	Descriptor Size		Class	
4	Orientation		Reserved	
6	Left Offset			
8	Top Offset			
10	Character Width			
12	Character Height			
14	Delta X			
16	Character Data:			
	(in bytes)			
	•			
	•			
	•			

Figure 14.12. Bit-mapped character descriptor format.

➤ **Format**. Specifies the format of the descriptor and the data following. The value used by the LaserJet III printer is 4.

> ➤ **Continuation**. Because the PCL printer language escape sequences are limited to 32,767 bits of data per block of data transmitted, large characters must be sent in more than one block of data. You can do this by sending a single character descriptor with the first block of data and preceding the subsequent blocks of data for the same character with a truncated descriptor that indicates the data is a continuation of the previous block and for the same character. The continuation block is shown in Figure 14.13.

Byte	15 - MSB	8	7	LSB - 0
0	Format		Continuation (1)	
2	Character Data:			
	•			
	•			
	•			

Figure 14.13. A bit-mapped continuation descriptor format.

> ➤ **Descriptor Size**. Declares the size of the character descriptor in bytes. The LaserJet III uses a 14-byte descriptor.

> ➤ **Class**. Declares the format of the character data. The LaserJet III printer uses the data format specified as numbers 1 or 2, where 1 refers to normal bit-mapped data and 2 refers to bit-mapped data compressed using the run-length encoding.

> ➤ **Orientation**. Specifies the orientation of the character and must match the orientation declared for the font.

> 0 Portrait
>
> 1 Landscape
>
> 2 Reverse portrait
>
> 3 Reverse landscape

➤ **Left Offset**. Specifies the distance from the left edge of the character cell as described in the font descriptor to the left-most edge of the actual character. (See Figure 14.14.) The offset is specified in dots and can range from –16,384 to 16,384.

➤ **Top Offset**. Specifies the distance from the baseline to the top-most point of the character. (See Figure 14.14.) The offset is specified in dots and can range from –16,384 to 16,384.

➤ **Character Width**. Specifies the width of the individual character in dots up to 16,384. (See Figure 14.14.) Specifying an individual character width larger than the cell width declared in the font descriptor will invalidate the character download.

➤ **Character Height**. Specifies the height of the individual character in dots up to 16,384. (See Figure 14.14.) Specifying an individual character height larger than the cell height declared in the font descriptor will invalidate the character download.

➤ **Delta** X. Specifies the actual horizontal cursor movement required to properly space proportional fonts. This differs from the character width in that it includes the left offset and any space following the printed character. (See Figure 14.14.) The Delta X is specified in units of 1/4 of a dot from 0 to 32,767.

➤ **Character Data**. The decimal equivalents of the bit-mapped image in discrete bytes. The data is transmitted sequentially row by row starting in the upper left of the character as it will be printed. Therefore, landscape characters are actually transmitted sideways because they will be printed sideways.

To download the Courier 10 pitch lowercase character "p" (12-point upright, portrait, medium) shown in Figure 14.15, you would send the following commands:

```
Ec*c112E

Ec(144W
```

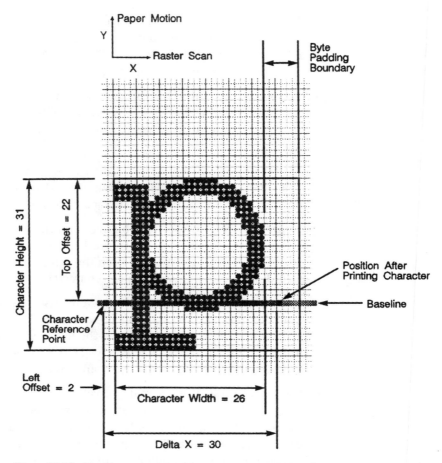

Figure 14.14. Character positioning in portrait orientation.

The character descriptor data is shown in table 14.6 and the character data is shown in Figure 14.15.

TABLE 14.6. CHARACTER DESCRIPTOR

Field	Value	Description
Format	4	
Continuation	0	
Descriptor size	14	

Field	Value	Description
Class	1	
Orientation	0	Portrait
Reserved	0	
Left offset	2	
Top offset	22	
Character width	27	
Character height	32	
Delta X	120	30 dots

Dot Row	Bit Map				Decimal Equivalent			
01	00000000	00001111	11000000	00000000	0	15	192	0
02	11111100	01111111	11111000	00000000	252	127	249	0
03	11111100	11111111	11111100	00000000	252	255	252	0
04	11111101	11110000	00111110	00000000	253	240	62	0
05	00011111	11000000	00001111	00000000	31	192	15	0
06	00011111	10000000	00000111	00000000	31	128	7	0
07	00011111	00000000	00000111	10000000	31	0	7	128
08	00011110	00000000	00000011	10000000	30	0	3	128
09	00011110	00000000	00000011	11000000	30	0	3	192
10	00011100	00000000	00000001	11000000	28	0	1	192
11	00011100	00000000	00000001	11000000	28	0	1	192
12	00011100	00000000	00000001	11000000	28	0	1	192
13	00011100	00000000	00000001	11000000	28	0	1	192
14	00011100	00000000	00000001	11000000	28	0	1	192
15	00011110	00000000	00000001	11000000	30	0	1	192
16	00011110	00000000	00000011	11000000	30	0	3	192
17	00011110	00000000	00000011	10000000	30	0	3	128
18	00011111	00000000	00000111	10000000	31	0	7	128
19	00011111	10000000	00001111	00000000	31	128	15	0
20	00011111	11000000	00011111	00000000	31	192	31	0
21	00011101	11110000	01111110	00000000	29	240	126	0
22	00011100	11111111	11111100	00000000	28	255	252	0
23	00011100	00111111	11110000	00000000	28	63	240	0
24	00011100	00001111	11000000	00000000	28	15	192	0
25	00011100	00000000	00000000	00000000	28	0	0	0
26	00011100	00000000	00000000	00000000	28	0	0	0
27	00011100	00000000	00000000	00000000	28	0	0	0
28	00011100	00000000	00000000	00000000	28	0	0	0
29	11111111	11111100	00000000	00000000	255	252	0	0
30	11111111	11111100	00000000	00000000	255	252	0	0
31	11111111	11111100	00000000	00000000	255	252	0	0

Figure 14.15. Bit-mapped image of the letter "p."

Macros

Macros are collections of individual printer commands that are frequently performed together. Rather than transmit the entire series of commands each time they are used, you can store them as a macro in the printer's memory and execute them as a set with a single command. This saves a great deal of time. PCL uses a series of commands to control the downloading, storing, naming, and executing of macros.

Defining a Macro

To begin the definition of a macro, you need to establish an ID number using the Macro ID command. You must then indicate the beginning of the macro definition by issuing the following start macro definition command:

```
Ec&f3Y      Set macro ID to 3
Ec&f0X      Starts macro definition
```

These commands can be combined into a single command as follows:

```
Ec&f3y0X
```

You would then transmit the commands and data to be contained in the macro and terminate the definition mode with the following command:

```
Ec&f1X
```

Running the Macro

There are three methods of running a macro: execution, calling, and overlaying. When you execute a macro, it alters the setting of the Current Defaults, just as if the commands were individually sent. When you call a macro, the macro commands are executed by starting with the Current Default Environment. The Current Default Environment then resets its values before running the macro. When you overlay a macro, it is run as the final task before printing each page. The overlay process stores the values of the Current Default Environment in memory, and restores the User Default Environment before starting. After finishing, the overlay process resets the values of the Current Default Environment to its values before starting the overlay.

To execute the current macro, you use the following command:

Ec&f2X

To call it, you use the following command:

Ec&f3X

To enable it for overlay, you use the following command:

Ec&f4X

Because the overlay process is a continuous process—once for each page—you must turn it off with the following command:

Ec&f5X

Deleting a Macro

You can delete macros one at a time, by type, or all at once. To delete the current macro, you use the following command:

Ec&f8X

To delete all temporary macros—macros that have been given the designation temporary so that they can be deleted and overwritten—you use the following command:

Ec&f7X

To delete all macros, you use the following command:

Ec&f6X

You can change the status of a macro to permanent—that prevents them from being deleted or overwritten—by using the following command:

Ec&f10X

You can return a macro to the default temporary status with the following command:

Ec&f9X

To set up a macro to create a 1-by-6-inch shaded box at the current position, assign it the ID #4 and execute it, you would enter and run the following BASIC program:

```
LPRINT CHR$(27);"&f1Y"Specify the ID #
LPRINT CHR$(27);"&f0X"Start macro definition
LPRINT CHR$(27);"*c300A"Set horizontal size
LPRINT CHR$(27);"*c1800B"Set vertical size
LPRINT CHR$(27);"*c25G"Selects shading percentage
LPRINT CHR$(27);"*c2P"Starts drawing with shading
LPRINT CHR$(27);"&f1X"Stop macro definition
LPRINT CHR$(27);"&f2X"Execute macro
```

The cursor position is not considered to be part of the Current Default Environment and is not restored after a macro is called. When you want to return the cursor to the starting position after calling a macro, you must store the coordinates of the current cursor position by using the Push command and restore the cursor to that position at the end of the macro by using the Pop command. In other words, the first macro command should be the Push command—Ec&f0S—and the last command should be the Pop command—Ec&f1S.

You can nest two layers of macros by having one macro call, or execute another macro as part of its command file. Be sure that both macros are properly loaded and identified before running the calling macro. You cannot run a macro overlay command from within a macro.

You also cannot use any font management or HP-GL/2 commands in a macro. For example, you can't change the status of a font from temporary to permanent from within a macro.

Status Readback

With the introduction of the LaserJet 4, Hewlett-Packard added bi-directional communication capabilities—the printer can talk back to the computer, telling it about its current status, and warning it about problems that require user intervention. To enable this feature, you need a printer and hardware interface capable of bidirectional communication, and you also need an operating environment and printer driver capable of interrogating and accepting solicited and/or unsolicited status reports. Because the creation of operating environments and printer drivers is beyond the interest and/or programming capabilities of most readers, the topic will be covered only in summary.

The LaserJet 4 and other printers supporting PJL and the PCL status readback commands are capable of reporting their status back to the computer via the bidirectional port. This ability to report statuses back to the computer is what makes the port bidirectional. For the bidirectional feature to work, however, the computer needs to be properly configured to receive information from, as well as send information to, the printer port. This capability is controlled by the printer driver used by your application or operating environment. At the time of this printing, Hewlett-Packard has provided drivers for many of the popular application software products—WordPerfect, Lotus 1-2-3, WordStar—as well as most of the popular operating environments—Windows 3.0 and 3.1, OS/2 and Macintosh. Within the constraints of their respective drivers, you have access to the new bidirectional communication ability. Unfortunately, at the time of this printing, the applications have not yet integrated the bidirectional features. One exception is the new Windows Printing System (see Appendix C) that provides extensive printer status information in the form of displayed messages, animated graphics, and even voice synthesis. LaserTools offers similar features with its latest release of their PrintCache product.

Solicited and Unsolicited Printer Status Information

PCL 5 and PJL support two kinds of printer status information, solicited and unsolicited. Solicited status information is provided only when specifically requested, and unsolicited status information is generated automatically.

Unsolicited Status Information

The transmission of unsolicited status information is governed by the PJL command USTATUS. By setting USTATUS to ON or VERBOSE, you are instructing the printer to send various levels of informational and error messages back to the computer without you requesting them.

The status code is preceded by a five-digit number from 10-000 to 50-999. The codes range upward in such a way that 10-000 to 10-999 are informational messages, and 50-000 to 50-999 represent hardware failures that require immediate operator attention.

To set your printer to provide unsolicited status information, you must first insure that you have your printer port set up for bidirectional communication. This means that the printer driver must be capable of recieving as well as sending information. Then you need to send a PJL command similar to the following:

```
<ESC>%-12345X@PJL <CR><LF>
@PJL USTATUS DEVICE = VERBOSE <CR><LF>
```

After the printer is set for sending unsolicited status reports, it will report any change in status in a form similar to the following:

```
@PJL USTATUS DEVICE<CR><LF>
CODE=40021<CR><LF>
DISPLAY="12 PRINTER OPEN"<CR><LF>
ONLINE=FALSE<CR><LF>
<FF>
```

The ability of your application or operating environment to display or act on this message is totally dependent on the installed print driver and the application/environment.

Solicited Status Information

PCL 5 and PJL also support the explicit request for status information via a series of status readback commands. In essence, the commands enable the computer to request specific information about the printer's status. The printer responds by placing its answers in the output buffer for the requesting port. Again, the ability to use the readback commands depends on the printer driver and application software's ability to not only request the information but to accept and act on the response.

There are two methods for requesting status information from your printer: you can use the PJL INQUIRE or DINQUIRE commands, or you can use the PCL status readback command. The PJL inquiry commands enable you to determine the state of the Default Menu Settings or their current value. The INQUIRE command provides information about the current operating environment, while the DINQUIRE command provides the default status for the requested status.

To use the PJL INQUIRE command, you need to only specify the setting you are interested in with a command of the following form:

```
<ESC>%-12345X@PJL  <CR><LF>
@PJL INQUIRE RESOLUTION <CR><LF>
<ESC>%-12345X
```

The printer will respond with the following:

```
@PJL INQUIRE RESOLUTION<CR><LF>
600 <CR><LF>
<FF>
```

You can also request information about the state of your printer by using a sequence of PCL readback commands. Like the PJL commands, you must not only issue the commands, but you must be capable of listening to and responding to the answers. The readback commands interrogate the status of a particular entity (font, symbol set, macro or user-defined pattern) stored in a particular location type (RAM, ROM, add on module (SIMM) or cartridge) and the specific unit of that type. The required sequence of commands is as follows:

1. Specify the location type   (RAM, ROM and so on)

2. Specify the location unit   (Permanent, left cartridge and so on)

3. Inquire about a specific entity   (Font, symbols set)

For example, you could request the names of the permanently down-loaded soft fonts with the following commands:

Ec*s4T	Set location to downloaded RAM
Ec*s2U	Set unit to permanently downloaded
Ec*s0I	Inquire about fonts

To which the printer would respond in the following form:

```
PCL
SELECT="<Esc>(8U<Esc>(s1p__v0s0b4197T<Esc>(9X"
SELECT="<Esc>(10U<Esc>(s1p__v0s0b4140T<Esc>(13X"
```

The first select line indicates that Marigold font (4197) has been permanently downloaded as font number 9, and the second indicates that Clarendon (4140) has been permanently downloaded as font number 13.

In addition to the status of downloaded fonts, you could inquire about the available fonts on loaded font cartridges or SIMMs, the available macros, symbol sets and user-defined patterns.

The value of such readback statuses is not immediately apparent to some users primarily because the commands work at a relatively low level of printer operation. Everyone can appreciate the value of a printer jam or out of paper message, but who really cares whether font X is located in a cartridge or temporary RAM? The answer becomes apparent if you have ever waited for a large bit-mapped font to download to your printer. You can readily see the advantage of interrogating the printer about the current availability of a particular downloaded font before redownloading the same font. By using the status readback command, intelligent drivers will only download specified fonts if they are not available on an installed cartridge or have not previously been downloaded and remain available. By submitting the correct sequence of status readback commands and interpreting the responses, the driver can often save considerable time without having to make dangerous assumptions.

Summary

At this point, you know all of the basic rules for writing even the most complex PCL printer language command strings. However, regardless of your intended use for PCL and the complexity of the strings you write, precision is most important. A single uppercase letter entered in lowercase form or vice versa causes the command to be ignored by the printer. Neither DOS or your laser printer will give you any clues as to why.

After you have tried to debug a lengthy PCL command string a couple of times, your chances of picking up the error diminish considerably. One of your great strengths—the ability to recognize patterns—is also your greatest weakness when it comes to programming. The solution? If you cannot make a command work on the first or second try, have someone read you the code as you type it into the computer. Then read it back to verify that it is correct.

15

PCL 5 Printer Language Reference Guide

This chapter consists of two parts. The first is a summary reference chart (see table 15.1) that organizes all PCL 5 printer language commands by functional areas, and presents information on the command's parameters, code, and ASCII decimal equivalent. Following the table, you will find detailed information about each PCL 5 printer language command. The commands are also organized by functional area corresponding to table 15.1. Use table 15.1 to select the commands you are interested in, and then turn to the individual guides to learn how to use the command in PCL 5 printer language strings. Each guide presents information on a command's functional group, application, decimal code, hexadecimal code, variables, and usage. In addition, a BASIC example is provided, with important cautions and notes.

TABLE 15.1. PCL CONTEXT PRINTER COMMANDS

Function	Parameter/ Description	PCL Code	Decimal Code Job
Job Control Commands			
Reset			
Reset	—	EcE	027 069
Number of copies	# of copies (1-99)	Ec&l#X	027 038 108 ### 088
Simplex/duplex operation			
Simplex/duplex print (IID, IIID)	Simplex	Ec&l0S	027 038 108 048 083
	Duplex		
	Long-edge binding	Ec&l1S	027 038 108 049 083
	Short-edge binding	Ec&l2S	027 038 108 050 083
Long-edge (left) offset registration	# of decipoints (1/720)	Ec&l#U	027 038 108 ### 085
Short-edge (top) offset registration	# of decipoints (1/720)	Ec&l#Z	027 038 108 ### 090
Page side selection	Next Side	Ec&a0G	027 038 097 048 071
	Front Side	Ec&a1G	027 038 097 049 071
	Back Side	Ec&a2G	027 038 097 050 071
Page Control Commands			
Page length and size			
Paper source	Eject page	Ec&l0H	027 038 108 048 072
	Upper tray, Lower Cassette (LJ 4)	Ec&l1H	027 038 108 049 072
	Manual feed	Ec&l2H	027 038 108 050 072
	Manual envelope feed	Ec&l3H	027 038 108 051 072
	Lower tray, MP Tray (LJ 4)	Ec&l4H	027 038 108 052 072
	Paper deck, Optional Tray (LJ 4)	Ec&l5H	027 038 108 053 072
	Envelope feeder	Ec&l6H	027 038 108 054 072

Function	Parameter/ Description	PCL Code	Decimal Code Job
Page and envelope sizes	Executive	Ec&l1A	027 038 108 049 065
	Letter	Ec&l2A	027 038 108 050 065
	Legal	Ec&l3A	027 038 108 051 065
	A4	Ec&l26A	027 038 108 050 054 065
	B5	Ec&l00A	027 038 108049 048 048 065
	Monarch	Ec&l80A	027 038 108 056 048 065
	COM 10	Ec&l81A	027 038 108 056 049 065
	DL	Ec&l90A	027 038 108 057 048 065
	C5	Ec&l91A	027 038 108 057 049 065
Page length	# of lines	Ec&l#P	027 038 108 ### 080

Orientation

Function	Parameter/ Description	PCL Code	Decimal Code Job
Orientation	Portrait	Ec&l0O	027 038 108 048 079
	Landscape	Ec&l1O	027 038 108 049 079
	Reverse portrait	Ec&l2O	027 038 108 050 079
	Reverse landscape	Ec&l3O	027 038 108 051 079
Print direction	# degrees of rotation (counterclockwise, 90 increments only)	Ec&a#P	027 038 097 ### 080
Top margin	# of lines	Ec&l#E	027 038 108 ### 069
Text length	# of lines	Ec&l#F	027 038 108 ### 070
Left margin	# of columns	Ec&a#L	027 038 097 ### 076
Right margin	# of columns	Ec&a#M	027 038 097 ### 077
Clear horizontal margins	—	Ec9	027 057

Perforation skip mode

Function	Parameter/ Description	PCL Code	Decimal Code Job
Perforation skip mode	Disable	Ec&l0L	027 038 108 048 076
	Enable	Ec&l1L	027 038 108 049 076

continues

TABLE 15.1. CONTINUED

Function	Parameter/ Description	PCL Code	Decimal Code Job
Horizontal column spacing			
Horizontal motion index (HMI)	# of 1/20 increments	Ec&k#H	027 038 107 ### 072
Vertical line spacing			
Vertical motion index (VMI)	# of 1/48 increments	Ec&l#C	027 038 108 ### 067
Line spacing (lines per inch)	1	Ec&l1D	027 038 108 049 068
	2	Ec&l2D	027 038 108 050 068
	3	Ec&l3D	027 038 108 051 068
	4	Ec&l4D	027 038 108 052 068
	6	Ec&l6D	027 038 108 054 068
	8	Ec&l8D	027 038 108 056 068
	12	Ec&l12D	027 038 108 049 050 068
	16	Ec&l16D	027 038 108 049 054 068
	24	Ec&l24D	027 038 108 050 052 068
	48	Ec&l48D	027 038 108 052 056 068
Cursor Positioning			
Vertical and horizontal			
Vertical position	# of rows	Ec&a#R	027 038 097 ### 082
	# of units	Ec*p#Y	027 042 112 ### 089
	# of decipoints	Ec&a#V	027 038 097 ### 086
Horizontal position	# of columns	Ec&a#C	027 038 097 ### 067
	# of units	Ec*p#X	027 042 112 ### 088
	# of decipoints	Ec&a#H	027 038 097 ### 072
Half line feed		Ec=	027 061

Function	Parameter/ Description	PCL Code	Decimal Code Job
End-of-line termination			
Line termination 048 071	CR=CR; LF=LF; FF=FF	Ec&k0G	027 038 107
	CR=CR+LF; LF=LF; FF=FF	Ec&k1G	027 038 107 049 071
	CR=CR; LF=CR+LF; FF=CR+FF	Ec&k2G	027 038 107 050 071
	CR=CR+LF; LF=CR+LF; FF=CR+FF	Ec&k3G	027 038 107 051 071
Push/pop position			
Push/pop position	Push	Ec&f0S	027 038 102 048 083
	Pop	Ec&f1S	027 038 102 049 083

Font Selection

Function	Parameter/ Description	PCL Code	Decimal Code Job
Symbol set selection			
Primary symbol set	ISO 60: Norwegian 1	Ec(0D	027 040 048 068
	ISO 4: United Kingdom	Ec(1E	027 040 049 069
	Windows 3.1 Latin 2	Ec(9E	027 040 057 069
	ISO 69: French	Ec(1F	027 040 049 070
	ISO 21: German	Ec(1G	027 040 049 071
	ISO 15: Italian	Ec(0I	027 040 048 073
	ECMA-94 Latin 1	Ec(0N	027 040 048 078
	ISO 8859-9 Latin 5	Ec(5N	027 040 053 078
	ISO 11: Swedish	Ec(0S	027 040 048 083
	ISO 17: Spanish	Ec(2S	027 040 050 083
	ISO 6: ASCII	Ec(0U	027 040 048 085
	Roman-8	Ec(8U	027 040 056 085
	PC-8	Ec(10U	027 040 049 048 085
	PC-8 D/N	Ec(11U	027 040 049 049 085
	PCX-850	Ec(12U	027 040 049 050 085
	PS Math	Ec(5M	027 040 053 077
	Ventura Math	Ec(6M	027 040 054 077
	Math 8	Ec(8M	027 040 056 077

continues

TABLE 15.1. CONTINUED

Function	Parameter/ Description	PCL Code	Decimal Code Job
	MS Pubs	Ec(6J	027 040 054 074
	MC Text	Ec(12J	027 040 049 050 074
	Wing Dings	Ec(19M	027 040 053 055 057 076
	Symbol	Ec(19M	027 040 049 057 077
	Windows 3.1 Latin 5	Ec(5T	027 040 057 084
	PC Turkish	Ec(9T	027 040 057 084
	Legal	Ec(1U	027 040 049 085
	PC-852	Ec(17U	027 040 049 055 085
	Windows 3.1 Latin 1	Ec(17U	027 040 049 057 085
	Desktop	Ec(7J	027 040 055 074
	PS Text	Ec(10J	027 040 049 048 074
	Ventura Intl	Ec(13J	027 040 049 051 074
	Ventura US	Ec(14J	027 040 049 052 074
	Pi Font	Ec(15U	027 040 049 053 085
	Windows 3.0 Latin 1	Ec(9U	027 040 057 085
Spacing			
Primary spacing	Fixed	Ec(s0P	027 040 115 048 080
	Proportional	Ec(s1P	027 040 115 049 080
Pitch			
Primary pitch	# characters/inch	Ec(s#H	027 040 115 ### 072
Set pitch mode	10.0	Ec&k0S	027 038 107 048 083
	Compressed (16.5-16.7)	Ec&k2S	027 038 107 050 083
	Elite (12.0)	Ec&k4S	027 038 107 052 083
Point size			
Primary height	# points	Ec(s#V	027 040 115 ### 086
Style			
Primary style	Upright (solid)	Ec(s0S	027 040 115 048 083
	Italic	Ec(s1S	027 040 115 049 083
	Condensed	Ec(s4S	027 040 115 052 083

Function	Parameter/ Description	PCL Code	Decimal Code Job
	Condensed italic	Ec(s5S	027 040 115 053 083
	Compressed (extra condensed)	Ec(s8S	027 040 115 056 083
	Expanded	Ec(s24S	027 040 115 050 052 083
	Outline	Ec(s32S	027 040 115 051 050 083
	Inline	Ec(s64S	027 040 115 054 052 083
	Shadowed	Ec(s128S	027 040 115 049 050 056 083
	Outline shadowed	Ec(s160S	027 040 115 049 054 048 083
Stroke weight			
Primary font stroke weight	Ultra thin	Ec(s-7B	027 040 115 045 055 066
	Extra thin	Ec(s-6B	027 040 115 045 054 066
	Thin	Ec(s-5B	027 040 115 045 053 066
	Extra light	Ec(s-4B	027 040 115 045 052 066
	Light	Ec(s-3B	027 040 115 045 051 066
	Demi light	Ec(s-2B	027 040 115 045 050 066
	Semi light	Ec(s-1B	027 040 115 045 049 066
	Medium (book or text)	Ec(s0B	027 040 115 048 066
	Semi bold	Ec(s1B	027 040 115 049 066
	Demi bold	Ec(s2B	027 040 115 050 066
	Bold	Ec(s3B	027 040 115 051 066
	Extra bold	Ec(s4B	027 040 115 052 066
	Black	Ec(s5B	027 040 115 053 066
	Extra black	Ec(s6B	027 040 115 054 066
	Ultra black	Ec(s7B	027 040 115 055 066

continues

TABLE 15.1. CONTINUED

Function	Parameter/ Description	PCL Code	Decimal Code Job
Primary Typeface Family			
Fixed pitch fonts			
Courier	Ec(s3T		027 040 115 051 084
Line Printer	Ex(s0T		027 040 115 048 084
Scalable fonts			
Albertus	Ec(s4362T		027 040 115 052 051 054 050 084
Antique Olive	Ec(s4168T		027 040 115 052 049 054 056 084
Clarendon	Ec(s4140T		027 040 115 052 049 052 048 084
Coronet	Ec(s4116T		027 040 115 052 049 049 054 084
Courier	Ec(s4099T		027 040 115 052 048 057 057 084
Garamond	Ec(s4197T		027 040 115 052 049 057 055 084
Letter Gothic	Ec(s4102T		027 040 115 052 049 048 050 084
Marigold	Ec(s4297T		027 040 115 052 050 057 055 084
CG Omega	Ec(s4113T		027 040 115 052 049 049 051 084
CG Times	Ec(s4101T		027 040 115 052 049 048 049 084
Univers	Ec(s4148T		027 040 115 052 049 052 056 084
Arial	Ec(s16602T		027 040 115 049 054 054 048 050 084
Times New Roman	Ec(s16901T		027 040 115 049 054 057 048 049 084
Symbol	Ec(s16686T		027 040 115 049 054 054 056 054 084
Wingdings	Ec(s31402T		027 040 115 051 049 052 048 050 084

Function	Parameter/ Description	PCL Code	Decimal Code Job
Font default			
Font default	Primary font	Ec(3@	027 040 051 064
	Secondary font	Ec)3@	027 041 051 064
Underline			
Underline	Enable fixed	Ec&d0D	027 038 100 048 068
	Enable floating	Ec&d3D	027 038 100 051 068
	Disable	Ec&d@	027 038 100 064
Transparent print			
Transparent print data	# of bytes	Ec&p#X [Data]	027 038 112 ### 088 [Data]
Font management			
Assign font ID	Font ID #	Ec*c#D	027 042 099 ### 068
Font and character control	Delete all fonts	Ec*c0F	027 042 099 048 070
	Delete all temporary fonts	Ec*c1F	027 042 099 049 070
	Delete last font ID specified	Ec*c2F	027 042 099 050 070
	Delete last character specified	Ec*c3F	027 042 099 051 070
	Make font temporary	Ec*c4F	027 042 099 052 070
	Make font permanent	Ec*c5F	027 042 099 053 070
	Copy/Assign the currently invoked font as temporary	Ec*c6F	027 042 099 054 070
Font selection by ID number			
Selection font	ID # primary font	Ec(#X	027 040 ### 088
	ID # secondary font	Ec)#X	027 041 ### 088

continues

TABLE 15.1. CONTINUED

Function	Parameter/ Description	PCL Code	Decimal Code Job
Soft font creation			
Font descriptor (font header)	# of bytes	Ec)#W [Data]	027 041 115 ### 087 [Data]
Download character	# of bytes	Ec(s#W [Data]	027 040 115 ### 087 [Data]
Character code	Character code #	Ec*c#E	027 042 099 ### 069

Graphics

Function	Parameter/ Description	PCL Code	Decimal Code Job
PCL vector graphics switching/set-up			
Enter PCL mode	Use previous PCL cursor position	Ec%0A	027 037 048 65
	Use current HP-GL/2 pen position for cursor position	Ec%1a	027 037 048 65
Enter HP-GLl2 mode	Use previous HP-GL/2 pen position	Ec%0B	027 037 048 066
	Use current PCL cursor position	Ec%1B	027 037 049 066
HP-GL/2 plot horizontal size	Horizontal size in inches	Ec*c#K	027 042 099 ### 075
HP-GL/2 plot vertical size	Vertical size in inches	Ec*c#L	027 042 099 ### 076
Set picture frame anchor point	Set anchor point to cursor position	Ec*c0T	027 042 099 048 084
Picture frame horizontal size	Decipoints	Ec*c#X	027 042 99 ### 088
Picture frame vertical size	Decipoints	Ec*c#Y	027 042 099 ### 089
Raster graphics			
Raster resolution	75	Ec*t75R	027 042 116 055 053 082
(dots/inch)	100	Ec*t100R	027 042 116 049 048 048 082
	150	Ec*t150R	027 042 116 049 053 048 082
	300	Ec*t300R	027 042 116 051 048 048 082

Function	Parameter/ Description	PCL Code	Decimal Code Job
	600	Ec*t600	027 042 116 054 048 048 082

Raster graphics creation

Function	Parameter/ Description	PCL Code	Decimal Code Job
Raster graphics presentation	Rotate image	Ec*r0F	027 042 114 048 070
	LaserJet landscape compatible	Ec*r3F	027 042 114 051 070
Start raster graphics	Left raster graphics margin	Ec*r0A	027 042 114 048 065
	Current cursor	Ec*r1A	027 042 114 049 065
Raster Y offset	# of raster lines of vertical movement	Ec*b#Y	027 042 098 ### 089
Set raster compression mode	Uncoded	Ec*b0M	027 042 098 048 077
	Run-length uncoded	Ec*b1M	027 042 098 049 077
	Tagged image file format	Ec*b2M	027 042 098 050 077
	Delta row	Ec*b3M	027 042 098 051 077
Transfer raster data	# of bytes	Ec*b#W [Data]	027 042 098 ### 087
End raster graphics	Old Version	Ec*rB	027 042 114 066
	Preferred	Ec*rC	027 042 114 067
Raster height	# raster rows	Ec*r#T	027 042 114 ### 084
Raster width	# pixels in the specified resolution	Ec*r#S	027 042 114 ### 083

The Print Model

Imaging

Function	Parameter/ Description	PCL Code	Decimal Code Job
Select pattern	Solid black (default)	Ec*v0T	027 042 118 048 084
	Solid white	Ec*v1T	027 042 118 049 084
	HP-defined shading pattern	Ec*v2T	027 042 118 050 084
	HP-defined cross-hatched pattern	Ec*v3T	027 042 118 051 084
	User-Defined pattern	Ec*V4T	027 042 118 052 084
Select source transparency mode	Transparent	Ec*v0N	027 042 118 048 078
	Opaque	Ec*v1N	027 042 118 049 078
Select pattern transparency mode	Transparent	Ec*v0O	027 042 118 048 079
	Opaque	Ec*v1O	027 042 118 049 079

continues

TABLE 15.1. CONTINUED

Function	Parameter/ Description	PCL Code	Decimal Code Job
Rectangle dimensions			
Rectangle width (horizontal size)	# of dots	Ec*c#A	027 042 099 ### 065
	# of decipoints	Ec*c#H	027 042 099 ### 072
Rectangle height (vertical size)	# of dots	Ec*c#B	027 042 099 ### 066
	# of decipoints	Ec*c#V	027 042 099 ### 086
Rectangular area fill			
Fill rectangular area	Solid black	Ec*c0P	027 042 099 048 080
	Erase (solid white fill)	Ec*c1P	027 042 099 049 080
	Shaded fill	Ec*c2P	027 042 099 050 080
	Cross-hatched fill	Ec*c3P	027 042 099 051 080
	Current pattern	Ec*c5P	027 042 099 053 080
Pattern ID	% of shading or type of pattern	Ec*c#G	027 042 099 ### 071
Shading (% gray)	2	Ec*c2G	027 042 099 050 071
	10	Ec*c10G	027 042 099 049 048 071
	15	Ec*c15G	027 042 099 049 053 071
	30	Ec*c30G	027 042 099 051 048 071
	45	Ec*c45G	027 042 099 052 053 071
	70	Ec*c70G	027 042 099 055 048 071
	90	Ec*c90G	027 042 099 057 048 071
	100	Ec*c100G	027 042 099 049 048 048 071
Pattern	1 Horizontal lines	Ec*c1G	027 042 099 049 071
	2 Vertical lines	Ec*c2G	027 042 099 050 071
	3 Diagonal lines	Ec*c3G	027 042 099 051 071
	4 Diagonal lines	Ec*c4G	027 042 099 052 071
	5 Square grid	Ec*c5G	027 042 099 053 071
	6 Diagonal grid	Ec*c6G	027 042 099 054 071

Function	Parameter/ Description	PCL Code	Decimal Code Job
User-defined Pattern			
Define Pattern	# of Bytes	Ec*c#W [data]	027 042 ### 087 [Data]
Pattern Control	Delete all paterns	Ec*c0Q	027 042 099 048 081
	Delete temporary patterns	Ec*c1Q	027 042 099 049 081
	Delete current pattern	Ec*c2Q	027 042 099 050 081
	Make pattern temporary	Ec*c4Q	027 042 099 052 081
	Make pattern temporary	Ec*c5Q	027 042 099 053 081
Set pattern reference	Rotate with orientation	Ec*p0R	027 042 112 048 082
Point	Follow physical page	Ec*p1R	027 042 112 049 082

Macros

Function	Parameter/ Description	PCL Code	Decimal Code Job
Macro ID	Marco ID #	Ec&f#Y	027 038 102 ### 089
Macro control	Start macro definition	Ec&f0X	027 038 102 048 088
	Stop macro definition	Ec&f1X	027 038 102 049 088
	Execute macro	Ec&f2X	027 038 102 050 088
	Call macro	Ec&f3X	027 038 102 051 088
	Enable overlay	Ec&f4X	027 038 102 052 088
	Disable overlay	Ec&f5X	027 038 102 053 088
	Delete macros	Ec&f6X	027 038 102 054 088
	Delete all temporary macros	Ec&f7X	027 038 102 055 088
	Delete macro ID	Ec&f8X	027 038 102 056 088
	Make temporary	Ec&f9X	027 038 102 057 088
	Make permanent	Ec&f10X	027 038 102 049 048 088

Programming Tools

Function	Parameter/ Description	PCL Code	Decimal Code Job
End-of-line-wrap	Enabled	Ec&s0C	027 038 115 048 067
	Disabled	Ec&s1C	027 038 115 049 067
Display Functions	On	EcY	027 089
	Off	EcZ	027 090

continues

TABLE 15.1. CONTINUED

Function	Parameter/ Description	PCL Code	Decimal Code Job
Status readback			
Set status readback location type	Invalid location	Ec*s0T	027 042 115 048 084
	Currently selected	Ec*s1T	027 042 115 049 084
	All locations	Ec*s2T	027 042 115 050 084
	Internal	Ec*s3T	027 042 115 051 084
	Downloaded	Ec*s4T	027 042 115 052 084
	Cartridge	Ec*s5T	027 042 115 053 084
	User-Installed ROM	Ec*s7T	027 042 115 055 084
Set status readback location Unit	All entities of the type	Ec*s0U	027 042 115 048 085
	Entity #1 or Temporary	Ec*s1U	027 042 115 049 085
	Entity #2 or Permanent	Ec*s2U	027 042 115 050 085
	Entity #3	Ec*s3U	027 042 115 051 085
	Entity #4	Ec*s4U	027 042 115 052 085
Inquire status			
Readback entity	Font	Ec*s0I	027 042 115 048 073
	Macro	Ec*s1I	027 042 115 049 073
	User-defined pattern	Ec*s2I	027 042 115 050 073
	Symbol Set	Ec*s3I	027 042 115 051 073
	Font Extender	Ec*s4I	027 042 115 052 073
Flush all pages	Flush completed pages	Ec&r0F	027 038 114 048 070
	Flush all page data	Ec&r1F	027 038 114 049 070
Free memory space	—	Ec*s1M	027 042 115 049 077
Echo	# = echo value	Ec*s#X	027 042 115 ### 088

Print Job Control

The print job control commands are used to set the overall environment for the print job. The most frequently used PCL 5 command is the EcE reset command. This command returns the printer to its default settings enabling you to set individual parameters from a known base environment. Other common print job control commands control the number of copies of each page printed and the binding offset. The binding offset enables you to distinguish between left and right page positions so that you can control the center gutter on bound documents. For users with LaserJet IIID printers, additional commands enable you to select simplex or duplex operations, and the side of the page upon which to print.

With the introduction of the LaserJet 4, Hewlett-Packard has added a new job control language called Print Job Language or PJL. PJL sits above PCL and other printer languages such as PostScript. (See Chapter 12 for a complete description of PJL.)

Reset Printer

Function group	Print job control
Application	Reset the printer to the User Defaults.
PCL 5 Command	EcE
Decimal Code	027 069
Hexadecimal Code	1B 45
Variables	None

Usage

To reset the printer to the User Defaults, issue the following command:

```
EcE
```

BASIC Example

To reset the printer from BASIC, you would enter and run the following BASIC program:

```
LPRINT CHR$(27);"E"
```

Cautions

A printer reset deletes all temporary soft fonts and temporary macros from the printer's memory. It also causes all data stored in the print buffer to be immediately printed and the page ejected, therefore you cannot issue a printer reset within a given page.

Notes

You will need to issue a printer reset *before* and *after* each print job. This ensures that subsequent commands will act from a known environment and will produce consistent results. (See Chapter 8 for a complete discussion of PJL and the Universal Edit Language.)

Number of Copies

Function group	Print job control
Application	Sets the number of each page to be printed.
PCL 5 Command	Ec&l#5
Decimal Code	027 038 108 ### 088
Hexadecimal Code	1B 26 6C ## 58
Variables	The # of copies: default = 1; range = 1799.

Usage

Number of Pages specifies the number of each page that will be printed. As with all PCL 5 commands, it will remain in effect until reset to 1 by reissuing the command, or resetting the printer. The printer prints multiple copies of the same page together, therefore specifying multiple copies of a long document will require that you collate the output. However, the printer will only have to compose the page once, and will print the subsequent copies at its top-rated output speed. To print five copies of each page, issue the following command:

```
Ec&l5X
```

BASIC Example

To print 12 copies of each page, you enter and run the following BASIC program:

```
LPRINT CHR$(27);"&l12X"
```

Cautions

To improve the printing speed, the laser printer prints the multiple copies of each page together so the final documents will be inter-mingled, and will have to be recollated.

Notes

You can issue the command anywhere in the current page and it will affect the printing of the current and all subsequent pages until set again or the printer is reset.

Simplex/Duplex (LaserJet IIID)

Function group	Print job control
Application	Selects one- or two-sided printing for LaserJet IIID only.
PCL 5 Command	Ec&l#S
Decimal Code	027 038 108 ### 083
Hexadecimal Code	1B 26 6C ## 53
Variables	# = 0 Simplex Printing (default)
	# = 1 Duplex, long–edge binding
	# = 2 Duplex, short-edge binding

Usage

When you are printing with duplex printers such as the LaserJet IIID, you can print on either the front side of each sheet—simplex—or on both sides—duplex. When you select duplex, you must specify how you plan to bind the sheets together—long edge or short edge. This will determine how the LaserJet IIID rotates and positions the back side of each sheet relative to the front side. The Simplex/Duplex command interacts with the orientation selection, and the left/top offset commands.

For example, when you select long-edge binding and print in portrait orientation, you will lay out each pair of pages as in a typical book with the left edge offset determining the center gutter. However, when you select short-edge binding and portrait orientation, you will print in a fashion typical for a flip chart with the top edge offset determining the center gutter. To select simplex printing, you use the following command:

```
Ec&l0S
```

BASIC Example

To select long-edge binding for duplex printing, you enter and run the following BASIC program:

```
LPRINT CHR$(27);"&l1S"
```

Notes

The simplex printing command is ignored by printers that cannot print on both sides of the paper.

Left Edge (Long) Offset

Function group	Print job control
Application	Positions the logical page on the physical page relative to the left edge of the page.
PCL 5 Command	Ec&l#U
Decimal Code	027 038 108 ### 085
Hexadecimal Code	1B 26 6C ## 55
Variables	# of decipoints (1/720 inch) offset. Positive values displace the logical page to the right, negative values to the left. Default = 0; range = –32767 to 32767.

Usage

Left Edge (Long) Offset is mostly used to control the variable left margin of duplexed print jobs that are intended to be bound along the left edge. By changing the left offset page by page, you can control the center gutter of the bound document without having to alter the actual left and right margins for each page. To shift the printed page to the right for a right-hand—odd-numbered—page, issue the following command:

```
Ec&l360U
```

BASIC Example

To move the printed page to the left 1/4-inch for a left-hand—even-numbered—page, you enter and run the following BASIC program:

```
LPRINT CHR$(27);"&l-180U"
```

Cautions

Moving the logical page outside the printable area will cause loss of data.

Notes

The offset direction is absolute and is not affected by the page orientation. You will use left offset for portrait orientation, and top offset in landscape orientation.

Top Edge (Short) Offset

Function group	Print job control
Application	Positions the logical page on the physical page relative to the top edge of the page.
PCL 5 Command	Ec&l#Z
Decimal Code	027 038 108 ### 090

Hexadecimal Code   1B 26 6C ## 5A

Variables   # of decipoints (1/720 inch) offset.
                          Positive values displace the logical
                          page down, negative values up. Default
                          = 0; range = –32767 to 32767.

Usage

Top Edge (Short) Offset is mostly used to control the variable left margin of duplexed print jobs that are intended to be bound along the short—for example, documents printed in landscape orientation. When you are printing in landscape orientation, you can control the center gutter of the bound document by changing the top offset page by page, without having to alter the actual left and right margins for each page. To shift the printed page half an inch to the right in landscape orientation for a right-hand—odd-numbered—page, you need to move the logical page down the physical page and issue the following command:

```
Ec&l360X
```

BASIC Example

To move the printed page to the left 1/4 inch for a left-hand—even-numbered—landscape orientation page, you enter and run the following BASIC program:

```
LPRINT CHR$(27);"&l-180U"
```

Cautions

Moving the logical page outside the printable area will cause a loss of data.

Notes

The offset direction is absolute and is not affected by the page orientation. You will use the left offset for portrait orientation, and the top offset in landscape orientation.

Page Side Selection (LaserJet IIID)

Function group	Print job control
Application	Determines which side of the paper to print the next page with duplex printers such as the LaserJet IIID.
PCL 5 Command	Ec&a#G
Decimal Code	027 038 097 ### 071
Hexadecimal Code	1B 26 61 ## 47
Variables	# = 0 Print on next side (default)
	# = 1 Print on front side
	# = 2 Print on back side

Usage

When you are printing on a duplex printer such as the LaserJet IIID, you can control on which side the next page is printed. For example, you need to start each chapter of a book on a right-hand—odd-numbered—page. You can force this by issuing the following command to print on the front side of the paper regardless of the last page printed.

    Ec&a1G

BASIC Example

To print the next page on the side that is next to be printed, you enter and run the following BASIC program:

```
LPRINT CHR$(27);"&a0G"
```

Notes

When you issue a side selection command in the middle of a page, the printer terminates the current page, ejects it, and starts on the new page as specified even if it is assigned to the same side as the current page.

Page Control

The page control commands control the source of paper, page dimensions and margins, print orientation and direction, and line spacing. Because many of these commands are interrelated, changing one setting will effect other settings. Changing the orientation of the logical page, for instance, will also change the starting direction for the Printing Direction command, because the rotation values for the print direction are relative to the logical page. Similarly, the left and right margins are related to the page dimension. Commands that place the left margin to the right of the right margin and vice versa are ignored. Finally, several commands perform the same function. The line spacing command and the vertical motion index command set the size of a row of text. The former in terms of lines per inch, and the latter in increments of 1/48th-of-an inch.

Eject Page/Form Feed

Function group	Page control
Application	Forces the current page to be immediately printed and the page ejected from the printer.
PCL 5 Command	Ec&l0H
Decimal Code	027 038 108 048 072
Hexadecimal Code	1B 26 6C 30 48
Variables	None

Usage

When you force the current page to be immediately printed, you will only print the data that has already been transmitted to the printer. Any subsequent data for that page will be printed on the next page.

To force the printing of the current page, you use the following command:

```
Ec&l0H
```

BASIC Example

To print and eject the current page, you enter and run the following BASIC program:

```
LPRINT CHR$(27);"&l0H"
```

Cautions

Forcing the printing of the current page can cause difficulty with proper pagination in some software. For example, issuing this command as an embedded print command from Lotus 1-2-3 will not reset the 1-2-3 line count, and will cause 1-2-3 to paginate incorrectly for the rest of that print job.

Paper Source

Function group	Page control
Application	Selects the source of paper for printing.
PCL 5 Command	Ec&l#H
Decimal Code	027 038 108 ### 072
Hexadecimal Code	1B 26 6C ## 48
Variables	# = 0 Page eject
	# = 1 Feed from paper tray
	# = 2 Manual paper feed
	# = 3 Manual envelope feed
	# = 4 Feed from lower paper tray
	# = 5 Feed from paper deck
	# = 6 Feed envelope from envelope feeder on IID or IIID

Usage

When you designate a manual feed, the printer will pause until you feed the requested paper into the manual feed slot or press the Continue button to override the request and print from the installed paper tray. To request a manual paper feed, issue the following command

```
Ec&l2H
```

BASIC Example

To reset the printer to feed from the internal paper tray, you enter and run the following BASIC program:

```
LPRINT CHR$(27);"&l1H"
```

Notes

This command is the same as the Form Feed or Page Eject command when used with a variable value of zero.

Page Size

Function group	Page control
Application	Sets the physical page size.
PCL 5 Command	Ec&l#A
Decimal Code	027 038 108 ### 065
Hexadecimal Code	1B 26 6C ## 41
Variables	Pages
	# = 1 Executive
	# = 2 Letter (default)
	# = 3 Legal
	# = 26 A4
	Envelopes
	# = 80 Monarch

# = 81	Commercial 10
# = 90	International DL
# = 91	International C5

Usage

The logical page size is set according to the dimensions of the paper selected. When you select a paper size, you also need to set the logical page size according to the orientation selected. Selecting legal paper in landscape orientation, for example, will set the logical page length to 2,550 dots or 8 1/2 inches. Figure 15.1 shows the dimensions in portrait orientation.

The number of lines of text that will print are determined by the page length less the margin settings, or by the text length setting (see Margins and Text Length commands).

To set the page size to legal, enter the following command:

```
Ec&l3A
```

BASIC Example

To set a page size to executive paper, enter and run the following BASIC program:

```
LPRINT CHR$(27);"&l1A"
```

Notes

The default page size is determined by the installed paper tray. The tray engages sensors in the printer that allow the printer to ascertain the size of the paper tray. If no tray is inserted, the default is set to letter-sized paper.

If the page size is set to a size different from the installed tray, the printer will stop and request the specified paper. Either insert the correct paper tray and press the Continue button or manually feed the specified paper.

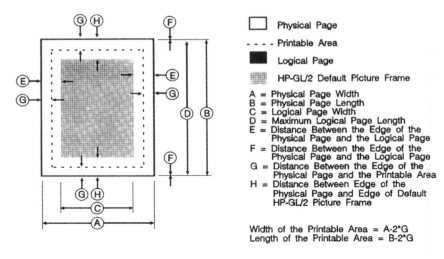

All dimensions are in dots.

PAPER SIZE	A	B	C	D	E	F	G	H
LETTER	2550	3300	2400	3300	75	0	50	150
LEGAL	2550	4200	2400	4200	75	0	50	150
EXECUTIVE	2175	3150	2025	3150	75	0	50	150
A4	2480	3507	2338	3507	71	0	50	150
COM-10	1237	2850	1087	2850	75	0	50	150
MONARCH	1162	2250	1012	2250	75	0	50	150
C5	1913	2704	1771	2704	71	0	50	150
DL	1299	2598	1157	2598	71	0	50	150

Figure 15.1. Page dimensions in portrait orientation.

Page Length

Function group	Page control
Application	Sets the physical page length.
PCL 5 Command	Ec&l#P
Decimal Code	027 038 108 ### 080

Hexadecimal Code	1B 26 6C ## 50
Variables	# of lines

Usage

The page length is used to specify the physical page size and is set in terms of the number of lines at the current setting of lines per inch. For example, an 8 1/2-by-11-inch piece of paper would be specified as 66 lines long at 6 lines per inch ($6 \times 11 = 66$) or 88 lines long at 8 lines per inch ($8 \times 11 = 88$). You can also set page size directly on most laser printers with the Page Size menu setting.

The number of lines of text that will print are determined by the page length less the margin settings or by the text length setting (see Margins and Text Length).

To set the page length, determine the number of lines by multiplying the length of the paper in inches by the number of lines per inch as determined by your choice of type fonts. (See Font Selection and Vertical Line Spacing.) The resulting value is inserted in place of the # sign in the PCL 5 printer language command. For example, the command for 66 lines would be as follows:

```
Ec&l66P
```

BASIC Example

To set a page length for 8 1/2-by-14-inch paper with 8 lines per inch, first calculate the total number of lines:

14-×-8 = 112 lines

Then, enter and run the following BASIC program:

```
LPRINT CHR$(27);"&l112P"
```

Cautions

A command setting a page length that equates to greater than 14 inches is ignored by the printer.

Sending a Page Length command causes the printer to print any data in the print buffer and eject the current page before it requests a paper change. Therefore, you need to issue the page length command before any data to be printed or your text will be split onto two pages.

When you change the page size through the control panel, you will also change the current Vertical Motion Index (VMI). When you subsequently issue a page length command, it will use the new VMI that may result in your specifying a page size other than the one intended.

Notes

The default page length is determined by the installed paper tray. The tray engages sensors in the printer that enable the printer to ascertain the size of the paper tray. When no tray is inserted, the default is set to letter-sized paper.

When the page length is set to a size different from the installed tray, the printer stops and requests the specified paper. You need to insert the correct paper tray and press the Continue button, or manually feed the specified paper.

Orientation

Function group	Page control
Application	Selects portrait (lengthwise) or landscape (widthwise) printing.
PCL 5 Command	Ec&l#O
Decimal Code	027 38 108 ### 079
Hexadecimal Code	1B 26 6C ## 4F
Variables	# = 0 Portrait (default)
	# = 1 Landscape
	# = 2 Reverse portrait
	# = 3 Reverse landscape

Usage

Orientation defines the alignment of the logical page with the physical page. It can be set to portrait or landscape, corresponding to lengthwise or widthwise printing. The LaserJet III and beyond can also print in Reverse Portrait and Reverse Landscape. See Figure 15.2.

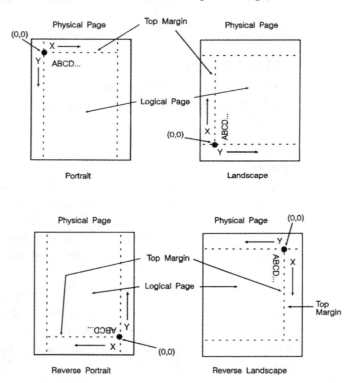

Figure 15.2. Page orientations.

When you set the orientation for a page, the LaserJet III and 4 rotate all of the fonts to the new orientation. Previous LaserJet printers and most compatibles would select the closest font available in the new orientation, often changing the font in the process.

You can only set the orientation once for a single page. Issuing a second orientation command within a page causes the data transmitted to the printer to be printed, and the page is ejected with the subsequent data printed on a second page. To change the direction of a portion of the type on a single page, use the Print Direction command (see below). The Print Direction command is relative to the logical page as set by the orientation command. When you change the orientation, you also change the base print direction.

To set the orientation to landscape, you issue the following command:

```
Ec&l1O
```

BASIC Example

To select the portrait orientation, you enter and run the following BASIC program:

```
LPRINT CHR$(27);"&l0O"
```

Notes

The Factory Default orientation is the portrait orientation. You can select a different default orientation through the control panel. Unlike previous versions of PCL, selecting a User Default font with landscape orientation in PCL 5 will not cause the User Default orientation to change to landscape. Rather, the printer will rotate the selected default font to the default orientation.

When you issue an orientation command with data in the buffer, it is printed and the page is ejected before setting the new orientation. Because you can only issue a single orientation command per page, you must use the Print Direction command to print in multiple directions on a single page.

Unlike previous versions of PCL where Orientation was the highest priority characteristic of a font, the ability of PCL 5 to rotate any font has reduced it to the lowest priority. This means that you can not use orientation to distinguish between two available fonts, because the printer will just rotate the current font rather than switch to the font defined in the new orientation.

Print Direction

Function group	Page control
Application	Used to print in multiple directions on a single page.
PCL 5 Command	Ec&a#P
Decimal Code	027 038 097 ### 080
Hexadecimal Code	1B 26 61 ## 50
Variables	# = 0 Portrait (default)
	# = 90 Landscape
	# = 180 Reverse portrait
	# = 270 Reverse landscape

Usage

The Print Direction command rotates the logical page coordinate system relative to the current orientation without issuing a page eject. This enables you to rotate text within the current page and print in all four orientations on the same page. The Print Direction command can rotate text in 90 degree increments. See Figure 15.3.

BASIC Example

To rotate the print direction to reverse landscape, you enter and run the following BASIC program:

```
LPRINT CHR$(27);"&a270P"
```

Notes

The margins and logical page coordinate system are rotated with the current font. The cursor remains in the same Physical location, but it is assigned the coordinates of its position relative to the new logical page.

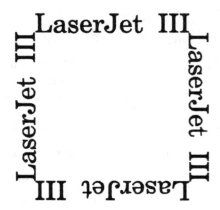

Figure 15.3. Using the Print Direction command to print in four directions on a single page.

Text Length

Function group	Page control
Application	Sets the length of printable text.
PCL 5 Command	Ec&l#F
Decimal Code	027 038 097 ### 070
Hexadecimal Code	1B 26 6C ## 46
Variables	# of lines

Usage

The Text Length defines the printable area between the top margin and the bottom margin. PCL 5 has no command for setting the bottom margin, and uses the text length command instead. See Figure 15.4.

The Text Length is set in lines. The actual space in inches will depend on the current setting for lines per inch or VMI. Commands setting a Text Length greater than the Page Length less the Top Margin are ignored. To set a Text Length of 60 lines, the command would be as follows:

    Ec&l60F

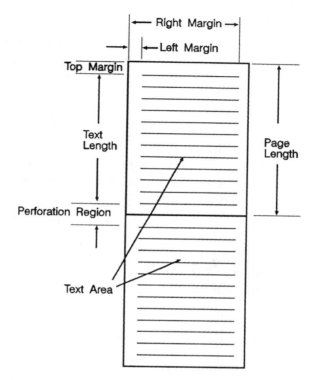

Figure 15.4. The relationship between the page length, top margin, and text length.

To set a bottom margin of 1 inch, you first need to determine the top margin and the number of lines per inch. If the top margin were set to 2 inches for an 8 1/2-by-11-inch page and the current lines per inch setting is 6, the text length would be set as follows:

(Page Length – (Top Margin + Bottom Margin)) × LPI
(11"–(2)+1")) × 6 LPI = 48 lines

The command would be as follows:

```
Ec&l48F
```

BASIC Example

To set a text length of 4 inches, you would first need to determine the number of lines per inch. If the current setting were 8 lines per inch, you would enter and run the following BASIC program:

```
LPRINT chr$(27);"&l32F"
```

Cautions

Resetting the Top Margin will also reset the Text Length to the following, where the 1/2 inch represents the unprintable area at the bottom of the page.

(Logical Page Length (in inches) – Top Margin – 1/2))

Margin, Top

Function group	Page control
Application	Sets top margin.
PCL Command	Ec&l#E
Decimal Code	027 038 108 ### 069
Hexadecimal Code	1B 26 6C ## 45
Variables	# of lines

Usage

The top margin is determined from the top of the logical page to the top of the text area. Although the top margin is set in lines, it represents a fixed physical distance in inches, and does not change when the number of lines per inch, or the vertical size of a line—as represented by the VMI—is subsequently altered. The logical page runs from the top edge of the physical page both in portrait and landscape orientation. Once the physical page size and/or the page length are set (note that these are mutually dependent settings), setting the top margin will determine the text length. The text length will be set to the following, where the 1/2 inch represents the unprintable area at the bottom of the page.

Logical Page Length (in inches) – Top Margin – 1/2

It is important to note that setting the top margin effectively resets a previously defined text length. If you want to limit the text length, you must set it again after setting the top margin.

To set the top margin to two inches, first determine the number of lines per inch as set either by the VMI or by the number of lines per page. (See Page Length.) If the current line spacing is 6 LPI, you would set a two-inch top margin as 12 lines, with the following command:

```
Ec&l12E
```

BASIC Example

To set a one-inch top margin, using 8 lines per inch, you would set the margin to 8 by entering and running the following BASIC program:

```
LPRINT CHR$(27);"&l8E"
```

Cautions

Any top margin command that exceeds the logical page length is ignored.

Margin, Left

Function group	Page control
Application	Sets left margin.
PCL 5 Command	Ec&a#L
Decimal Code	027 038 097 ### 076
Hexadecimal Code	1B 26 61 ## 4C
Variables	Column #

Usage

The left margin is determined from the leftmost printable character. The leftmost printable character is given the margin position zero. The margin is specified by the number of columns from the leftmost printable character. The size of a column is determined by the pitch of a fixed pitch type—10 pitch type has 10 columns per inch, and 12 pitch type has 12 columns per inch. The width of a column is set to the width of the Space character for proportional type fonts. Note that the width of the Space character can be affected by changing the Horizontal Motion Index.

To set a one-inch left margin, using Courier 10 point type (12 pitch), you need to first determine the number of columns by multiplying the margin in inches by the number of columns per inch:

$$1 \times 12 = 12 \text{ columns}$$

Insert the column number in the command as follows:

```
Ec&a12L
```

BASIC Example

To set a one-inch left margin using Courier 10 point type (12 pitch), first determine the number of columns by multiplying the margin in inches by the number of columns per inch:

$$\times 12 = 12 \text{ columns}$$

Then, enter and run the following BASIC program:

```
LPRINT CHR$(27);"&a12L"
```

Cautions

Any margin command that places the left margin to the right of the right margin (or vice versa) will be ignored.

Margin, Right

Function group	Page control
Application	Sets right margin.
PCL 5 Command	Ec&a#M
Decimal Code	027 038 097 ### 077
Hexadecimal Code	1B 26 61 ## 4D
Variables	Column #

Usage

The right margin is determined from the leftmost printable character. The leftmost printable character is given the margin position zero. The margin is specified by the number of columns from the leftmost printable character. The size of a column is determined by the pitch of a fixed pitch type (10 Pitch type has 10 columns per inch, while 12 Pitch type has 12 columns per inch). The width of a column is set to the width of the Space character for proportional type fonts. Note that the width of the Space character can be affected by changing the Horizontal Motion Index.

To set an eight-inch right margin, using Courier 10 point type (12 pitch), first determine the number of columns by multiplying the margin in inches by the number of columns per inch:

$8 \times 12 = 96$ columns

Insert the column number in the command as follows:

```
Ec&a96M
```

BASIC Example

To set an eight-inch right margin, using Courier 10 point type (12 pitch), first determine the number of columns by multiplying the margin in inches by the number of columns per inch, as follows:

$8 \times 12 = 96$ columns

Then, enter and run the following BASIC program:

```
LPRINT CHR$(27);"&a96M"
```

Cautions

Any margin command that places the right margin to the left of the left margin—or vice versa—will be ignored.

Margin Clear

Function group	Page control
Application	Clears side margins back to defaults.
PCL 5 Command	Ec9
Decimal Code	027 057
Hexadecimal Code	1B 39
Variables	None

Usage

The margin clear command will reset the horizontal margins back to the left and right most printable characters.

BASIC Example

To clear the left and right margins back to their default positions enter and run the following BASIC program:

```
LPRINT CHR$(27);"9"
```

Cautions

The margin clear command leaves the cursor at the right margin. You need to issue a carriage return command to return the cursor to its customary starting position at the left margin.

Notes

The command does not affect the top or bottom margins.

Perforation Skip

Function group	Page control
Application	Sets Perforation Skip on and off.
PCL 5 Command	Ec&l#L

Decimal Code	027 038 108 ### 076	
Hexadecimal Code	1B 26 6C ## 4C	
Variables	# = 0	Turn On
	# = 1	Turn Off

Usage

The Perforation Region is the area between the bottom of the Text Area of one page, and the top of the Text Area of the next. (See Figure 15.5.) It is defined by the Page Length, Top Margin, and the Text Length. All three of these settings determine the bottom of the text area of the current page, and the Top Margin determines the top of the text area of the next page.

When Perforation Skip is turned on—enabled—any line feed command that moves the cursor into the Perforation Region causes the cursor to be moved to the top of the text area of the next page. This forces the current page to be printed and ejected.

To turn Perforation Skip off, you issue the following command:

```
Ec&l0L
```

BASIC Example

To turn Perforation Skip on, you enter and run the following BASIC program:

```
LPRINT CHR$(27);"&l1L"
```

Cautions

If you set Perforation Skip off, and try to print outside of the printable area at the bottom or top of a page, you will lose data.

Notes

The Factory Default for Perforation Skip is enabled—turned on.

Horizontal Motion Index (HMI)

Function group	Page control
Application	Used to set the column width in 1/120 of an inch.
PCL 5 Command	Ec&k#H
Decimal Code	027 038 107 ### 072
Hexadecimal Code	1B 26 6B ## 48
Variables	# of 1/120th of an inch

Usage

The column width is called the Horizontal Motion Index (HMI) and is set in 1/120 of an inch. The HMI is the reciprocal of the number of characters per inch (cpi) because the number of characters you can fit into an inch of text will be the inverse of the horizontal size of each character or the column width. When you select a fixed pitch font, you automatically set the HMI. To manually set the appropriate HMI for 12 characters per inch, first determine the correct HMI value by dividing the cpi into 120, as follows:

12 CPI " 120 = 10 HMI

Then issue the following command:

Ec&k10H

BASIC Example

To send the same example in BASIC, you enter and run the following BASIC program:

```
LPRINT CHR$(27);"&k10H"
```

Notes

When you select a fixed pitch font, you automatically set the HMI to the pitch. The HMI is constant for all characters in a fixed pitch font, making it *fixed*. If you set the HMI for a variable pitch—proportional—font, it only affects the control code space character.

Vertical Motion Index (VMI)

Function group	Page control
Application	Used to set the line height in 1/48th-of-an-inch.
PCL 5 Command	Ec&l#C
Decimal Code	027 038 108 ### 067
Hexadecimal Code	1B 26 6C ## 43
Variables	# of 1/48th of an inch

Usage

The line height is called the Vertical Motion Index (VMI) and is set in 1/48 of an inch. The VMI is the reciprocal of the number of lines per inch (lpi), because the number of lines you can fit into an inch of text will be the inverse of the vertical size of each line. To set the VMI for six to eight lines per inch, you issue the following command:

```
Ec&l6C
```

BASIC Example

To send the same example in BASIC, you enter and run the following BASIC program:

```
LPRINT CHR$(27);"&l6C"
```

Notes

The VMI is similar to the typesetting concept of leading, although it is set at intervals of 1/48 of an inch, and leading is set in points that are 1/72 of an inch.

You can also set the User Default for the VMI through the Control Panel Menu System, by setting the FORM. The FORM is set in lines per page and is related to the VMI. To determine the VMI, you need to know the logical page length, the top margin, and the FORM setting in lines per inch. The VMI is calculated as follows:

$$VMI = (\text{Page Length} - \text{Top Margin} - 1/2))/\text{FORM}$$

The 1/2 inch represents the unprintable area at the top and bottom of the page.

Line Spacing, Lines per Inch

Function group	Page control
Application	Sets the vertical height of a line of text (VMI) in lines per inch.
PCL 5 Command	Ec&l#D
Decimal Code	027 038 108 ### 068
Hexadecimal Code	1B 26 6C ## 44
Variables	# of lines per inch

Usage

This command sets the vertical size of a line of text (VMI) in the more common form of lines per inch. The size of an individual line of text will be inversely proportional to the number of lines of text in one inch. To set six lines per inch, use the following command:

```
Ec&l6D
```

BASIC Example

To set eight lines per inch, you enter and run the following BASIC program:

```
LPRINT CHR$(27);"&l8D"
```

Cautions

You need to set a vertical line spacing appropriate for the size of the type you are using, or you will cause the type to overlap or be too widely spaced.

Notes

The VMI is similar to the typesetting concept of leading, although it is set in 1/48th-inch intervals, and leading is set in points that are 1/72nd-of-an-inch.

Cursor Positioning

The PCL 5 command language treats the printed page like the word processor's screen display, instructing the printer to place a cursor at a particular location on the page and printing a specified item. The printer does not have a physical cursor, but the metaphor makes understanding the process so much easier that Hewlett-Packard has defined many of its positioning commands as cursor commands. These are used to position the items to be printed. When you issue a cursor positioning command, you are instructing the printer where to place the subsequent item—text or image—on the logical page.

All positions are relative to the 0,0 point of the logical page—top left corner in portrait orientation. Most cursor positioning commands can accept absolute or relative position arguments. When you specify an absolute position, it is determined relative to the 0,0 point. When you specify a relative movement by preceding the position with a positive or negative sign, the cursor is moved from its current position in the specified direction for the specified distance.

Move Cursor Vertically by Row

Function group	Cursor movement
Application	Positioning the cursor for text printing.
PCL 5 Command	Ec&a#R
Decimal Code	027 038 097 ### 082
Hexadecimal Code	1B 26 61 ## 52
Variables	# of row(s). Preceding the # with a + (plus) or – (minus) will move the cursor the specified number of rows relative to the current position.

Usage

To position the cursor in a particular row relative to the top margin of the page, enter the command without a leading plus or minus sign. The top margin of the logical page is defined as row zero.

To position the cursor in a row a specified number of rows before or after the current row, precede the row number in the command with a plus sign to move down the page, or a minus sign to move up the page.

Any request to position the cursor outside of the logical page places the cursor at the corresponding edge of the logical page with the exception of positive relative positioning—includes a plus sign—that will move the cursor to the specified number of rows beyond the current page. The perforation skip mode is ignored during vertical cursor positioning, enabling the cursor to be placed in the perforation area.

To place the cursor in row 40, use the following command:

```
Ec]&a40R
```

To move the cursor 5 rows down, use the following command

```
Ec&a+5R
```

BASIC Example

To position the cursor in row 55, you enter and run the following BASIC program:

```
100 LPRINT CHR$(27);"&a55R"
```

To move the cursor six lines up the page from the current position, you enter and run the following BASIC program:

```
LPRINT CHR$(27);"&a-6R"
```

Notes

This command is accurate to four decimal places.

Move Cursor Vertically by Dots

Function group	Cursor movement
Application	Positioning the cursor for graphics printing.
PCL 5 Command	Ec*p#Y
Decimal Code	027 042 112 ### 086
Hexadecimal Code	1B 2A 70 ## 59
Variables	# of dots (1/300th of an inch). Preceding the # with a + (plus) or – (minus) will move the cursor the specified number of dots relative to the current position.

Usage

To position the cursor relative to the top margin of the page, enter the command without a leading plus or minus sign. The top margin of the logical page is defined as vertical position zero.

To position the cursor a specified number of dots before or after the current position, precede the number of dots in the command with a plus sign to move down the page, or a minus sign to move up the page. Any request to position the cursor outside the logical page will place the cursor at the corresponding edge of the logical page.

To place the cursor in position 400, use the following command:

```
Ec*p400Y
```

To move the cursor 50 dots down, use the following command:

```
Ec*p+50Y
```

BASIC Example

To place the cursor in position 550, you enter and run the following BASIC program:

```
LPRINT CHR$(27);"*p550Y"
```

To move the cursor 60 dots up the page from the current position, you enter and run the following BASIC program:

```
LPRINT CHR$(27);"*p-60Y"
```

Notes

This command is accurate to two decimal places.

Move Cursor Vertically by Decipoints

Function group	Cursor movement
Application	Positioning the cursor for graphics printing.
PCL 5 Command	Ec&a#V
Decimal Code	027 038 097 ### 086
Hexadecimal Code	1B 26 61 ## 56
Variables	# of decipoints (1/720th of an inch). Preceding the # with a + (plus) or – (minus) will move the cursor the specified number of decipoints relative to the current position.

Usage

To position the cursor relative to the top margin of the page, enter the command without a leading plus or minus sign. The top margin of the logical page is defined as vertical position zero.

To position the cursor a specified number of decipoints before or after the current position, precede the number of decipoints in the command with a plus sign to move down the page or a minus sign to move up the page. Any request to position the cursor outside the logical page will place the cursor at the corresponding edge of the logical page.

To place the cursor in position 400, use the following command:

```
Ec&a400V
```

To move the cursor 50 decipoints down, use the following command:

```
Ec&a+50V
```

BASIC Example

To place the cursor in position 550, you enter and run the following BASIC program:

```
LPRINT CHR$(27);"&a550V"
```

To move the cursor 60 decipoints up the page from the current position, you enter and run the following BASIC program:

```
LPRINT CHR$(27);"&a-60V"
```

Notes

This command is accurate to two decimal places.

Move Cursor Horizontally by Column

Function group	Cursor movement
Application	Positioning the cursor for text printing.
PCL 5 Command	Ec&a#C
Decimal Code	027 038 097 ### 067
Hexadecimal Code	1B 26 61 ## 43
Variables	# of column(s). Preceding the # with a + (plus) or – (minus) will move the cursor the specified number of columns relative to the current position.

Usage

To position the cursor in a column relative to the edge of the page, enter the command without a leading plus or minus sign. The left edge of the logical page is defined as column zero.

To position the cursor in a column, a specified number of columns before or after the current cursor location, precede the column number in the command with a plus sign to move to the right or a minus sign to move to the left. When you are positioning the cursor with this command, it ignores any margin settings; however, it does respect the edges of the logical page. Any request to position the cursor outside the logical page will place the cursor at the corresponding edge of the logical page.

To place the cursor in column 40, use the following command:

```
Ec&a40C
```

To move the cursor 5 columns to the right, use the following command:

```
Ec&a+5C
```

BASIC Example

To position the cursor in column 55, you enter and run the following BASIC program:

```
LPRINT CHR$(27);"&a55C"
```

To move the cursor six spaces to the left of the current position, you would enter and run the following BASIC program:

```
LPRINT CHR$(27);"&a-6C"
```

Notes

This command is accurate to four decimal places.

Move Cursor Horizontally by Dots

Function group	Cursor movement
Application	Positioning the cursor for graphics printing.

PCL 5 Command	Ec*p#x
Decimal Code	027 042 112 ### 088
Hexadecimal Code1	B 2A 70 ## 58
Variables	# of dots (1/300th of an inch). Preceding the # with a + (plus) or – (minus) will move the cursor the specified number of dots relative to the current position.

Usage

To position the cursor relative to the edge of the page, enter the command without a leading plus or minus sign. The left edge of the logical page is defined as horizontal position zero.

To position the cursor a specified number of dots before or after the current cursor location, precede the dot number in the command with a plus sign to move to the right or a minus sign to move to the left.

When you are positioning the cursor with this command, it ignores any margin settings; however, it does respect the edges of the logical page. Any request to position the cursor outside the logical page will place the cursor at the corresponding edge of the logical page.

To place the cursor in position 400, use the following command:

    Ec*p400X

To move the cursor 50 dots to the right, use the folowing command:

    Ec*p+50X

BASIC Example

To position the cursor in position 550, you enter and run the following BASIC program:

    LPRINT CHR$(27);"*p550X"

To move the cursor 60 dots to the left of the current position, you enter and run the following BASIC program:

```
LPRINT CHR$(27);"*p-60X"
```

Notes

This command is accurate to two decimal places.

Move Cursor Horizontally by Decipoints

Function group	Cursor movement
Application	Positioning the cursor for graphics printing.
PCL 5 Command	Ec&a#H
Decimal Code	027 038 097 ### 072
Hexadecimal Code1	B 26 61 ## 48
Variables	# of decipoints (1/720th of an inch). Preceding the # with a + (plus) or – (minus) will move the cursor the specified number of decipoints relative to the current position.

Usage

To position the cursor relative to the edge of the page, enter the command without a leading plus or minus sign. The left edge of the logical page is defined as horizontal position zero.

To position the cursor a specified number of decipoints before or after the current cursor location, precede the decipoint number in the command with a plus sign to move to the right or minus sign to move to the left.

This command ignores any margin settings; however, it does respect the edges of the logical page. Any request to position the cursor outside of the logical page will place the cursor at the corresponding edge of the logical page.

To place the cursor in position 400, use the following command:

Ec&a400H

To move the cursor 50 decipoints to the right, use the following command:

Ec&a+50H

BASIC Example

To position the cursor in position 550, you would enter and run the following BASIC program:

LPRINT CHR$(27);"&a550H"

To move the cursor 60 decipoints to the left of the current position, you enter and run the following BASIC program:

LPRINT CHR$(27);"&a-60H"

Notes

This command is accurate to two decimal places.

Half Line Feed

Function group	Cursor positioning
Application	Moves the cursor down one half of the current line spacing.
PCL 5 Command	Ec=
Decimal Code	027 061
Hexadecimal Code	1B 3D
Variables	None

Usage

The vertical distance of half a line feed is set to half of the current Vertical Motion Index (VMI). The VMI can be set directly, or by setting the number of lines per inch (lpi). For example, if the current lpi setting is six lines per inch, the VMI is 6/48 = 8 VMI units—remember that VMI is set in 48ths of an inch. Therefore, a half line feed would move the cursor down 4 VMI units, or 4/48 (1/12) of an inch. To move the cursor down half a line, you would issue the following command:

```
Ec=
```

BASIC Example

To issue a half line feed, you enter and run the following BASIC program:

```
LPRINT CHR$(27);"="
```

Line Termination

Function group	Miscellaneous
Application	Instructs the print how to handle various standard printer control codes such as carriage return (CR), line feed (LF), and form feed (FF).
PCL 5 Command	Ec&k#G
Decimal Code	027 038 107 ### 071
Hexadecimal Code	1B 26 6B ## 47
Variables	# = 0 CR=CR, LF=LF, FF=FF
	# = 1 CR=CR+LF, LF=LF, FF=FF
	# = 2 CR=CR, LF=CR+LF, FF=CR+FF
	# = 3 CR+CR+LF, LF+CR+LF,FF=CR+FF

Usage

Most software packages issue standard formatting control codes with the text that they control. For example, a word processor will transmit a carriage return at the end of a line of text to indicate that the next word appears in the leftmost position of the next line.

Some word processors expect the printer to interpret the single command code CR (ASCII 13) as the command to move to the left margin, and the command to move to the next line. Others do not and will send a CR and a LF command.

The line termination command enables you to match the LaserJet's interpretation of the various line termination commands sent by your software with their intended operation. For example, suppose your software intended the CR command code to represent both a carriage return and a line feed. You would send the following command:

```
Ec&k1G
```

BASIC Example

If you found that all of your printouts were being double spaced because the software was sending a line feed and the printer was supplying one for the CR, you might be able to correct the problem by entering and running the following BASIC program that resets the printer's line termination to CR=CR, LF=LF and FF=FF.

```
LPRINT CHR$(27);"&k0G"
```

Notes

The factory default line termination is CR=CR, LF=LF and FF=FF, or a value of zero.

Push/Pop Cursor Position

Function group	Cursor positioning
Application	Used to store the current cursor position for future return.
PCL 5 Command	Ec&f#S
Decimal Code	027 038 102 ### 083
Hexadecimal Code	1B 26 66 ## 53

Variables	# = 0	Store current cursor position
	# = 1	Return to last stored cursor position

Usage

The Push/Pop command combination works with a type of memory called a stack. The stack is capable of storing 20 cursor positions. When you push the current cursor position onto the stack, each position previously stored in the stack is moved up one level and the top value is pushed out the top and lost.

Each time you pop a position from the stack, the cursor is moved to the position described by the bottom-most position description in the stack. That description is removed and the entire stack is moved down one level, with the top level left blank. You can store many positions and keep track of them in memory by remembering the order in which they were stored. The most recent position pushed is always the first popped, the next most recent pushed will be the second popped and so on.

The push and pop commands are most often used with overlapping graphic elements such as lines and boxes where you want to restart many different elements from the same position. If you want to return the cursor to a particular location twice, you must remember to push it twice since the process of popping removes the position from the stack. You can push/push/pop/pop or push/pop/push/pop.

To push the current cursor position, you use the following command:

```
Ec&f0S
```

BASIC Example

To pop the most recent position pushed, you would enter and run the following BASIC program:

```
LPRINT CHR$(27);"&f1S"
```

Font Selection

The LaserJet III, 4, and compatibles, support bit-mapped and scalable fonts; and they are capable of rotating to any of the four printing directions. In the case of scalable fonts, the printer is capable of creating characters between 0.25 and 999.75 points in 0.25 point increments. The introduction of rotatable fonts has changed the hierarchy by which font characteristics are used to select a font. In previous versions of PCL, orientation was the highest characteristic used to differentiate two fonts. This often caused problems when users changed the print orientation, and the selected font was not available in the new orientation. For example, if you were printing a letter in Times Roman 12 point type on a LaserJet Series II, and you attempted to print the address in landscape orientation, you would find that your envelope would print out in Courier, because it was the closest font available in landscape orientation. With the LaserJet III and 4, using PCL 5, this is no longer a problem, because the printer will automatically rotate your 12 point Times into landscape orientation.

In PCL 5, a font is specified by nine characteristics, and a particular font is selected for printing by matching the available fonts—internal, cartridge based, or downloaded—against the current font specification. The match is made in the following hierarchy, eliminating nonmatching fonts until a single font is left which is then selected:

Symbol Set

Spacing

Pitch

Point Size

Height

Style

Stroke Weight

Typeface Family

Orientation

In the case of multiple fonts matching all criteria, the font is selected based on its location in the following order:

> Bit-mapped soft font with the lowest ID
>
> Scalable soft font with the lowest ID
>
> Left cartridge bit-mapped font
>
> Right cartridge bit-mapped font
>
> Left cartridge scalable font
>
> Right cartridge scalable font
>
> Internal bit-mapped font
>
> Internal scalable font

You can designate two separate fonts called primary and secondary. The font characteristic commands use the open parenthesis "(" to specify a characteristic for the primary font and the close parenthesis ")" for the secondary font. After you have specified your primary and secondary fonts, you can switch between these two fonts with the Shift In (ASCII 15) and ShiftOut (ASCII 14) control codes. Alternatively, you can assign a soft font an ID number when it is downloaded, and select the font based on its assigned number. When specifying a font, you need to only specify those characteristics that differ from the currently selected font. When you first start your printer or issue a printer reset—either from the control panel or through the EcEcommand—both the primary and the secondary fonts are set to the default font—initially Courier 10 or as otherwise specified through the control panel.

Symbol Set

Function group	Font selection
Application	Used to select the set of special characters and symbols used for a given font.

PCL 5 Command	Ec(## selects primary font symbol set; Ec)## selects secondary font symbol set.
Decimal Code	027 040 ### ###; 027 041 ### ###
Hexadecimal Code	1B 28 ## ##; 1B 29 ## ##
Variables	The combination of one number and a letter select a specific font according to table 15.2.

TABLE 15.2. SYMBOL SET VALUES.

Symbol Set Name	Symbol Set ID
Default set	0@
Math-7	0A
Line Draw-7	OB
HP Large Characters (264x Terminals)	OC
ISO 60: Danish/Norwegian	0D
ISO 61: Norwegian Version 2	1D
Roman Extensions	0E
ISO 4: United Kingdom	1E
ISO 25: French	0F
ISO 69: French	1F
HP German	0G
ISO 21: German	1G
Greek-8	8G
Hebrew-7	0H
Hebrew-8	8H
ISO 15: Italian	0I
Microsoft Publishing	6J
DeskTop	7J
Document	8J
PS Text	10J
Ventura International	13H
Ventura US	14J
ISO 14: JIS ASCII	0K
ISO 13: Katakana	1K
ISO 57: Chinese	2K

continues

TABLE 15.2. CONTINUED

Symbol Set Name	Symbol Set ID
Kana-8	8K
Korean-8	9K
Line Draw-7 (Same as OB)	0L
HP Block Characters	1L
Tax Line Draw	2L
Line Draw-8	8L
Ventura ITC Zapf Dingbats	9L
PS ITC Zapf Dingbats	10L
ITC Zapf Dingbats Series 100	11L
ITC Zapf Dingbats Series 200	12L
ITC Zapf Dingbats Series 300	13L
Math-7 (Same as 0A)	0M
Tech-7	1M
PS Math	5M
Ventura Math	6M
Math-8	8M
ECMA-94 Latin 1 (ISO 8859/1)	0N
ECMA-94 Latin 2 (ISO 8859/2)	2N
ECMA-128 Latin 5 (ISO 8859/9)	5N
ECMA-113/88 Latin/Cyrillic (ISO 8859/5.2)	10N
OCR A	0O
OCR B	1O
OCR M	2O
APL (Typewriter Paired)	0P
APL (Bit Paired)	1P
Specials	xQ
Cyrillic ASCII (ECMA-113/86, ISO 8859/5)	0R
Cyrillic	1R
PC Cyrillic	3R
ISO 11: Swedish for Names	0S
HP Spanish	1S
ISO 17: Spanish	2S
ISO 10: Swedish	3S
ISO 16: Portuguese	4S
ISO 84: Portuguese	5S
ISO 85: Spanish	6S

Symbol Set Name	Symbol Set ID
HP European Spanish	7S
HP Latin Spanish	8S
HP-GL Download	16S
HP-GL Drafting	17S
HP-GL Special Symbols	18S
Thai-8	0T
Turkish-8	8T
ISO 6: ASCII	0U
Legal 1U	
ISO 2: International Reference Version	2U
HPL Language Set	5U
OEM-1	7U
Roman-8	8U
Windows	9U
PC-8 10U	
PC-8 D/N (Danish/Norwegian)	11U
PC-850	12U
PC-852	17U
Pi Font	15U
Arabic (McKay's Version)	0V
Arabic-8	8V
3 of 9 Barcode	0Y
Industrial 2 of 5 Barcode	1Y
Matrix 2 of 5 Barcode	2Y
Interleaved 2 of 5 Barcode	4Y
CODABAR Barcode	5Y
MSI/Plessey Barcode	6Y
Code 11 Barcode	7Y
UPC/EAN Barcode	8Y
USPS Zip	15Y

Usage

The symbol set defines which letters, numbers, and special characters are contained in a particular font. The basic symbol sets are USASCII, the Hewlett-Packard Roman Extension set for USASCII, and

Roman-8—combining the first two. Special symbol sets include: foreign language sets with special characters and accented character; special purpose sets such as legal or math with special symbols; and special function sets such as Line Draw composed of graphics characters. Roman-8 is the most common symbol set used for the Hewlett-Packard resident fonts and cartridge fonts. Roman-8 is also the factory default symbol set. Many users find it advantageous to change these to PC-8, giving up some seldom used foreign characters for the PC line draw characters.

The symbol set is the highest priority characteristic of a font. Since fonts are symbol set specific, you must select a symbol set for which you have a font available. To select the Roman-8 Symbol Set for the primary font, you would use the following command:

```
Ec(8U
```

BASIC Example

To select the PC-8 character set for the secondary font, you would enter and run the following BASIC program:

```
LPRINT CHR$(27);")10U"
```

Notes

The User Default symbol set is implicitly defined by the selection of a User Default font.

Spacing

Function group	Font selection
Application	Used to select inter-character spacing.
PCL 5 Command	Ec(s#P sets primary font spacing; Ec)s#P sets secondary font spacing.
Decimal Code	027 040 115 ### 080; 027 041 115 ### 080
Hexadecimal Code	1B 28 73 ## 50; 1B 29 73 ## 50
Variables	# = 0 Fixed spacing
	# = 1 Proportional spacing

Usage

This command is used to select fixed or proportional spacing according to the font selected. Type fonts, that are bit-mapped and scalable, are specified as fixed or proportionally spaced. If you select proportional spacing, and a proportionally spaced font is not available, the fixed pitch font with the current pitch setting will be selected. To select a fixed pitch spacing for a fixed pitch font as the primary font, you use the following command:

```
Ec(s0P
```

BASIC Example

To select proportional spacing for a proportional font as the secondary font, you enter and run the following BASIC program:

```
LPRINT CHR$(27);")s1P"
```

Notes

The factory default spacing is fixed. The User Default spacing set is implicitly defined by the selection of a User Default font.

Pitch

Function group	Font selection
Application	Used to set horizontal character spacing for fixed pitch fonts.
PCL 5 Command	Ec(s#H sets primary font pitch; Ec)s#H sets secondary font pitch.
Decimal Code	027 040 115 ### 072; 027 041 115 ### 072
Hexadecimal Code	1B 28 73 ## 48; 1B 29 73 ## 48
Variables	# of characters per inch (cpi)

Usage

Pitch sets the horizontal character spacing for fixed pitch fonts —bit-mapped or scalable—in characters per inch (cpi). The most common pitches are 10 cpi for Courier 10 type and 12 cpi for Prestige Elite 12 type. If you select a pitch for a font that is not available, the next larger available pitch is used. When no larger pitch fonts are available, the next lower is used.

To select 10 cpi for the pitch of the primary font, you use the following command:

```
Ec(s10H
```

BASIC Example

To select 12 CPI for the secondary font, you would enter and run the following BASIC program:

```
LPRINT CHR$(27);")s12H"
```

Notes

The Factory Default pitch is 10 cpi. The User Default pitch is implicitly set by the selection of the User Default font. The pitch can be specified with two decimals accuracy.

Height (Point Size)

Function group	Font selection
Application	Selects the vertical size of the primary and secondary fonts.
PCL 5 Command	Ec(s#V selects primary font point size; Ec)s#V selects secondary font point size.
Decimal Code	027 040 115 ### 086; 027 041 115 ### 086
Hexadecimal Code	1B 28 73 ## 56; 1B 29 73 ## 56
Variables	# of points high

Usage

The point size determines the vertical size of the font selected. For fixed pitch fonts, this will generally require a reciprocal change in the pitch. For proportionally spaced fonts, the horizontal spacing will be determined for each character. If you set a vertical height for a bit-mapped font that isn't available, the next closest height font will be selected.

For scalable fonts, you can select a height from 0.25 to 999.75 points in increments of 0.25 point. To select a font of 14.4 points for the primary font, you would use the following command:

```
Ec(s14.4V
```

BASIC Example

To set the vertical height of the secondary font to 10 points, you enter and run the following BASIC program:

```
LPRINT CHR$(27);")s10V"
```

Notes

The Factory Default point size is 12 points. The User Default point size is set by the selection of the User Default font.

If you select a scalable font by ID number, and do not specify its height, it will be scaled to the same height as the last specified font.

Style

Function group	Font selection
Application	Selects upright, italics, or other style.
PCL 5 Command	Ec(s#S selects primary font style; Ec)s#S selects secondary font style.
Decimal Code	027 040 115 ### 083; 027 041 115 ### 083
Hexadecimal Code	1B 28 73 ## 53; 1B 29 73 ## 53

Variables	# = 0	Upright/Roman style
	# = 1	Italic style
	# = 4	Condensed
	# = 5	Condensed italics
	# = 8	Compressed
	# = 24	Expanded
	# = 32	Outline
	# = 64	Inline
	# = 128	Shadowed
	# = 160	Outlined shadow

Usage

This command is used to select the style of the primary or secondary fonts. To specify italic style for the primary font, use the following command:

```
Ec(s1S
```

BASIC Example

To specify the upright style for the secondary font, you enter and run the following BASIC program:

```
LPRINT CHR$(27);")s0S"
```

Notes

The Factory Default style is upright. The User Default style is set by the selection of the User Default font.

If the requested style is not available at the time the command is issued, the command appears to be ignored; however, the parameter in the current environment has been changed. If the font is made available by downloading or by cartridge addition, it will be selected as the default font.

Stroke Weight

Function group	Font selection
Application	Used to select the weight of print—light, medium, or bold.
PCL 5 Command	Ec(s#B sets primary font stroke weight; Ec)s#B sets secondary font stroke weight.
Decimal Code	027 040 115 ### 066; 027 041 115 ### 066
Hexadecimal Code	1B 28 73 ## 42; 1B 29 73 ## 42
Variables	# = −7 to +7 where

−7 = Ultra thin

−6 = Extra thin

−5 = Thin

−4 = Extra light

−3 = Light

−2 = Demi light

−1 = Semi light

 0 = Medium

+1 = Semi bold

+2 = Demi bold

+3 = Bold

+4 = Extra bold

+5 = Black

+6 = Extra black

+7 = Ultra black

Usage

This command selects the thickness or heaviness of the lines used to make up the characters. The plus sign of the positive settings is optional. To select a bold primary font, you would use one of the following commands:

```
Ec(s+3B
```

```
Ec(s3B
```

BASIC Example

To select a light secondary font, you would enter and run the following BASIC program:

```
LPRINT CHR$(27);")s-3B"
```

Notes

The Factory Default stroke weight is medium. The User Default stroke weight is set by the selection of the User Default font.

If the stroke weight is not available, the closest available weight is used. When the weight parameter is negative, the system will look for a thinner stroke weight first. If no thinner font is available the system will look for the nearest thicker font. When the weight parameter is positive, the system will first look for a thicker font, and then a thinner font.

Typeface

Function group	Font selection
Application	Selects the face of the type.
PCL 5 Command	Ec(s#T selects the primary font face; Ec)s#T selects the secondary font face.
Decimal Code	027 040 115 ### 084; 027 041 115 ### 084
Hexadecimal Code	1B 28 73 ## 54; 1B 29 73 ## 54
Variables	# of typeface from table 15.3

Usage

The Typeface command is used to select the face of the primary or secondary font. If the specified face is not available, the command is ignored when selecting a font. With the introduction of the LaserJet IID, Hewlett-Packard expanded the typeface specification to two bytes which identify the vendor, and their version of the typeface. In many cases, you can specify a font either by its two byte representation shown in table 15.3 or by its one byte specification supported by earlier models shown in table 15.4. In practice, you should use the two byte technique, because that is the path that Hewlett-Packard intends to follow in the future. A computer list and typeface value can be found in the Hewlett-Packard technical reference manual.

TABLE 15.3. TYPEFACE TWO-BYTE VALUES

Two-Byte Value	Typeface Family
4362	Albertus
16602	Ariel
4168	Antique Olive
4127	ITC Avant Garde
4135	Baskerville
4158	ITC Benguiat
4149	CG Bodoni
4143	ITC Bookman
4128	Brush
4119	CG Century Schoolbook
4159	ITC Cheltenham
4140	Clarendon
4135	ITC Clearface
4142	Cooper
4116	Coronet
4099	Courier
4157	Dom Casual
4172	ITC Eras
4110	Futura II
4126	ITC Galliard
4197	Garamond

continues

TABLE 15.3. CONTINUED

Two-Byte Value	Typeface Family
4147	Gill Sans
4138	CG Goudy Old Style
4123	ITC Korina
4102	Letter Gothic
4174	ITC Lubalin Graph
4297	Marigold
4151	CG Melliza
4175	Microstyle
4113	CG Omega
4111	CG Palacio
4155	Park Avenue
4193	Revue
4150	Rockwell
4112	ITC Souvenir
16686	Symbol
4152	ITC Tiffany
4101	CG Times
16901	Times New Roman
4100	CG Triumvirate
4169	Uncial
4148	Universe
31402	Wingdings

TABLE 15.4. TYPFACE VALUES

One-Byte Value	Typeface Family
0	Line Printer
1	Pica
2	Elite
3	Courier
4	Helvetica
5	Times Roman
6	Letter Gothic
7	Script

One-Byte Value	Typeface Family
8	Prestige
9	Caslon
10	Orator
11	Presentation
12	Helvetica Condensed
13	Serifa
14	Futura
15	Palatino
16	ITC Souvenir
17	Optima
18	ITC Garamond
19	Cooper Black
20	Coronet
21	Broadway
22	Bauer Bodoni Black Condensed
23	Century Schoolbook
24	University Roman
25	Helvetica Outline
26	Futura Condensed
27	ITC Korinna
28	Naskh
29	Cloister Black
30	ITC Galliard
31	ITC Avant Garde Gothic
32	Brush
33	Blippo
34	Hobo
35	Windsor
36	Helvetica Compressed
37	Helvetica Extra Compressed
38	Peignot
39	Baskerville
40	ITC Garamond Condensed
41	Trade Gothic
42	Goudy Old Style
43	ITC Zapf Chancery
44	Clarendon

continues

TABLE 15.4. CONTINUED

One-Byte Value	Typeface Family
45	ITC Zapf Dingbats
46	Cooper
47	ITC Bookman
48	Stick
49	HP-GL Drafting
50	IIP-GL Spline
51	Gill Sans
52	Univers
53	Bodoni
54	Rockwell
55	Melior
56	ITC Tiffany
57	ITC Clearface
58	Amelia
59	Park Avenue
60	Handel Gothic
61	Dom Casual
62	ITC Benguiat
63	ITC Cheltenham
64	Century Expanded
65	Franklin Gothic
66	Franklin Gothic Expressed
67	Franklin Gothic Extra Condensed
68	Plantin
69	Trump Mediaeval
70	Futura Black
72	Antique Olive
73	Uncial
74	ITC Bauhaus
75	Century Oldstyle
76	ITC Eras
77	Friz Ouadrata (ITC)
78	ITC Lubalin Graph
79	Eurostile
80	Mincho
81	ITC Serif Gothic

One-Byte Value	Typeface Family
82	Signet Roundhand
83	Souvenir Gothic
84	Stymie
87	Bernhard Modern
89	Excelsior
90	Gando Ronda Script
91	Ondine
92	P.T. Barnum
93	Kaufman
94	ITC Bolt Bold
96	Helvetica Monospaced
97	Revue
101	Garamond (Stempel)
102	Garth Graphic
103	ITC Ronda
104	OCR-A
106	Englische Schreibschrift
107	Flash
108	Gothic Outline (URW)
109	Stencil (ATF)
110	OCR-B
111	Akzidenz-Grotesk
112	TD Logos
113	Shannon
114	ITC Century
152	Maru Gosikku
153	Gossikku
154	Socho
155	Kyokasho
156	Kaisho
157	Traditional Arabic Script
158	Arabic News
160	Devanagari (Hindi)
161	Krishna (Gujarati)
162	Ranjit (Gurmukhi)
163	Raj Raja (Tamil)

continues

TABLE 15.4. CONTINUED

One-Byte Value	Typeface Family
164	Gyosho
164	Hebrew
166	Nork
167	Ousbouh
168	Koufi
261	Greek Times

To specify the CG Times (Times Roman) for the primary font, you use the following command:

```
Ec(s4101T
```

BASIC Example

To specify CG Triumvirate (Helvetica) for the secondary font, you would enter and run the following BASIC program:

```
LPRINT CHR$(27);")s4100T"
```

Notes

The Factory Default face is Courier. The UserDefault face is implicitly set by the selection of the User Default font.

Select the Default Font

Function group	Font selection
Application	Used to select the User Default Font as the primary or secondary font.
PCL 5 Command	Ec(3@ selects the default font as primary; Ec)3@ selects the default font as secondary.
Decimal Code	027 040 051 064; 027 041 051 064
Hexadecimal Code	1B 28 33 40; 1B 29 33 40

Variables	None

Usage

The User Default Font is set through the control panel menu system. If it has not been explicitly set, it is the same as the Factory Default font—Courier 10 portrait. You can use this command to assign the User Default to the primary font or the secondary font. Subsequent commands can then refer to the designated font simply as the primary or secondary font. This enables you to create generic command sequences that can be applied to any font, including the User Default font by assigning it to the status of primary or secondary fonts prior to use. For example, to specify the User Default font as the secondary font, you use the following command:

```
Ec)3@
```

Thereafter, any request for the secondary font will call the User Default font.

BASIC Example

To select the User Default font as the primary font, you enter and run the following BASIC program:

```
LPRINT CHR$(27);"(3@"
```

Underline

Function group	Font selection
Application	Sets text underline on and off.
PCL 5 Command	Ec&d#D starts underline; Ec&d@ stops underline.
Decimal Code	027 038 100 ### 068; 027 038 100 064
Hexadecimal Code	1B 26 64 ## 44; 1B 26 64 40
Variables	# = 0 Fixed position
	# = 3 Floating position

Usage

There are two modes of underlining, fixed and floating. Fixed underlining places the underline stroke at a fixed distance—5 dots—under the baseline of all the characters. Floating underlining, available on the LaserJet III, determines the placement distance below the characters based on the largest font printed on the current line. Each font contains a preferred underline distance in its description file.

To underline text, insert the appropriate starting code before the text and the terminating code after the text. For example to underline the text *Red Bicycle* with a fixed distance underline, the command structure would be as follows:

```
Ec&d0D Red Bicycle Ec&d@
```

BASIC Example

To issue the above example in BASIC, enter and run the following program:

```
LPRINT CHR$(27);"&d0D"

LPRINT "Red Bicycle"

LPRINT CHR$(27);"&d@"
```

Font Management

The font management commands are used to control downloaded soft fonts. With these commands, you can assign a soft font an ID number that can be used to select the soft font as the primary or secondary font. You can classify a downloaded soft font as permanent or temporary. Permanent soft fonts reside in the printer's memory until they are explicitly deleted. Temporary soft fonts, however, will be overwritten if they are not currently selected and the memory is required for another soft font or print data. You can selectively delete all of the soft fonts, all of the temporary soft fonts, or only the last soft font specified.

Assign Font ID

Function group	Font management
Application	Assigns an ID # to downloaded soft font.
PCL 5 Command	Ec*c#D
Decimal Code	027 042 099 ### 068
Hexadecimal Code	1B 2A 63 ## 44
Variables	Assigned ID # (0 to 32767)

Usage

When a soft font is downloaded from the computer to the printer, it must be assigned an ID number. This number can be used to specify the font later in the printing session more efficiently than specifying it by its full characteristic description. The font ID command must be sent to the printer immediately BEFORE transmitting the soft font file.

For example, to download a soft font contained in the file named MYFONT and assign it ID number 6, you would use the following command:

```
Ec*c6D
```

Then you need to download the file containing the soft font by using the DOS COPY command or some other transmission command. When using the DOS COPY command, you need to include the /B option to indicate that the file contains binary data, as follows:

```
COPY /B MYFONT LPT1:
```

BASIC Example

To download the font contained in the file MYFONT to your printer and assign it the ID #2, you enter and run the following BASIC program:

```
LPRINT CHR$(27);"*c2D"

SHELL "COPY /B MYFONT LPT1:"
```

Cautions

Each font ID # must be unique. If you assign an ID # that had previously been assigned, the previous font is deleted from the printer's memory.

Font Control

Function group	Font management
Application	Used to delete soft fonts from memory and change their status.
PCL 5 Command	Ec*c#F
Decimal Code	027 042 099 ### 070
Hexadecimal Code	1B 2A 63 ## 46
Variables	# = 0 Delete all soft fonts.
	# = 1 Delete all temporary soft fonts.
	# = 2 Delete last soft font specified.
	# = 4 Make last soft font specified temporary.
	# = 5 Make last soft font specified permanent.

Usage

This series of commands is used to manage soft fonts in the printer's memory. They delete specific soft fonts or types of soft fonts, and change the status of the fonts from temporary to permanent or vice versa. To delete all soft fonts from the printer's memory, you use the following command:

    Ec*c0F

To delete all temporary soft fonts and retain all permanent soft fonts, you use the following command:

    Ec*c1F

And to make a temporary font permanent, you specify its ID and issue the following command:

```
Ec*c#D
```

To make it permanent, issue the following command:

```
Ec*c5F
```

BASIC Example

To change the permanent font number 32 to temporary, you enter and run the following BASIC program:

```
LPRINT CHR$(27);"*c32D"

LPRINT CHR$(27);"*c4F"
```

Notes

Commands 2, 4, and 5, apply to the last soft font specified. You can use the Font ID command to specify any currently available soft font by ID number.

Designate Font as Primary

Function group	Font management
Application	Designates which of the available fonts is to be used as the Primary Font.
PCL 5 Command	Ec(#x
Decimal Code	027 040 ### 068
Hexadecimal Code1	B 28 ## 58
Variables	Soft Font ID #

Usage

This command is used to select the font designated by the ID # as the primary font. Subsequent commands can refer to the designated font as the primary font. This enables you to create generic command sequences that can be applied to any font or any font ID number by assigning it the status of primary font prior to use.

For example, to specify font ID #6 as the primary font, you use the following command:

```
Ec(6X
```

Thereafter, any command or request for the primary font will act on, or call the font number 6.

BASIC Example

To select font number 32 as the primary font, you enter and run the following BASIC program:

```
LPRINT CHR$(27);"(32X"
```

Designate Font as Secondary

Function group	Font management
Application	Designates which of the available fonts is to be used as the secondary font.
PCL 5 Command	Ec)#x
Decimal Code	027 041 ### 068
Hexadecimal Code	1B 29 ## 58
Variables	Soft Font ID #

Usage

This command selects the font designated by the ID # as the secondary font. Subsequent commands can refer to the designated font as the secondary font. This enables you to create generic command sequences that can be applied to any font or any font ID number by assigning it the status of a secondary font prior to use.

For example, to specify font ID #6 as the secondary font, you use the following command:

```
Ec)6X
```

Thereafter, any command or request for the secondary font will act on or call font number 6.

BASIC Example

To select font number 32 as the secondary font, you enter and run the following BASIC program:

```
LPRINT CHR$(27);")32X"
```

Soft Font Creation

The soft font creation commands are used to create a soft font by describing the characteristics of the font and downloading the data describing each character of the font. These commands are not commonly used in everyday printing sessions. The soft font creation commands can be used to create bit-mapped or scalable soft fonts. This section only discusses their use with bit-mapped fonts as the creation of scalable fonts is beyond the scope of this book.

Font Descriptor and Data

Function group	Soft font creation
Application	Used to transmit the font description data to the printer.
PCL 5 Command	Ec)s#W data
Decimal Code	027 041 115 ### 087 data
Hexadecimal Code	1B 29 73 ## 57 data
Variables	# of bytes of data

Usage

When you are creating a new font, you must first assign it an ID number by using the Font ID Number command. Then you must transmit a font description to the printer. This information is contained in the font descriptor. Finally you must transmit the individual characters using the character commands. To transmit the font descriptor, you must tell the printer how much data is to be transmitted. This is the function of the variable in this command. To send the

64 byte font descriptor used for bit-mapped fonts, you use the following command:

```
Ec)s64W data
```

BASIC Example

To send this command in BASIC, you would enter and run the following BASIC program:

```
LPRINT CHR$(27);")s64W"
```

followed by the data.

Notes

You must send the font ID code before sending the descriptor file. This command is also used to send the 80 byte font descriptor used for scalable fonts. Please refer to the Hewlett-Packard Technical Reference manual for details on creating scalable soft fonts.

Character Descriptor and Data

Function group	Soft font creation
Application	Used to download the character's description and data.
PCL 5 Command	Ec(s#W data
Decimal Code	027 040 115 ### 087 data
Hexadecimal Code	1B 28 73 ## 57 data
Variables	# of bytes of data

Usage

This command precedes the data that describes the actual character. The variable tells the printer how much data follows the command in numbers of bytes. To send a character description that is 144 bytes long, you would use the following command:

```
Ec(s144W data
```

BASIC Example

To send this command in BASIC, you would enter and run the following BASIC program, followed by the data.

```
LPRINT CHR$(27);"(s144W"
```

Cautions

You must send the character code to the printer before sending the data.

Notes

This command is also used to send the 120-byte character descriptor used for scalable fonts. Refer to the Hewlett-Packard Technical Reference manual for details on creating scalable soft fonts.

Character Code

Function group	Soft font creation
Application	Used to set the decimal code assigned to the next character downloaded.
PCL 5 Command	Ec*c#E
Decimal Code	027 042 099 ### 069
Hexadecimal Code	1B 2A 63 ## 45
Variables	Decimal code # assigned to character

Usage

When creating characters, you must assign each one a decimal code. The code is used to call that character for printing before downloading its data. If you assign one of the codes of the current symbol set's printable characters, you will replace the existing character with your own.

To assign the code usually assigned to the @ character (ASCII 064) to your new character, you would use the following command:

```
Ec*c64E
```

BASIC Example

To send this example in BASIC, you would enter and run the following BASIC program:

```
LPRINT CHR$(27);"*c64E"
```

Graphics

The graphics commands fall into two categories, those that support the new HP-GL/2 vector graphics printing mode, and those that support the direct printing of raster graphics. The details of the HP-GL/2 vector graphics commands are beyond the scope of this book. Readers interested in HP-GL/2 should refer to the Hewlett-Packard Technical Reference Manual. This section only discusses the PCL 5 commands uses to access the HP-GL/2 mode and define the HP-GL/2 picture frame, which in turn can be used to print predefined HP-GL/2 graphics within a PCL 5 page. The following materials also covers the raster graphics commands in detail, since they can be used directly within PCL 5 to print raster-based images.

Enter PCL Mode

Function group	Graphics
Application	Returns printer to PCL mode from Hewlett-Packard-GL/2 mode.
PCL 5 Command	Ec%#A
Decimal Code	027 037 ### 065
Hexadecimal Code	1B 25 ## 41
Variables	# = 0 Use previous PCL 5 cursor position for current PCL 5 cursor position.
	# = 1 Use current HP-GL/2 cursor position for current PCL 5 cursor position.

Usage

After completing a HP-GL/2 graphics command series, you will want to return to PCL 5 to resume the print job. This command makes that conversion with two options. You can specify that PCL 5 should resume with the cursor located at the same spot as it was located before the HP-GL/2 session was started, or you can specify that the current HP-GL/2 cursor position should be used for the following PCL 5 session. To return to PCL 5 mode using the previous PCL 5 cursor position, you would use the following command:

```
Ec%0A
```

BASIC Example

To return to PCL 5 mode using the current HP-GL/2 cursor position, you enter and run the following BASIC program:

```
LPRINT CHR$(27);"%1A"
```

Notes

Entering and exiting HP-GL/2 mode does not change any of the PCL 5 variables; however, changing PCL 5 variables will affect the corresponding HP-GL/2 settings.

For example, executing a PCL 5 reset (EcE) will execute a HP-GL/2 initialization (IN), and will reset the PCL 5 picture frame size, anchor point, logical page orientation, and the HP-GL/2 plot size to their defaults.

Enter HP-GL/2 Mode

Function group	Graphics
Application	Switches from PCL 5 to HP-GL/2 mode.
PCL 5 Command	Ec%#B
Decimal Code	027 037 ### 066
Hexadecimal Code	1B 25 ## 42

Variables	# = 0	Use previous HP-GL/2 cursor position for current HP-GL/2 cursor position.
	# = 1	Use current PCL 5 cursor position for HP-GL/2 cursor position.

Usage

To print vector graphics, you need to switch from PCL 5 mode to HP-GL/2 mode. You can access all of the HP-GL/2 vector graphic commands. When you are switching from PCL 5 into HP- GL/2 mode, you can specify whether to use the PCL 5 cursor position as the starting cursor position for the HP-GL/2 session, or, if resuming a previous HP-GL/2 session, you can use the last HP-GL/2 cursor position as the starting point. To switch into HP-GL/2 with the current PCL 5 cursor position, use the following command:

    Ec%1B

BASIC Example

To switch into HP-GL/2 mode using the last HP-GL/2 cursor position, you would enter and run the following BASIC program:

    LPRINT CHR$(27);"%0B"

HP-GL/2 Plot Horizontal Size

Function group	Graphics
Application	Specifies the original horizontal size of a graphic image to be printed.
PCL 5 Command	Ec*c#K
Decimal Code	027 042 099 ### 075
Hexadecimal Code1	B 2A 63 ## 4B
Variables	# = horizontal size in inches

Usage

When printing a HP-GL/2 graphic in a PCL 5 picture frame that is smaller than the original image, HP-GL/2 automatically scales the image to fit the picture frame. To do this properly, HP-GL/2 needs to know the original size of the image. This command is used to specify the horizontal size. For example, if the original HP-GL/2 plot size is eight inches wide and the picture frame is only two inches wide, the horizontal scaling factor would be 4:1. To specify an eight-inch horizontal size, use the following command:

```
Ec*c8K
```

BASIC Example

To specify a four-inch horizontal size, you enter and run the following BASIC program:

```
LPRINT CHR$(27);"*c4K"
```

Notes

Resetting the printer or using a horizontal size of zero will set the horizontal size to the size of the picture frame.

HP-GL/2 Plot Vertical Size

Function group	Graphics
Application	Specifies the original vertical size of a graphic image to be printed.
PCL 5 Command	Ec*c#L
Decimal Code	027 042 099 ### 076
Hexadecimal Code	1B 2A 63 ## 4C
Variables	# = vertical size in inches

Usage

When printing an HP-GL/2 graphic in a PCL 5 picture frame that is smaller than the original image, HP-GL/2 scales the image to fit the picture frame. To do this properly, HP-GL/2 needs to know the original size of the image. This command is used to specify the vertical size.

If, for example, the original HP-GL/2 plot size would be four inches high and the picture frame is only two inches high, the vertical scaling factor would be 2:1. To specify a four-inch horizontal size, use the following command:

```
Ec*c4L
```

BASIC Example

To specify a six-inch vertical size, you enter and run the following BASIC program:

```
LPRINT CHR$(27);"*c6L"
```

Notes

Resetting the printer or using a vertical size of zero will set the vertical size to the size of the picture frame.

Set Picture Frame Anchor Point

Function group	Graphics
Application	Positions the top left corner of the PCL 5 picture frame.
PCL 5 Command	Ec*c0T
Decimal Code	027 042 099 048 084
Hexadecimal Code	1B 2A 63 30 54
Variables	Although the parameter zero is a variable, only the value of zero is recognized

Usage

When you enter HP-GL/2 mode to print an existing vector graphic, HP-GL/2 uses the PCL 5 picture frame to position and scale the vector graphic. The size of the picture frame as compared to the HP-GL/2 plot size determines the scaling factor, and the location of the PCL 5 picture frame's anchor point determines the position on the page.

To set the anchor point, you must first position the PCL 5 cursor at the desired location and then issue Ec*c0T command. If you do not issue the anchor point command, the anchor point will default to the left edge and top margin of the logical page. To set the anchor point two inches to the right of the left margin and three inches below the top margin use the following commands, where the first half of the command position the cursor 600 dots (2 inches) to the right and 900 dots (3 inches) down from the top left corner of the logical page and the second half sets the anchor point.

```
Ec*p600x900YEc*c0T
```

```
BASIC Example
```

To set the anchor point at five inches down and two inches over, you enter and run the following BASIC program:

```
LPRINT CHR$(27);"*p600x1500Y"
```

```
LPRINT CHR$(27);"*c0T"
```

Picture Frame Horizontal Size

Function group	Graphics
Application	Sets the horizontal size of the PCL 5 picture frame.
PCL 5 Command	Ec*c#x
Decimal Code	027 042 099 ### 088
Hexadecimal Code	1B 2A 63 ## 58
Variables	# = horizontal size in decipoints (1/720th of an inch)

Usage

When you enter HP-GL/2 mode to print an existing vector graphic, HP-GL/2 uses the PCL 5 picture frame to position and scale the vector graphic. The size of the picture frame as compared to the HP-GL/2 plot size determines the scaling factor, and the location of the PCL 5 picture frame's anchor point determines the position on the page.

This command is used to specify the horizontal dimension of the picture frame. For example, to specify a picture frame four inches wide you would use the following command, where 2,880 equals 4 × 720. If the original graphic were specified as being eight inches wide, this would produce a scaling factor of 2:1.

```
Ec*c2880X
```

BASIC Example

To set the horizontal dimension of the picture frame to five inches, you enter and run the following BASIC program:

```
LPRINT CHR$(27);"*c3600X"
```

Picture Frame Vertical Size

Function group	Graphics
Application	Sets the vertical size of the PCL 5 picture frame.
PCL 5 Command	Ec*c#Y
Decimal Code	027 042 099 ### 089
Hexadecimal Code	1B 2A 63 ## 59
Variables	# = vertical size in decipoints (1/720th of an inch)

Usage

When you enter HP-GL/2 mode to print an existing vector graphic, HP-GL/2 uses the PCL 5 picture frame to position and scale the vector graphic. The size of the picture frame as compared to the HP-GL/2 plot size determines the scaling factor, and the location of the PCL 5 picture frame's anchor point determines the position on the page.

This command is used to specify the vertical dimension of the picture frame. For example, to specify a picture frame five inches high you would use the following command, where 3,600 equals 5 × 720. If the original graphic were specified as being eight inches wide, this would produce a scaling factor of 8:5.

```
Ec*c3600Y
```

BASIC Example

To set the vertical dimension of the picture frame to six inches, you would enter and run the following BASIC program:

```
LPRINT CHR$(27);"*c4320Y"
```

Raster Graphics Resolution

Function group	Graphics
Application	Sets the resolution of graphics in dots per inch (dpi).
PCL 5 Command	Ec*t#R
Decimal Code	027 042 116 ### 082
Hexadecimal Code	1B 2A 74 ## 52
Variables	# = 75 for 75 DPI
	# = 100 for 100 DPI
	# = 150 for 150 DPI
	# = 300 for 300 DPI
	Note that the actual decimal values —150— are entered in the code, not the ASCII representation of their digits.

Usage

This command sets the resolution of all graphics printed on a page. The resolution must be set before transmitting graphics data to the printer. Because the printer always outputs with a physical resolution of 300 dpi, lower resolution settings are simulated by substituting patterned squares of 300 dpi dots for each dot of the lower resolution image. In this way, the lower resolution image can take up less memory in the printer, and still print at 300 dpi.

To set the resolution to 150 dpi you use the following command:

```
Ec*t150R
```

BASIC Example

To set the resolution to 75 dpi in BASIC, you enter and run the following BASIC program:

```
LPRINT CHR$(27);"*t75R"
```

Notes

The Factory Default resolution is 75 dpi for graphics.

Raster Graphics Presentation

Function group	Graphics
Application	Set the orientation of the raster image on the logical page.
PCL 5 Command	Ec*r#F
Decimal Code	027 042 114 ### 070
Hexadecimal Code	1B 2A 72 ## 46
Variables	# = 0 Raster image is printed in the same orientation as the logical page.
	# = 3 Raster image is printed across the width of the physical page regardless of the orientation of the logical page (the default).

Usage

When you are printing raster images, you can specify whether the orientation should follow the orientation of the logical page, or the image should be printed across the physical page regardless of the logical page orientation. This becomes important when you are printing in landscape mode because the default mode is printed across the physical page—3—regardless of the orientation. You must explicitly set the presentation mode to follow the logical page orientation—0—to print graphics in the same orientation as the text in landscape. To do this, use the following command:

```
Ec*r0F
```

BASIC Example

To print graphics in the same orientation as the text, you would enter and run the following BASIC program:

```
LPRINT CHR$(27);"*r0F"
```

Raster Graphics Start

Function group	Graphics
Application	Start graphics mode at the left margin or at the current cursor position.
PCL 5 Command	Ec*r#A
Decimal Code	027 042 114 ### 065
Hexadecimal Code	1B 2A 72 ## 41
Variables	# = 0 Start graphics at left margin.
	# = 1 Start graphics at current position.

Usage

When you are initiating the graphics mode, you must first set the graphics resolution and the left margin, because they will remain fixed for the duration of the graphics mode (see Graphics Resolution).

To initiate graphics at the current cursor position, set the variable to 1. Set the variable to 0 to start the graphics mode at the left margin— position 0. To start the graphics mode at the current cursor position, you use the following command:

```
Ec*r1A
```

BASIC Example

To start the graphics mode at the left margin—position 0—you enter and run the following BASIC program:

```
LPRINT CHR$(27);"*r0A"
```

Notes

After you start raster graphics, the resolution, presentation mode, height, width, and left margin are fixed until the end of raster graphics command is executed.

Raster Graphics Y Offset

Function group	Graphics
Application	Moves the cursor vertically in raster mode.
PCL 5 Command	Ec*b#Y
Decimal Code	027 042 098 ### 089
Hexadecimal Code	1B 2A 62 ## 59
Variables	# = number of raster lines

Usage

This is used to move the cursor vertically within the raster print area. To move the cursor 50 lines vertically, use the following command:

```
Ec*b50Y
```

BASIC Example

To move the cursor 100 lines, you enter and run the following BASIC program:

```
100 LPRINT CHR$(27);"*b100Y"
```

Set Raster Graphics Compression Mode

Function group	Graphics
Application	Use to specify one of three raster graphic data compression modes.
PCL 5 Command	Ec*b#M
Decimal Code	027 042 098 ### 077
Hexadecimal Code	1B 2A 62 ## 4D
Variables	# = 0 Unencoded
	# = 1 Run-length encoding
	# = 2 Tagged image file format (TIFF)
	# = 3 Delta row compression

Usage

To speed up data transmission and conserve memory and storage space, PCL 5 supports three compressed data formats for raster graphics. The run-length and TIFF compression methods use the principal of transmitting a literal image of part of an image and a repetition count. The literal image is repeated the specified number of times. In this way, the repeated image only has to be transmitted one time. The delta row compression technique works on the premise that most of the data in each successive row of a raster image is the same, and it only transmits the changes.

Each technique has its advantages, and your selection will depend more on the available format of your image than anything else. If you have a choice, you will have to select the format based on the contents of the specific image.

To select TIFF data compression mode, use the following command:

```
Ec*b2M
```

BASIC Example

To select delta row compression mode, you enter and run the following BASIC program:

```
LPRINT CHR$(27);"*b3M"
```

Raster Graphics Data Transfer

Function group	Graphics
Application	Transfer raster graphics data.
PCL 5 Command	Ec*b#W data
Decimal Code	027 042 098 ### 087 data
Hexadecimal Code	1B 2A 62 ## 57 data
Variables	# of bytes of data following command

Usage

This command is used as the PCL 5 printer language prefix for the transfer of raster graphics data. The printer needs to know how many bytes of data will be transmitted to the printer for a particular line of the graphic image. The variable supplied in the command indicates the number of bytes of data that will follow.

To transmit 12 bytes of graphics data, for instance, you must set the printer in graphics mode (see Graphics Start), and issue the PCL 5 transfer graphics data command, followed by the 12 bytes of data. You need to use the following command:

```
Ec*b12W data
```

BASIC Example

To send 45 bytes of graphics data, you would enter and run the following BASIC program:

```
LPRINT CHR$(27);"*b45W"
```

Cautions

You must set the left margin and start the graphics mode before transmitting graphics data.

Notes

The graphics mode ignores the text area and perforation area limits. Graphics can print anywhere on the printable area of the logical page.

Raster Graphics End

Function group	Graphics
Application	Signals the end of the graphics data transfer.
PCL 5 Command	Ec*rB
Decimal Code	027 042 114 066
Hexadecimal Code	1B 2A 72 42
Variables	None

Usage

To stop graphics data transmission, you would use the following command:

```
Ec*rB
```

BASIC Example

To signal the end of graphics data transmission, you enter and run the following BASIC program:

```
LPRINT CHR$(27);"*rB"
```

Raster Graphics Height

Function group	Graphics
Application	Specifies the vertical height of the Raster Area.

PCL 5 Comman	dEc*r#T
Decimal Code	027 042 114 ### 084
Hexadecimal Code	1B 2A 72 ## 54
Variables	# = height in raster rows

Usage

The horizontal and vertical raster dimensions define the Raster Area. The raster area is used for two purposes. First, it can be used to reduce the amount of raster data transmission required since the entire raster area defaults to white or transparent (depending on the setting of source transparency mode).

With the raster area defaulting to white, you need to only transmit the lines that contain nonwhite data by using the raster Y offset to space down for intermediate blank rows. With some raster graphics, this can greatly reduce transmission times. The second use is to define the clipping area for the graphic. Any data that would fall outside of the raster area will be clipped. To set the vertical height to 40 rows, use the following command:

```
Ec*r40T
```

BASIC Example

To set the vertical height to 100 rows, you enter and run the following BASIC program:

```
100 LPRINT CHR$(27);"*r100T"
```

Notes

Setting the raster height outside of the logical page or printable area will not extend printing to these areas.

Raster Graphics Width

Function group	Graphics
Application	Specifies the width of the Raster Area.
PCL 5 Command	Ec*r#S
Decimal Code	027 042 114 ### 083
Hexadecimal Code	1B 2A 72 ## 53
Variables	# = pixels of the current resolution

Usage

The horizontal and vertical raster dimensions define the Raster Area. The raster area is used for two purposes. First, it can be used to reduce the amount of raster data transmission required because the entire raster area defaults to white or transparent—depending on the setting of source transparency mode.

With the raster area defaulting to white, you need to only transmit the lines that contain nonwhite data, by using the raster Y offset to space down for intermediate blank rows. With some raster graphics, this can greatly reduce transmission times. The second use is to define the clipping area for the graphic. Any data that falls outside the raster area will be clipped. To set the width to 400 pixels, use the following command:

```
Ec*r400S
```

BASIC Example

To set the width to 900 pixels, you enter and run the following BASIC program:

```
LPRINT CHR$(27);"*r900S"
```

Notes

Setting the raster width outside of the logical page or printable area will not extend printing to these areas.

The Print Model

The Print Model commands determine how raster graphics are printed. You can control the pattern of shading or cross-hatching used to fill the graphic, as well as the transparency of a graphic that overlaps previously defined text or graphics. The previously defined text and graphics are called the Destination Image because the new image—the Source image—will be laid on top of it. The combination of Pattern, Source Image, and respective transparencies will determine how they are overlaid on the Destination Image.

When the Source Image or Pattern is defined as opaque, the white portions of the Image or Pattern will overwrite the black portions of the Destination Image. When the Source Image or Pattern is defined as transparent, the white areas are ignored and the black portions of the underlying Destination Image will be allowed to show through.

Select Pattern

Function group	Print model
Application	Selects the pattern to be applied onto the destination.
PCL 5 Command	Ec*v#T
Decimal Code	027 042 118 ### 084
Hexadecimal Code	1B 2A 76 ## 54
Variables	# = 0 Solid black (default)
	# = 1 Solid white
	# = 2 Shading pattern
	# = 3 Cross-hatch pattern

Usage

When printing an image, you can define the shading or cross-hatching used to fill the image as well as the opacity of that shading. To select the solid black or solid white, you need to only use this command with the 0 or 1 variable. To specify shading or cross-hatching, you must first specify the desired shading with the Area Fill ID command. To select solid black pattern—the default—use the following command:

```
Ec*v0T
```

BASIC Example

To select a 10 percent shading, you enter and run the following BASIC program:

```
100 LPRINT CHR$(27);"*c10G"

200 LPRINT CHR$(27);"*v2T"
```

Select Source Transparency Mode

Function group	Print Model
Application	Defines whether new images are added to or overwrite existing images.
PCL 5 Command	Ec*v#N
Decimal Code	027 042 118 ### 078
Hexadecimal Code	1B 2A 76 ## 4E
Variables	# = 0 Source treated as transparent
	# = 1 Source treated as opaque

Usage

When printing a new image on top of an existing image, you can specify that the entire image should overwrite the existing image (opaque) or that it should be added to the existing image (transparent).

This distinction is accomplished by looking only at the white areas of the new image. If you specify opaque, the white area will obscure any black areas of the underlying image. If you specify transparent, the white areas of the new image are ignored, enabling the underlying image to show through. You can specify that the entire image should be treated as opaque or transparent—this command—or that only the defined fill area of the image be treated as opaque or transparent—next command. Figure 15.5 shows the results of each of these settings.

To specify that the entire source image is to be treated as opaque, use the following command:

```
Ec*v1N
```

BASIC Example

To specify that the source image is to be treated as transparent, you enter and run the following BASIC program:

```
LPRINT CHR$(27);"*v0N"
```

Select Pattern Transparency Mode

Function group	Print model
Application	Determines whether the pattern assigned to an image is to be treated as transparent or opaque.
PCL 5 Command	Ec*v#O
Decimal Code	027 042 118 ### 079
Hexadecimal Code	1B 2A 76 ## 4F
Variables	# = 0 Treat pattern as transparent
	# = 1 Treat pattern as opaque

Usage

When you are printing a new image on top of an existing image, you can specify that the pattern assigned to the image should overwrite the existing image (opaque), or that it should be added to the existing image (transparent). You can do this by looking only at the white areas of the new image's pattern. If you specify opaque, the white area will obscure any black areas of the underlying image. If you specify transparent, the white areas of the new image are ignored, allowing the underlying image to show through.

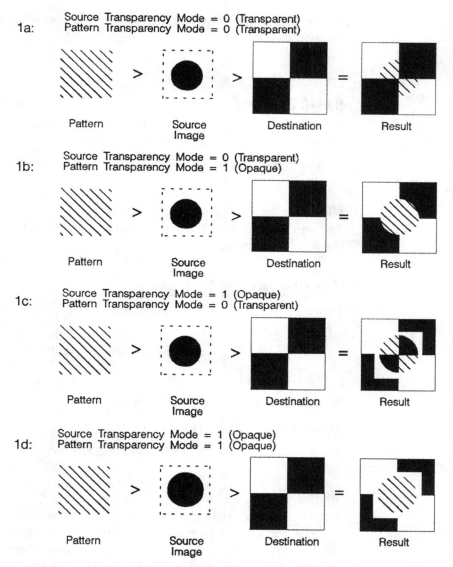

Figure 15.5. The transparency mode and its effect on combined images.

You can specify that the entire image should be treated as opaque or transparent (the previous command), or that only the defined fill area of the image be treated as opaque or transparent (this command). Figure 15.5 (above) shows the results of each of these settings.

To specify that the pattern is to be treated as opaque, use the following command:

```
Ec*v1O
```

BASIC Example

To specify that the pattern is to be treated as transparent, you would enter and run the following BASIC program:

```
LPRINT CHR$(27);"*vOO"
```

Notes

The terminal character of this command is a capital O. Make sure you distinguish it from a zero.

Rectangle Width in Dots

Function group	Print model
Application	Sets the horizontal size of a rectangular graphic element such as a rule or box.
PCL 5 Command	Ec*c#A
Decimal Code	027 042 099 ### 065
Hexadecimal Code	1B 2A 63 ## 41
Variables	# of dots (300 dots per inch)

Usage

To describe a rectangular graphic element such as a rule or box, you need to define its shape and size by setting its horizontal and vertical dimensions relative to the current cursor position. You also need to define the type of pattern or shading density you used to fill the rectangular space. To set a horizontal dimension of four inches in terms of dots (1/300th inch), you would first calculate the total number of dots as follows:

$$4" \times 300 \text{ DPI} = 1,200 \text{ Dots}$$

Enter the following command:

```
Ec*c1200A
```

BASIC Example

To set the horizontal dimension to three inches, you enter and run the following BASIC program:

```
LPRINT CHR$(27);"*c900A"
```

Notes

You must also specify the vertical dimension and the fill pattern. After setting all three specifications, you need to issue an Area Fill command to initiate the drawing process.

Rectangle Width in Decipoints

Function group	Print model
Application	Sets the horizontal size of a rectangular graphic element such as a rule or box.
PCL 5 Command	Ec*c#H
Decimal Code	027 042 099 ### 072
Hexadecimal Code	1B 2A 63 ## 48
Variables	# of decipoints (720 decipoints per inch)

Usage

To describe a rectangular graphic element such as a rule or a box, you need to define its shape and size by setting its horizontal and vertical dimensions relative to the current cursor position. You also need to define the type of pattern or shading density you used to fill the rectangular space. To set a horizontal dimension of four inches in terms of decipoints (1/720th inch), you first calculate the total number of decipoints as follows:

$$4" \times 720 \text{ DPI} = 2,880 \text{ Decipoints}$$

Enter the following command:

```
Ec*c2880H
```

BASIC Example

To set the horizontal dimension to three inches, you enter and run the following BASIC program:

```
LPRINT CHR$(27);"*c2160H"
```

Notes

You also need to specify the vertical dimension and the fill pattern. After setting all three specifications, you need to issue an Area Fill command to initiate the drawing process.

Although the graphics resolution of the printer is only 300 dpi, the dimension set in decipoints—720 per inch—is rounded up to the nearest dot—75 decipoints equals 31.25 dots, that would be rounded up to 32 dots.

Rectangle Height in Dots

Function group	Print model
Application	Sets the horizontal size of a rectangular graphic element such as a rule or box.
PCL 5 Command	Ec*c#B
Decimal Code	027 042 099 ### 066
Hexadecimal Code	1B 2A 63 ## 42
Variables	# of dots (300 dots per inch)

Usage

To describe a rectangular graphic element such as a rule or box, you must define its shape and size by setting its horizontal and vertical dimensions relative to the current cursor position. You need to also define the type of pattern or shading density you used to fill the rectangular space. To set a vertical dimension of four inches in terms of dots—1/300th inch—you would first calculate the total number of dots as follows:

$$4" \times 300 \text{ DPI} = 1,200 \text{ Dots}$$

Then enter the following command:

```
Ec*c1200B
```

BASIC Example

To set the vertical dimension to three inches, you enter and run the following BASIC program:

```
LPRINT CHR$(27);"*c900B"
```

Notes

You also need to specify the horizontal dimension and the fill pattern. After setting all three specifications, you need to issue an Area Fill command to initiate the drawing process.

Rectangle Height in Decipoints

Function group	Print model
Application	Sets the horizontal size of a rectangular graphic element such as a rule or box.
PCL 5 Command	Ec*c#V
Decimal Code	027 042 099 ### 086
Hexadecimal Code	1B 2A 63 ## 56
Variables	# of decipoints (720 decipoints per inch)

Usage

To describe a rectangular graphic element such as a rule or box, you need to define its shape and size by setting its horizontal and vertical dimensions relative to the current cursor position. You also need to define the type of pattern or shading density used to fill the rectangular space. To set a vertical dimension of four inches in terms of decipoints—1/720th inch—you would first calculate the total number of decipoints as follows:

$$4" \times 720 \text{ DPI} = 2,880 \text{ Decipoints}$$

Then enter the following command:

```
Ec*c2880V
```

BASIC Example

To set the vertical dimension to three inches, you enter and run the following BASIC program:

```
LPRINT CHR$(27);"*c2160V"
```

Notes

You also need to specify the horizontal dimension and the fill pattern. After setting all three specifications, you need to issue an Area Fill draw command to initiate the drawing process.

Although the graphics resolution of the printer is only 300 dpi, the dimension set in decipoints—720 per inch—is rounded up to the nearest dot—75 decipoints equals 31.25 dots, that would be rounded to 32 dots.

Fill Rectangle Area

Function group: Print model

Application	Used to initiate the drawing process for rectangular graphic elements by specifying the type of fill.
PCL 5 Command	Ec*c#P
Decimal Code	027 042 099 ### 080

Hexadecimal Code	1B 2A 63 ## 50	
Variables	# = 0	Solid black fill
	# = 1	Solid white fill (erases area)
	# = 2	Shaded fill
	# = 3	Patterned fill
	# = 4	User Defined Pattern
	# = 5	Fill with current pattern

Usage

The Rectangle Fill command is used to initiate the drawing process after the size and the fill pattern have been defined. If the solid fill # equals 0, or 1 is selected, no shading or fill pattern needs to be defined. The rectangle's upper left corner will be placed at the current cursor position.

To draw a 4-by-5-inch box with #6 cross-hatch fill pattern at the current position, you issue the following sequence of commands:

Ec*c1200A	Sets the width.
Ec*c1500B	Sets the height.
Ec*c6G	Selects fill pattern #6.
Ec*3P	Starts drawing with a cross-hatch fill pattern.

BASIC Example

To draw a 2-by-3-inch box with 25 percent gray shading starting at position 300,600 dots—one inch over, two inches down—from the upper left corner of the logical page, you enter and run the following BASIC program:

100 LPRINT CHR$(27);"*p300x400Y"	Positions cursor.
200 LPRINT CHR$(27);"*c600A"	Sets horizontal size.
300 LPRINT CHR$(27);"*c900B"	Sets vertical size.
400 LPRINT CHR$(27);"*c25G"	Selects shading percentage.
500 LPRINT CHR$(27);"*c2P"	Starts drawing with shading.

Cautions

You must specify the starting position, horizontal and vertical size, and the shading or fill pattern before initiating the drawing process. You must select the correct variable corresponding to the shading percentage or fill pattern defined by the fill designation command.

Graphic Element: Fill Pattern or Shading

Function group	Print model
Application	Specifies the pattern or shading used to fill a defined rectangular area or images.
PCL 5 Command	Ec*c#G
Decimal Code	027 042 099 ### 071
Hexadecimal Code	1B 2A 63 ## 47
Variables	Pattern number or percentage of gray.

The distinction between patterns and percentages with the same value is determined by the Rectangle Area Fill command (for rectangles), or the Select Current Pattern (for images).

Usage

To draw a rectangular graphic element, you need to define its dimensions and the pattern or shading to be used to fill the rectangle. This command is used to set the cross-hatch pattern or the shading level. The cross-hatch pattern can be selected by number from Figure 15.6. The shading level can be defined as any percentage shading from 1–100 percent. The actual shading used will correspond to one of the eight levels shown in Figure 15.7, depending on the value of the percentage requested.

Although the numbers are used to designate the fill patterns (1–6) also correspond to shading percentages, another method must be used to distinguish them from each other. The Fill Rectangle Area command uses a variable that distinguishes between filled or shaded rectangles.

See Fill Rectangle Area. To select a fill pattern of vertical lines—pattern #2—you would use the following command:

```
Ec*c2G
```

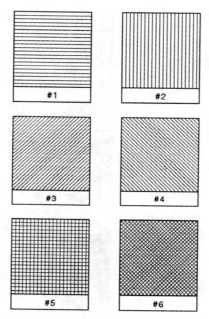

Figure 15.6. Cross-hatch patterns.

BASIC Example

To specify a 25 percent shading level, you enter and run the following BASIC program:

```
LPRINT CHR$(27);"*c25G"
```

Notes

You also need to specify the horizontal and vertical sizes of the rectangle, and issue a fill command to create a graphic element.

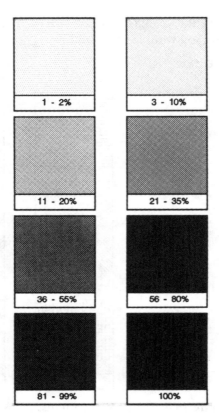

Figure 15.7. Shading patterns.

User-Defined Pattern

Function group	Print model
Application	Enables the user to define a unique pattern for area filling.
PCL 5 Command	Ec*c#W [Data]
Decimal Code	027 042 ### 087 [Data]
Hexidecimal Code	1B 2A 63 ## 57 [Data]
Variables	Number of bytes of pattern data

Usage

To create your own pattern for filling areas, you must first design the pattern and reduce it to hexidecimal data. The logic is the same for creating a soft font—first representing each pixel of the pattern as a binary 1 or 0 and then encoding the binary data as hexidecimal code. In addition to the hexidecimal code defining the pattern, the data must contain an 8–10 byte header defining the the size and resolution of the pattern. The header file contains the following data:

Byte	15 - 8	7 - 0
0	Format (0)	Continuation (0)
2	Pixel Encoding (1)	Reserved (0)
4	Height in pixels	
6	Width in pixels	
8	X resolution	
10	Y resolution	
12	Pattern image ...	

BASIC Example

To create a user-defined pattern, you enter and run the following BASIC programs:

```
LPRINT CHR$(27);"*c10G"
```
Specify the pattern number

```
LPRINT CHR$(27);"*c76W"
```
Specify the data as 76 bytes — 8 bytes for the header and 68 bytes of data

Then copy the pattern data to the printer. The following data creates an hour glass pattern.

00 00 01 00 00 10 00 20	Pattern header
FF FF FF FF	Pattern data
7F FF FF FE	
3F FF FF FC	
1F FF FF F8	

```
OF FF FF F0
07 FF FF E0
03 FF FF C0
01 FF FF 80
00 FF FF 00
01 FF FF 80
03 FF FF C0
07 FF FF E0
OF FF FF F0
1F FF FF F8
3F FF FF FC
7F FF FF FE
FF FF FF FF
```

Pattern Reference Point

Function group	Print model
Application	Sets the rotation of the pattern relative to the current print direction or fixed.
PCL 5 Command	Ec*p#R
Decimal Code	027 042 112 ### 082
Hexidecimal Code	1B 2A 70 ## 52
Variables	# = 0 Rotate with print orientation
	# = 1 Remain fixed relative to physical page

Usage

After you have specified a single instance of a particular pattern, you must specify how it is to be replicated for areas larger than a single instance of the pattern. You can specify that the pattern is to be rotated along with any changes in the print direction—0 is the default—or is to remained fixed relative to the physical page.

BASIC Example

To set the pattern to remain fixed relative to the physical paper, you enter and run the following program:

```
LPRINT CHR$(27);"*p1R"
```

Pattern Control

Function group	Print Model
Application	Controls the storage of user defined patterns.
PCL 5 Command	Ec*c#Q
Decimal Code	027 042 099 ### 081
Hexidecimal Code	1B 2A 63 ## 51
Variables	# = 0 Delete all patterns
	# = 1 Delete all temporary patterns
	# = 2 Delete last specified pattern
	# = 3 Reserved
	# = 4 Make last specified pattern temporary
	# = 5 Make last specified pattern permanent

Usage

This series of commands is used to control the patterns in the printer's memory. They delete specific patterns or types of patterns and change the status of a pattern from temporary to permanent and vice versa. To delete all of the patterns, you use the following command:

```
Ec*c0Q
```

To delete all of the temporary patterns, you use the following command:

```
Ec*c1Q
```

BASIC Example

To change the last specified pattern to temoprary, you enter and run the following BASIC progam:

```
LPRINT CHR$(27);"*c4Q"
```

Macros

PCL 5 macros can be used to store frequently used PCL 5 command sequences in the printer's memory, assign them a unique ID number, and reexecute them by executing the macro. This process can reduce transmission times for repetitive PCL 5 commands. Macros stored in the printer's memory reduce the amount of memory available for soft fonts and print data.

Macro ID # Specification

Function group	Macro commands
Application	Used to set the macro ID number before downloading a macro to the printer.
PCL 5 Command	Ec&f#Y
Decimal Code	027 038 102 ### 089
Hexadecimal Code	1B 26 66 ## 59
Variables	Macro ID # (0732,767)

Usage

Before you begin downloading a macro to the printer's memory, you need to assign it an ID number. Thereafter, you can execute or manipulate the macro by referring to its ID number. To set the macro ID number of the next macro to be downloaded to 12, you use the following command:

```
Ec&f12Y
```

BASIC Example

To establish this ID number through BASIC, you enter and run the following BASIC program:

```
100 LPRINT CHR$(27);"&f12Y"
```

Cautions

You need to establish the ID number for a macro before you begin to download it.

Macro Control

Function group	Macro commands
Application	Used to define, execute, or delete a macro.
PCL 5 Command	Ec&f#¥
Decimal Code	027 038 102 ### 088
Hexadecimal Code	1B 26 66 ## 58
Variables	# = 0 Start macro definition*
	# = 1 Stop macro definition
	# = 2 Execute macro*
	# = 3 Call macro*
	# = 4 Enable macro for automatic overlay*

# = 5	Disable automatic overlay
# = 6	Delete all macros
# = 7	Delete all temporary macros
# = 8	Delete specific macro*
# = 9	Convert macro to temporary*
# = 10	Convert macro to permanent*

* Acts upon the last macro ID specified by the Macro ID command.

Usage

This series of commands are used to control the definition, running, and deletion of printer macros.

Defining a Macro

To begin the definition of a macro, you must first establish an ID number using the Macro ID command. You need to indicate the beginning of the macro definition by issuing the start of the folowing macro definition command:

```
Ec&f3Y Sets macro ID to 3

Ec&f0X Starts macro definition
```

These commands can be combined into a single command as follows:

```
Ec&f3y0X
```

You would then transmit the commands and data to be contained in the macro and terminate the definition mode with the following command:

```
Ec&f1X
```

Running a Macro

There are three methods of running a macro: Execution, Calling, and Overlaying. When you execute a macro, it alters the setting of the Current Defaults, just as if the commands were individually sent. When you call a macro, the macro commands are executed starting with the Current Default Environment. The Current Default Environment resets to its values before running the macro.

When you overlay a macro, it is run as the final task before printing each page. The overlay process stores the values of the Current Default Environment in memory, and restores the User Default Environment before starting. After finishing, the overlay process resets the values of the Current Default Environment to its values before starting the overlay. To Execute the current macro, you would use the following command:

```
Ec&f2X
```

To call it, use the following command:

```
Ec&f3X
```

To enable it for overlay, use the following command:

```
Ec&f4X
```

Because the overlay process is a continuous process—once for each page—you must turn it off with the following command:

```
Ec&f5X
```

Remember that you need to precede any of the macro starting commands with a macro ID command.

Deleting a Macro

You can delete macros one at a time, by type or all at once. To delete the current macro, use the following command:

```
Ec&f8X
```

To delete all of the temporary macros, use the following command:

```
Ec&f7X
```

To delete all of the macros, use the following command:

```
Ec&f6X
```

You can change the status of a macro to permanent by using the following command:

```
Ec&f10X
```

You can return it to the default temporary status with the following command:

```
Ec&f9X
```

BASIC Example

To set up a macro to create an 1-by-6-inch shaded box at the current position, assign it the ID #4, and execute it, you enter and run the following BASIC program:

`LPRINT CHR$(27);"&f4Y"`	Specifies the ID #
`LPRINT CHR$(27);"&f0X"`	Starts macro definition
`LPRINT CHR$(27);"*c300A"`	Sets horizontal size
`LPRINT CHR$(27);"*c1800B"`	Sets vertical size
`LPRINT CHR$(27);"*c25G"`	Selects shading percentage
`LPRINT CHR$(27);"*c2P"`	Starts drawing with shading
`LPRINT CHR$(27);"&f1X"`	Stops macro definition
`LPRINT CHR$(27);"&f2X"`	Executes macro

Cautions

The cursor position is not considered to be part of the Current Default Environment and is not restored after a macro is called. If you want to return the cursor to the starting position after calling a macro, you must store the coordinates of the current cursor position using the Push command and restore the cursor to that position at the end of the macro using the Pop command. Therefore, the first macro command should be the Push command—Ec&f0S—and the last command should be the Pop command—Ec&f1S.

Notes

You can nest two layers of a macro by having one macro call or execute another macro as part of its command file. You need to make sure that both macros are properly loaded and identified before running the calling macro. You cannot run a macro overlay command from within a macro.

You also cannot use any font management commands in a macro. For example, you cannot change the status of a font from temporary to permanent from within a macro.

Programming Tools

PCL 5 provides several commands that facilitate the process of creating and debugging PCL 5 command sequences. For example, the Display Functions command causes the subsequent PCL 5 command to be printed, rather than executed, enabling you to confirm what is being sent to your printer.

End of Line Wrap

Function group	Programming tools
Application	Used to cause the printer to issue its own end of a line wrap command when the text would run past the right margin and be clipped.
PCL 5 Command	Ec&s#C
Decimal Code	027 038 115 ### 067
Hexadecimal Code	1B 26 73 ## 43
Variables	# = 0 Enable end of line wrap
	# = 1 Disable end of line wrap

Usage

Most word processors control their own end of line wrap so the default value for this option is disabled. When you are printing unformatted ASCII text or programs that might extend over the right margin of the page, you may not print the full line of text. That portion that extends past the right margin will be clipped. To ensure that all text is printed, enable the line wrapping function of the printer, and the extending portion will be printed on the next line. This function is often used in conjunction with the Display Functions Mode, which prints the control codes instead of executing them.

To enable line wrapping you use the following command:

```
Ec&s0C
```

BASIC Example

To disable line wrapping, you enter and run the following BASIC program:

```
LPRINT CHR$(27);"&s1C"
```

Cautions

Using line wrapping in conjunction with software that performs its own line wrapping can cause unpredictable results.

Display Functions Mode

Function group	Programming tools
Application	Used to debug graphics and macro control sequences, by printing the commands rather than executing them.
PCL 5 Command	EcY enables; EcZ disables.
Decimal Code	027 089; 027 090
Hexadecimal Code	1B 59; 1B 5A
Variables	None

Usage

When you are creating custom graphics or macros for the LaserJet III printer, it is often helpful to see the commands sent to the printer in typed form rather than have them executed. To do this, you enable the Display Functions Mode with the following command—note that you should always precede this command with the End of Line Wrap command to prevent lines of function commands from extending over the right margin of the page and being clipped.

Ec&s0C	Enable line wrapping
EcY	Starts display mode

DATA   Graphics or macro data

EcZ   End display mode

Ec&s1C   Disable line wrapping

BASIC Example

To send the same command sequence in BASIC, you enter and run the following BASIC program:

```
LPRINT CHR$(27);"&s0C"

LPRINT CHR$(27);"Y"

LPRINT DATA

LPRINT CHR$(27);"Z"

LPRINT CHR$(27);"&s1C
```

PART

Appendices

Glossary

Auto Continue	A feature on the LaserJet Series II that enables the printer to continue its operation despite an error message.
Baud Rate	A measure of the speed at which data is transferred serially. LaserJets can be configured to transmit at speeds between 300 baud and 19,200 baud.
Bit-Mapping	The process by which characters are described graphically as a series of ones and zeros, that corresponds to dots and white spaces.
Bond Paper	Any paper that consists of pure cellulose or cotton fiber.
C5	Envelopes that measure 162-by-229 mm.
COM-10	Commercial size (#10) envelope. Standard business size (4 1/2-by-9 1/2 inches).
Configuration	A setting that determines whether the printer is set up to receive data through a serial or parallel interface.

Cotton Bond Paper that consists of fibers made from rags. It has the finest feel and is used for letterhead stationery. Because it does not have the optimal electrical properties and tends to cause jamming problems with mechanical feeders, it is not recommended for laser printers.

CPI Characters per inch; also known as pitch.

DDL Document Description Language. DDL was created by Imagen Corporation and Xerox Corporation to control laser printers. It is similar to and competitive with PostScript. Some laser printers can support both page description languages.

Decipoint A unit of measurement that is used by the LaserJet for spacing characters and graphics, equal to 1/720th of an inch.

Default A feature setting that is used each time the printer is turned on.

DL Refers to envelopes that measure 110-by-220 mm.

Downloading A process by which soft fonts stored on a disk are transferred to the printer.

DPI Dots per inch. A measure of printing resolution based on the number of dots printed on a one square inch surface.

DTR Polarity The printer constantly emits a DTR (Data Terminal Ready) signal to the computer to indicate whether it is ready to receive data. Normally, high DTR polarity indicates that the printer buffer is empty, and low DTR tells the computer that the buffer is full and data transmission should be suspended.

EP Cartridge	A disposable Electrophotographic cartridge that contains a supply of toner, a light sensitive drum, a charging wire, and a cleaning assembly.
Escape Character	The nonprinting control character assigned to the decimal ASCII number 027. It is used by the Hewlett-Packard LaserJets and most other printers to indicate the beginning of a printer command.
Escape Sequence	A printer command beginning with the Escape Character.
Factory Default	A group of settings programmed into the printer's permanent ROM memory during manufacturing. The settings can be changed by altering dip switches on the classic LaserJet/LaserJet PLUS/LaserJet 500 Plus printers, or they can be overridden on the LaserJet Series II by changing the User Defaults through the Control Panel Menu System.
Font	A group of characters and symbols related by certain criteria—such as weight, style, and pitch. Fonts are available from three sources:

1. Resident-programmed into the computer's memory.
2. Plug-in cartridges.
3. Disk-based soft fonts.

Fuser Assembly	A mechanism with two high temperature rollers that melt the toner onto the paper, forming a permanent image.
Horizontal Motion Index (HMI)	Defines the distance between characters, measured in 1/120th of an inch.

HP-GL/2	HP's popular HP-GL/2 vector language. HP-GL/2 is used to create and print line drawings, and graphs. It is supported by many CAD/CAM systems and plotters. The PCL 5 command language supported by LaserJet III provides access to HP-GL/2.
Internal Fonts	The fonts that are programmed into the printer's memory at the factory. These are also called resident fonts.
I/O	An abbreviation for "Input/Output," that refers to a device's interface, for example, a serial or parallel connection.
I/O Buffer	The portion of the printer's memory that first stores the data when it is transmitted from the printer.
Landscape Orientation	Widthwise or sideways printing. Compare to portrait or lengthwise printing.
Laser	A highly focused monochromatic light source that is used to scan across the photosensitive drum. The laser is pulsed on and off in a pattern corresponding to the image on the page.
Logical Page	The portion of the page that can be printed—as distinct from the physical page.
Macro	A series of commands that are stored together so they can be easily recalled and rerun.
Monarch	Designation for envelopes sized at 3 7/8-by-7 1/2 inches.
Off-Line	A status in which the printer cannot accept data.
On-Line	"Ready" mode, when the printer can accept data from the computer.

Page Description Language   A specialty language used to tell page printers, such as the LaserJet, how to position and print characters and graphics. PostScript and DDL are common page description languages.

Page Orientation   Refers to whether a font will print in portrait or landscape orientation.

Page Printer   Printers that compose and print entire pages unlike line printers, that print one line at a time.

Paper Grain   The direction of the fibers in paper. For laser printing, long—lengthwise—grain is recommended.

Paper Path   The mechanism that guides the paper from the tray or manual feed through the imaging and fuser assemblies.

Parallel Interface   A communications channel between a computer and external peripheral devices—such as printers—referred to as LPT1: or LPT2:, in which data is transmitted eight bits at a time over eight separate data lines.

PCL   Printer Command Language. PCL commands are used to change margins, fonts, and other page formatting options.

Pitch   The number of characters per inch (cpi).

Point Size   The height of a character, measured in 1/72nd of an inch.

Portrait Orientation   Lengthwise printing.

PostScript   A powerful page description language developed by Adobe Systems, Inc. that is used to print type fonts and graphics on a laser printer or phototypesetter.

PPM	Pages per minute. The number of pages a printer can print under optimum conditions.
Primary Corona Wire	A wire in the EP cartridge that places a uniform electric charge on the photosensitive drum so that it will repell toner except in the areas discharged by the laser.
Print Density	The darkness of the print as it is laid down on the paper. The darker the print density, the quicker the toner is used up.
Print Driver	A file that is used to tell an application program how to control a particular printer. With printers that can be altered by adding font cartridges or soft fonts—such as the LaserJet—more than one print driver may be required.
RAM	Random-Access Memory (RAM) is high-speed memory in computers and printers, that is used to store data temporarily. RAM memory is lost when the printer or computer is turned off.
Rasterization	A process by which graphic elements are converted into dots. This is equivalent to the bit mapping.
Resolution	The measurement of the precision of a printing device such as a laser printer measured in dots per inch (dpi). The Hewlett-Packard LaserJets can print with 300 dpi resolution. Resolution can also be used to describe the dpi used to print a particular graphic element.
Resolution Enhancement	A system that modulates the Technology (RET) laser in LaserJets III and IIID so that dots are sized and placed in a fashion that smoothes jagged edges and gives the appearance of higher resolution.

Robust-XON

A "handshaking" signal that the printer sends to the computer to indicate that it is ready to receive data.

ROM

Read-Only Memory (ROM) is permanent memory that is used in computers and printers to store programs, data, and default settings that can be read, but never altered. Unlike RAM memory, ROM memory is not lost when the device is turned off.

Sans Serif Typeface

A typeface without serifs, such as Helvetica (see serifs).

Scalable Fonts

The font outlines stored as formulas, that can be scaled to any point size between 0.25 and 999.75 points. They can be stored as internal fonts on optional font cartridges, or as soft fonts.

Serial Interface

A communications channel between a computer and external peripheral devices—such as printers, modems and other computers—referred to as COM1:, COM2:, or COM3:, in which data is transmitted sequentially one bit at a time over a single data line. The speed of a serial interface is measured in baud. LaserJets use 9,600 baud as the default speed for serial interfaces.

Serif Typeface

A typeface that has fine horizontal strokes on the ascenders or descenders. The serifs help guide the eye along a line of type, and make the typeface more suitable for blocks of text than sans serif faces. Times Roman is a typical serif typeface.

Soft Font

Font images that are stored on a disk. Soft fonts must be downloaded to the printer before they can be used.

Status Indicator

Feedback from the printer, in the form of a code or message—LaserJet Series II—describing the operating conditions of the printer—for example, 02 -WARM UP.

Stroke Weight

The thickness of the strokes making up a character. The traditional stroke weights are light, medium—also called regular—or bold.

Style

Refers to whether a typeface is upright (regular or Roman) or slanted (italic).

Symbol Set

A group of special symbols that are part of a font. Symbols include such characters as accent marks and the legal paragraph symbol. Symbol sets are available for various foreign languages and specialized purposes, such as legal or mathematical typing.

Toner

A plastic-based powdered ink with a magnetic core. The toner is first attracted to the drum in the EP cartridge, and then transferred to the paper. The fuser assembly melts the toner into the paper and forms the permanent image.

Transfer Corona Wire

A thin steel wire that produces a uniform electrical charge on the paper before it passes into the imaging assembly. This charge enables the paper to attract the toner from the EP drum.

Typeface

A unique character design, such as Courier, Times Roman, and Helvetica.

User Default Environment

LaserJet Series II printer settings that a user enters through the Control Panel Menu System.

Vertical Motion Index (VMI)

A measure of the spacing between lines, measured in 1/48th of an inch.

Xerographic Paper   A type of bond paper with the best electrical properties for laser printing. It is precisely cut paper made for high-speed mechanical feeding.

B

Tables

TABLE B.1. ASCII TABLE FOR ROMAN-8 CHARACTER CONVERSIONS

Graphic	Hex	Dec	Oct	Description
	00	0	000	NUL (null)
	01	1	001	SOH (start of heading)
	02	2	002	STX (start of text)
	03	3	003	ETX (end of text)
	04	4	004	EOT (end of transmission)
	05	5	005	ENQ (enquiry)
	06	6	006	ACK (acknowledge)
	07	7	007	BEL (bell)
	08	8	010	BS (backspace)
	09	9	011	HT (horizontal tabulation)
	0A	10	012	LF (line feed)
	0B	11	013	VT (vertical tabulation)
	0C	12	014	FF (form feed)
	0D	13	015	CR (carriage return)
	0E	14	016	SO (shift out)
	0F	15	017	SI (shift in)

TABLE B.1. CONTINUED

Graphic	Hex	Dec	Oct	Description
	10	16	020	DLE (data link escape)
	11	17	021	DC1 (device control 1 or X-ON)
	12	18	022	DC2 (device control 2)
	13	19	023	DC3 (device control 3 or X-OFF)
	14	20	024	DC4 (device control 4)
	15	21	025	NAK (negative acknowledge)
	16	22	026	SYN (synchronous idle)
	17	23	027	ETB (end of transmission block)
	18	24	030	CAN (cancel)
	19	25	031	EM (end of medium)
	1A	26	032	SUB (substitute)
	1B	27	033	ESC (escape)
	1C	28	034	FS (file separator)
	1D	29	035	GS (group separator)
	1E	30	036	RS (record separator)
	1F	31	037	US (unit separator)
	20	32	040	Space
!	21	33	041	Exclamation point
" "	22	34	042	Quotation mark
#	23	35	043	Number sign (hash mark)
$	24	36	044	Dollar sign
%	25	37	045	Percent sign
&	26	38	046	Ampersand
'	27	39	047	Apostrophe (closing single quote)
(	28	40	050	Opening parenthesis
)	29	41	051	Closing parenthesis
*	2A	42	052	Asterisk
+	2B	43	053	Plus
,	2C	44	054	Comma
–	2D	45	055	Hyphen (minus)

Graphic	Hex	Dec	Oct	Description
.	2E	46	056	Period (point)
/	2F	47	057	Slant (solidus)
0	30	48	060	Zero
1	31	49	061	One
2	32	50	062	Two
3	33	51	063	Three
4	34	52	064	Four
5	35	53	065	Five
6	36	54	066	Six
7	37	55	067	Seven
8	38	56	070	Eight
9	39	57	071	Nine
:	3A	58	072	Colon
;	3B	59	073	Semicolon
<	3C	60	074	Less than sign
=	3D	61	075	Equal sign
>	3E	62	076	Greater than sign
?	3F	63	077	Question mark
@	40	64	100	Commercial at sign
A	41	65	101	Uppercase A
B	42	66	102	Uppercase B
C	43	67	103	Uppercase C
D	44	68	104	Uppercase D
E	45	69	105	Uppercase E
F	46	70	106	Uppercase F
G	47	71	107	Uppercase G
H	48	72	110	Uppercase H
I	49	73	111	Uppercase I
J	4A	74	112	Uppercase J
K	4B	75	113	Uppercase K
L	4C	76	114	Uppercase L
M	4D	77	115	Uppercase M
N	4E	78	116	Uppercase N

continues

TABLE B.1. CONTINUED

Graphic	Hex	Dec	Oct	Description
O	4F	79	117	Uppercase O
P	50	80	120	Uppercase P
Q	51	81	121	Uppercase Q
R	52	82	122	Uppercase R
S	53	83	123	Uppercase S
T	54	84	124	Uppercase T
U	55	85	125	Uppercase U
V	56	86	126	Uppercase V
W	57	87	127	Uppercase W
X	58	88	130	Uppercase X
Y	59	89	131	Uppercase Y
Z	5A	90	132	Uppercase Z
[	5B	91	133	Opening square bracket
\	5C	92	134	Reverse slant
]	5D	93	135	Closing square bracket
^	5E	94	136	Caret (circumflex)
_	5F	95	137	Underscore (low line)
"	60	96	140	Opening single quote
a	61	97	141	Lowercase a
b	62	98	142	Lowercase b
c	63	99	143	Lowercase c
d	64	100	144	Lowercase d
e	65	101	145	Lowercase e
f	66	102	146	Lowercase f
g	67	103	147	Lowercase g
h	68	104	150	Lowercase h
i	69	105	151	Lowercase i
j	6A	106	152	Lowercase j
k	6B	107	153	Lowercase k
l	6C	108	154	Lowercase l
m	6D	109	155	Lowercase m
n	6E	110	156	Lowercase n
o	6F	111	157	Lowercase o

Graphic	Hex	Dec	Oct	Description
p	70	112	160	Lowercase p
q	71	113	161	Lowercase q
r	72	114	162	Lowercase r
s	73	115	163	Lowercase s
t	74	116	164	Lowercase t
u	75	117	165	Lowercase u
v	76	118	166	Lowercase v
w	77	119	167	Lowercase w
x	78	120	170	Lowercase x
y	79	121	171	Lowercase y
z	7A	122	172	Lowercase z
{	7B	123	173	Opening brace (curly bracket)
|	7C	124	174	Vertical line
}	7D	125	175	Closing brace (curly bracket)
~	7E	126	176	Tilde
□	7F	127	177	Delete (rubout)
	80	128	200	--undefined control code--
	81	129	201	--undefined control code--
	82	130	202	--undefined control code--
	83	131	203	--undefined control code--
	84	132	204	--undefined control code--
	85	133	205	--undefined control code--
	86	134	206	--undefined control code--
	87	135	207	--undefined control code--
	88	136	210	--undefined control code--
	89	137	211	--undefined control code--
	8A	138	212	--undefined control code--
	8B	139	213	--undefined control code--
	8C	140	214	--undefined control code--
	8D	141	215	--undefined control code--
	8E	142	216	--undefined control code--
	8F	143	217	--undefined control code--

continues

TABLE B.1. CONTINUED

Graphic	Hex	Dec	Oct	Description
	90	144	220	--undefined control code--
	91	145	221	--undefined control code--
	92	146	222	--undefined control code--
	93	147	223	--undefined control code--
	94	148	224	--undefined control code--
	95	149	225	--undefined control code--
	96	150	226	--undefined control code--
	97	151	227	--undefined control code--
	98	152	230	--undefined control code--
	99	153	231	--undefined control code--
	9A	154	232	--undefined control code--
	9B	155	233	--undefined control code--
	9C	156	234	--undefined control code--
	9D	157	235	--undefined control code--
	9E	158	236	--undefined control code--
	9F	159	237	--undefined control code--
	A0	160	240	--undefined--
À	A1	161	241	Uppercase A grave accent
Â	A2	162	242	Uppercase A circumflex
È	A3	163	243	Uppercase E grave accent
Ê	A4	164	244	Uppercase E circumflex
Ë	A5	165	245	Uppercase E umlaut or diaeresis
Î	A6	166	246	Uppercase I circumflex
Ï	A7	167	247	Uppercase I umlaut or diaeresis
´	A8	168	250	Acute accent
`	A9	169	251	Grave accent
^	AA	170	252	Circumflex accent
¨	AB	171	253	Umlaut (diaeresis) accent
~	AC	172	254	Tilde accent
Ù	AD	173	255	Uppercase U grave accent
Û	AE	174	256	Uppercase U circumflex
£	AF	175	257	Italian Lira symbol

Graphic	Hex	Dec	Oct	Description
‾	B0	176	260	Over line (high line)
	B1	177	261	--undefined--
	B2	178	262	--undefined--
°	B3	179	263	Degree (ring)
Ç	B4	180	264	Uppercase C cedilla
ç	B5	181	265	Lowercase c cedilla
Ñ	B6	182	266	Uppercase N tilde
ñ	B7	183	267	Lowercase n tilde
¡	B8	184	270	Inverse exclamation mark
¿	B9	185	271	Inverse question mark
¤	BA	186	272	General currency symbol
£	BB	187	273	British pound sign
¥	BC	188	274	Japanese yen symbol
§	BD	189	275	Section sign
ƒ	BE	190	276	Dutch guilder symbol
¢	BF	191	277	U.S. cent symbol
â	C0	192	300	Lowercase a circumflex
ê	C1	193	301	Lowercase e circumflex
ô	C2	194	302	Lowercase o circumflex
û	C3	195	303	Lowercase u circumflex
á	C4	196	304	Lowercase a acute accent
é	C5	197	305	Lowercase e acute accent
ó	C6	198	306	Lowercase o acute accent
ú	C7	199	307	Lowercase u acute accent
à	C8	200	310	Lowercase a grave accent
è	C9	201	311	Lowercase e grave accent
ò	CA	202	312	Lowercase o grave accent
ù	CB	203	313	Lowercase u grave accent
ä	CC	204	314	Lowercase a umlaut or diaeresis
ë	CD	205	315	Lowercase e umlaut or diaeresis
ö	CE	206	316	Lowercase o umlaut or diaeresis
ü	CF	207	317	Lowercase u umlaut or diaeresis

continues

TABLE B.1. CONTINUED

Graphic	Hex	Dec	Oct	Description
Å	D0	208	320	Uppercase A degree
î	D1	209	321	Lowercase i circumflex
Ø	D2	210	322	Uppercase O crossbar
Æ	D3	211	323	Uppercase Æ ligature
å	D4	212	324	Lowercase a degree
í	D5	213	325	Lowercase i acute accent
ø	D6	214	326	Lowercase o crossbar
æ	D7	215	327	Lowercase ae ligature
Ä	D8	216	330	Uppercase A umlaut or diaeresis
ì	D9	217	331	Lowercase i grave accent
Ö	DA	218	332	Uppercase O umlaut or diaeresis
Ü	DB	219	333	Uppercase U umlaut or diaeresis
É	DC	220	334	Uppercase E acute accent
ï	DD	221	335	Lowercase i umlaut or diaeresis
ß	DE	222	336	Sharp s
Ô	DF	223	337	Uppercase O circumflex
Á	E0	224	340	Uppercase A acute accent
Ã	E1	225	341	Uppercase A tilde
ã	E2	226	342	Lowercase a tilde
Đ	E3	227	343	Uppercase D with stroke
đ	E4	228	344	Lowercase d with stroke
Í	E5	229	345	Uppercase I acute accent
Ì	E6	230	346	Uppercase I grave accent
Ó	E7	231	347	Uppercase O acute accent
Ò	E8	232	350	Uppercase O grave accent
Õ	E9	233	351	Uppercase O tilde
õ	EA	234	352	Lowercase o tilde
Š	EB	235	353	Uppercase S with caron
š	EC	236	354	Lowercase s with caron

Graphic	Hex	Dec	Oct	Description
Ú	ED	237	355	Uppercase U acute accent
Ÿ	EE	238	356	Uppercase Y umlaut or diaeresis
ÿ	EF	239	357	Lowercase y umlaut or diaeresis
Þ	F0	240	360	Uppercase thorn
þ	F1	241	361	Lowercase thorn
	F2	242	362	--undefined--
	F3	243	363	--undefined--
	F4	244	364	--undefined--
	F5	245	365	--undefined--
—	F6	246	366	Long dash (horizontal bar)
¼	F7	247	367	One fourth (one quarter)
½	F8	248	370	One half
ª	F9	249	371	Feminine ordinal indicator
º	FA	250	372	Masculine ordinal indicator
«	FB	251	373	Opening guillemets (angle quotes)
■	FC	252	374	Solid
»	FD	253	375	Closing guillemets (angle quotes)
±	FE	254	376	Plus/minus sign
	FF	255	377	--undefined--

TABLE B.2. PCL CONTEXT PRINTER COMMANDS

Function	Parameter/ Description	PCL Code	Decimal Code Job
		Job Control Commands		
Reset			
Reset	—	EcE	027 069
Number of copies	# of copies (1–99)	Ec&l#X	027 038 108 ### 088

continues

TABLE B.2. CONTINUED

Function	Parameter/ Description	PCL Code	Decimal Code Job
Simplex/duplex operation			
Simplex/duplex print	Simplex	Ec&l0S	027 038 108 048 083
(IID, IIID)	Duplex		
	Long-edge binding	Ec&l1S	027 038 108 049 083
	Short-edge binding	Ec&l2S	027 038 108 050 083
Long-edge (left) offset registration	# of decipoints (1/720)	Ec&l#U	027 038 108 ### 085
Short-edge (top) offset registration	# of decipoints (1/720)	Ec&l#Z	027 038 108 ### 090
Page side selection	Next Side	Ec&a0G	027 038 097 048 071
	Front Side	Ec&a1G	027 038 097 049 071
	Back Side	Ec&a2G	027 038 097 050 071

Page Control Commands

Function	Parameter/ Description	PCL Code	Decimal Code Job
Page length and size			
Paper source	Eject page	Ec&l0H	027 038 108 048 072
	Upper tray, Lower cassette (LJ 4)	Ec&l1H	027 038 108 049 072
	Manual feed	Ec&l2H	027 038 108 050 072
	Manual envelope feed	Ec&l3H	027 038 108 051 072
	Lower tray, MP Tray (LJ 4)	Ec&l4H	027 038 108 052 072
	Paper deck, Optional tray (LJ 4)	Ec&l5H	027 038 108 053 072
	Envelope feeder	Ec&l6H	027 038 108 054 072
Page and envelope sizes	Executive	Ec&l1A	027 038 108 049 065
	Letter	Ec&l2A	027 038 108 050 065
	Legal	Ec&l3A	027 038 108 051 065
	A4	Ec&l26A	027 038 108 050 054 065
	B5	Ec&l00A	027 038 108049 048 048 065

Function	Parameter/ Description	PCL Code	Decimal Code Job
	Monarch	Ec&l80A	027 038 108 056 048 065
	COM 10	Ec&l81A	027 038 108 056 049 065
	DL	Ec&l90A	027 038 108 057 048 065
	C5	Ec&l91A	027 038 108 057 049 065
Page length	# of lines	Ec&l#P	027 038 108 ### 080

Orientation

Function	Parameter/ Description	PCL Code	Decimal Code Job
Orientation	Portrait	Ec&l0O	027 038 108 048 079
	Landscape	Ec&l1O	027 038 108 049 079
	Reverse portrait	Ec&l2O	027 038 108 050 079
	Reverse landscape	Ec&l3O	027 038 108 051 079
Print direction	# degrees of rotation (counterclockwise, 90 increments only)	Ec&a#P	027 038 097 ### 080
Top margin	# of lines	Ec&l#E	027 038 108 ### 069
Text length	# of lines	Ec&l#F	027 038 108 ### 070
Left margin	# of columns	Ec&a#L	027 038 097 ### 076
Right margin	# of columns	Ec&a#M	027 038 097 ### 077
Clear horizontal margins	—	Ec9	027 057

Perforation skip mode

Function	Parameter/ Description	PCL Code	Decimal Code Job
Perforation skip mode	Disable	Ec&l0L	027 038 108 048 076
	Enable	Ec&l1L	027 038 108 049 076

Horizontal column spacing

Function	Parameter/ Description	PCL Code	Decimal Code Job
Horizontal motion index (HMI)	# of 1/20 increments	Ec&k#H	027 038 107 ### 072

continues

TABLE B.2. CONTINUED

Function	Parameter/ Description	PCL Code	Decimal Code Job
Vertical line spacing			
Vertical motion index (VMI)	# of 1/48 increments	Ec&l#C	027 038 108 ### 067
Line spacing (lines per inch)	1	Ec&l1D	027 038 108 049 068
	2	Ec&l2D	027 038 108 050 068
	3	Ec&l3D	027 038 108 051 068
	4	Ec&l4D	027 038 108 052 068
	6	Ec&l6D	027 038 108 054 068
	8	Ec&l8D	027 038 108 056 068
	12	Ec&l12D	027 038 108 049 050 068
	16	Ec&l16D	027 038 108 049 054 068
	24	Ec&l24D	027 038 108 050 052 068
	48	Ec&l48D	027 038 108 052 056 068

Cursor Positioning

Function	Parameter/ Description	PCL Code	Decimal Code Job
Vertical and horizontal			
Vertical position	# of rows	Ec&a#R	027 038 097 ### 082
	# of units	Ec*p#Y	027 042 112 ### 089
	# of decipoints	Ec&a#V	027 038 097 ### 086
Horizontal position	# of columns	Ec&a#C	027 038 097 ### 067
	# of units	Ec*p#X	027 042 112 ### 088
	# of decipoints	Ec&a#H	027 038 097 ### 072
Half line feed		Ec=	027 061

Function	Parameter/ Description	PCL Code	Decimal Code Job
End-of-line termination			
Line termination 048 071	CR=CR; LF=LF; FF=FF	Ec&k0G	027 038 107
	CR=CR+LF; LF=LF; FF=FF	Ec&k1G	027 038 107 049 071
	CR=CR; LF=CR+LF; FF=CR+FF	Ec&k2G	027 038 107 050 071

Function	Parameter/ Description	PCL Code	Decimal Code Job
	CR=CR+LF; LF=CR+LF; FF=CR+FF	Ec&k3G	027 038 107 051 071

Push/pop position

Push/pop position	Push	Ec&f0S	027 038 102 048 083
	Pop	Ec&f1S	027 038 102 049 083

Font Selection

Symbol set selection

Primary symbol set	ISO 60: Norwegian 1	Ec(0D	027 040 048 068
	ISO 4: United Kingdom	Ec(1E	027 040 049 069
	Windows 3.1 Latin 2	Ec(9E	027 040 057 069
	ISO 69: French	Ec(1F	027 040 049 070
	ISO 21: German	Ec(1G	027 040 049 071
	ISO 15: Italian	Ec(0I	027 040 048 073
	ECMA-94 Latin 1	Ec(0N	027 040 048 078
	ISO 8859-9 Latin 5	Ec(5N	027 040 053 078
	ISO 11: Swedish	Ec(0S	027 040 048 083
	ISO 17: Spanish	Ec(2S	027 040 050 083
	ISO 6: ASCII	Ec(0U	027 040 048 085
	Roman-8	Ec(8U	027 040 056 085
	PC-8	Ec(10U	027 040 049 048 085
	PC-8 D/N	Ec(11U	027 040 049 049 085
	PCX-850	Ec(12U	027 040 049 050 085
	PS Math	Ec(5M	027 040 053 077
	Ventura Math	Ec(6M	027 040 054 077
	Math 8	Ec(8M	027 040 056 077
	MS Pubs	Ec(6J	027 040 054 074
	MC Text	Ec(12J	027 040 049 050 074
	Wing Dings	Ec(19M	027 040 053 055 057 076
	Symbol	Ec(19M	027 040 049 057 077
	Windows 3.1 Latin 5	Ec(5T	027 040 057 084
	PC Turkish	Ec(9T	027 040 057 084

continues

TABLE B.2. CONTINUED

Function	Parameter/ Description	PCL Code	Decimal Code Job
	Legal	Ec(lU	027 040 049 085
	PC-852	Ec(17U	027 040 049 055 085
	Windows 3.1 Latin 1	Ec(17U	027 040 049 057 085
	Desktop	Ec(7J	027 040 055 074
	PS Text	Ec(10J	027 040 049 048 074
	Ventura Intl	Ec(13J	027 040 049 051 074
	Ventura US	Ec(14J	027 040 049 052 074
	Pi Font	Ec(15U	027 040 049 053 085
	Windows 3.0 Latin 1	Ec(9U	027 040 057 085
Spacing			
Primary spacing	Fixed	Ec(s0P	027 040 115 048 080
	Proportional	Ec(s1P	027 040 115 049 080
Pitch			
Primary pitch	# characters/inch	Ec(s#H	027 040 115 ### 072
Set pitch mode	10.0	Ec&k0S	027 038 107 048 083
	Compressed (16.5-16.7)	Ec&k2S	027 038 107 050 083
	Elite (12.0)	Ec&k4S	027 038 107 052 083
Point size			
Primary height	# points	Ec(s#V	027 040 115 ### 086
Style			
Primary style	Upright (solid)	Ec(s0S	027 040 115 048 083
	Italic	Ec(s1S	027 040 115 049 083
	Condensed	Ec(s4S	027 040 115 052 083
	Condensed italic	Ec(s5S	027 040 115 053 083
	Compressed (extra condensed)	Ec(s8S	027 040 115 056 083
	Expanded	Ec(s24S	027 040 115 050 052 083
	Outline	Ec(s32S	027 040 115 051 050 083
	Inline	Ec(s64S	027 040 115 054 052 083

Function	Parameter/ Description	PCL Code	Decimal Code Job
	Shadowed	Ec(s128S	027 040 115 049 050 056 083
	Outline shadowed	Ec(s160S	027 040 115 049 054 048 083

Stroke weight

Function	Parameter/ Description	PCL Code	Decimal Code Job
Primary font stroke weight	Ultra thin	Ec(s-7B	027 040 115 045 055 066
	Extra thin	Ec(s-6B	027 040 115 045 054 066
	Thin	Ec(s-5B	027 040 115 045 053 066
	Extra light	Ec(s-4B	027 040 115 045 052 066
	Light	Ec(s-3B	027 040 115 045 051 066
	Demi light	Ec(s-2B	027 040 115 045 050 066
	Semi light	Ec(s-1B	027 040 115 045 049 066
	Medium (book or text)	Ec(s0B	027 040 115 048 066
	Semi bold	Ec(s1B	027 040 115 049 066
	Demi bold	Ec(s2B	027 040 115 050 066
	Bold	Ec(s3B	027 040 115 051 066
	Extra bold	Ec(s4B	027 040 115 052 066
	Black	Ec(s5B	027 040 115 053 066
	Extra black	Ec(s6B	027 040 115 054 066
	Ultra black	Ec(s7B	027 040 115 055 066

Primary Typeface Family

Fixed pitch fonts

Courier	Ec(s3T		027 040 115 051 084
Line Printer	Ex(s0T		027 040 115 048 084

Scalable fonts

Albertus	Ec(s4362T		027 040 115 052 051 054 050 084

continues

TABLE B.2. CONTINUED

Function	Parameter/ Description	PCL Code	Decimal Code Job
Antique Olive	Ec(s4168T	027 040 115 052 049 054 056 084	
Clarendon	Ec(s4140T	027 040 115 052 049 052 048 084	
Coronet	Ec(s4116T	027 040 115 052 049 049 054 084	
Courier	Ec(s4099T	027 040 115 052 048 057 057 084	
Garamond	Ec(s4197T	027 040 115 052 049 057 055 084	
Letter Gothic	Ec(s4102T	027 040 115 052 049 048 050 084	
Marigold	Ec(s4297T	027 040 115 052 050 057 055 084	
CG Omega	Ec(s4113T	027 040 115 052 049 049 051 084	
CG Times	Ec(s4101T	027 040 115 052 049 048 049 084	
Univers	Ec(s4148T	027 040 115 052 049 052 056 084	
Arial	Ec(s16602T	027 040 115 049 054 054 048 050 084	
Times New Roman	Ec(s16901T	027 040 115 049 054 057 048 049 084	
Symbol	Ec(s16686T	027 040 115 049 054 054 056 054 084	
Wingdings	Ec(s31402T	027 040 115 051 049 052 048 050 084	
Font default			
Font default	Primary font	Ec(3@	027 040 051 064
	Secondary font	Ec)3@	027 041 051 064
Underline			
Underline	Enable fixed	Ec&d0D	027 038 100 048 068
	Enable floating	Ec&d3D	027 038 100 051 068
	Disable	Ec&d@	027 038 100 064

Function	Parameter/ Description	PCL Code	Decimal Code Job
Transparent print			
Transparent print data	# of bytes	Ec&p#X [Data]	027 038 112 ### 088 [Data]
Font management			
Assign font ID	Font ID #	Ec*c#D	027 042 099 ### 068
Font and character control	Delete all fonts	Ec*c0F	027 042 099 048 070
	Delete all temporary fonts	Ec*c1F	027 042 099 049 070
	Delete last font ID specified	Ec*c2F	027 042 099 050 070
	Delete last character specified	Ec*c3F	027 042 099 051 070
	Make font temporary	Ec*c4F	027 042 099 052 070
	Make font permanent	Ec*c5F	027 042 099 053 070
	Copy/Assign the currently invoked font as temporary	Ec*c6F	027 042 099 054 070
Font selection by ID number			
Selection font	ID # primary font	Ec(#X	027 040 ### 088
	ID # secondary font	Ec)#X	027 041 ### 088
Soft font creation			
Font descriptor (font header)	# of bytes	Ec)#W [Data]	027 041 115 ### 087 [Data]
Download character	# of bytes	Ec(s#W [Data]	027 040 115 ### 087 [Data]
Character code	Character code #	Ec*c#E	027 042 099 ### 069
Graphics			
PCL vector graphics switching/set-up			
Enter PCL mode	Use previous PCL cursor position	Ec%0A	027 037 048 65

continues

411

TABLE B.2. CONTINUED

Function	Parameter/ Description	PCL Code	Decimal Code Job
	Use current HP-GL/2 pen position for cursor position	Ec%1a	027 037 048 65
Enter HP-GLl2 mode	Use previous HP-GL/2 pen position	Ec%0B	027 037 048 066
	Use current PCL cursor position	Ec%1B	027 037 049 066
HP-GL/2 plot horizontal size	Horizontal size in inches	Ec*c#K	027 042 099 ### 075
HP-GL/2 plot vertical size	Vertical size in inches	Ec*c#L	027 042 099 ### 076
Set picture frame anchor point	Set anchor point to cursor position	Ec*c0T	027 042 099 048 084
Picture frame horizontal size	Decipoints	Ec*c#X	027 042 99 ### 088
Picture frame vertical size	Decipoints	Ec*c#Y	027 042 099 ### 089
Raster graphics			
Raster resolution	75	Ec*t75R	027 042 116 055 053 082
(dots/inch)	100	Ec*t100R	027 042 116 049 048 048 082
	150	Ec*t150R	027 042 116 049 053 048 082
	300	Ec*t300R	027 042 116 051 048 048 082
	600	Ec*t600	027 042 116 054 048 048 082
Raster graphics creation			
Raster graphics presentation	Rotate image	Ec*r0F	027 042 114 048 070
	LaserJet landscape compatible	Ec*r3F	027 042 114 051 070
Start raster graphics	Left raster graphics margin	Ec*r0A	027 042 114 048 065
	Current cursor	Ec*r1A	027 042 114 049 065
Raster Y offset	# of raster lines of vertical movement	Ec*b#Y	027 042 098 ### 089

Function	Parameter/ Description	PCL Code	Decimal Code Job
Set raster compression mode	Uncoded	Ec*b0M	027 042 098 048 077
	Run-length uncoded	Ec*b1M	027 042 098 049 077
	Tagged image file format	Ec*b2M	027 042 098 050 077
	Delta row	Ec*b3M	027 042 098 051 077
Transfer raster data	# of bytes	Ec*b#W [Data]	027 042 098 ### 087
End raster graphics	Old version	Ec*rB	027 042 114 066
	Preferred	Ec*rC	027 042 114 067
Raster height	# raster rows	Ec*r#T	027 042 114 ### 084
Raster width	# pixels in the specified resolution	Ec*r#S	027 042 114 ### 083

The Print Model

Imaging

Select pattern	Solid black (default)	Ec*v0T	027 042 118 048 084
	Solid white	Ec*v1T	027 042 118 049 084
	HP-defined shading pattern	Ec*v2T	027 042 118 050 084
	HP-defined cross-hatched pattern	Ec*v3T	027 042 118 051 084
	User-defined pattern	Ec*V4T	027 042 118 052 084
Select source transparency mode	Transparent	Ec*v0N	027 042 118 048 078
	Opaque	Ec*v1N	027 042 118 049 078
Select pattern transparency mode	Transparent	Ec*v0O	027 042 118 048 079
	Opaque	Ec*v1O	027 042 118 049 079

Rectangle dimensions

Rectangle width (horizontal size)	# of dots	Ec*c#A	027 042 099 ### 065
	# of decipoints	Ec*c#H	027 042 099 ### 072
Rectangle height vertical size)	# of dots	Ec*c#B	027 042 099 ### 066
	# of decipoints	Ec*c#V	027 042 099 ### 086

Rectangular area fill

Fill rectangular area	Solid black	Ec*c0P	027 042 099 048 080
	Erase (solid white fill)	Ec*c1P	027 042 099 049 080
	Shaded fill	Ec*c2P	027 042 099 050 080

continues

TABLE B.2. CONTINUED

Function	Parameter/ Description	PCL Code	Decimal Code Job
	Cross-hatched fill	Ec*c3P	027 042 099 051 080
	Current pattern	Ec*c5P	027 042 099 053 080
Pattern ID	% of shading or type of pattern	Ec*c#G	027 042 099 ### 071
Shading (% gray)	2	Ec*c2G	027 042 099 050 071
	10	Ec*c10G	027 042 099 049 048 071
	15	Ec*c15G	027 042 099 049 053 071
	30	Ec*c30G	027 042 099 051 048 071
	45	Ec*c45G	027 042 099 052 053 071
	70	Ec*c70G	027 042 099 055 048 071
	90	Ec*c90G	027 042 099 057 048 071
	100	Ec*c100G	027 042 099 049 048 048 071
Pattern	1 Horizontal lines	Ec*c1G	027 042 099 049 071
	2 Vertical lines	Ec*c2G	027 042 099 050 071
	3 Diagonal lines	Ec*c3G	027 042 099 051 071
	4 Diagonal lines	Ec*c4G	027 042 099 052 071
	5 Square grid	Ec*c5G	027 042 099 053 071
	6 Diagonal grid	Ec*c6G	027 042 099 054 071
User-defined pattern			
Define pattern	# of Bytes	Ec*c#W [data]	027 042 ### 087 [Data]
Pattern control	Delete all patterns	Ec*c0Q	027 042 099 048 081
	Delete temporary patterns	Ec*c1Q	027 042 099 049 081
	Delete current pattern	Ec*c2Q	027 042 099 050 081
	Make pattern temporary	Ec*c4Q	027 042 099 052 081
	Make pattern temporary	Ec*c5Q	027 042 099 053 081
Set pattern reference	Rotate with orientation	Ec*p0R	027 042 112 048 082
Point	Follow physical page	Ec*p1R	027 042 112 049 082

Function	Parameter/ Description	PCL Code	Decimal Code Job
Macros			
Macro ID	Marco ID #	Ec&f#Y	027 038 102 ### 089
Macro control	Start macro definition	Ec&f0X	027 038 102 048 088
	Stop macro definition	Ec&f1X	027 038 102 049 088
	Execute macro	Ec&f2X	027 038 102 050 088
	Call macro	Ec&f3X	027 038 102 051 088
	Enable overlay	Ec&f4X	027 038 102 052 088
	Disable overlay	Ec&f5X	027 038 102 053 088
	Delete macros	Ec&f6X	027 038 102 054 088
	Delete all temporary macros	Ec&f7X	027 038 102 055 088
	Delete macro ID	Ec&f8X	027 038 102 056 088
	Make temporary	Ec&f9X	027 038 102 057 088
	Make permanent	Ec&f10X	027 038 102 049 048 088
Programming Tools			
End-of-line-wrap	Enabled	Ec&s0C	027 038 115 048 067
	Disabled	Ec&s1C	027 038 115 049 067
Display functions	On	EcY	027 089
	Off	EcZ	027 090
Status readback			
Set status readback location type	Invalid location	Ec*s0T	027 042 115 048 084
	Currently selected	Ec*s1T	027 042 115 049 084
	All locations	Ec*s2T	027 042 115 050 084
	Internal	Ec*s3T	027 042 115 051 084
	Downloaded	Ec*s4T	027 042 115 052 084
	Cartridge	Ec*s5T	027 042 115 053 084
	User-installed ROM	Ec*s7T	027 042 115 055 084
Set status readback location unit	All entities of the type	Ec*s0U	027 042 115 048 085
	Entity #1 or temporary	Ec*s1U	027 042 115 049 085
	Entity #2 or permanent	Ec*s2U	027 042 115 050 085
	Entity #3	Ec*s3U	027 042 115 051 085
	Entity #4	Ec*s4U	027 042 115 052 085

continues

415

TABLE B.2. CONTINUED

Function	Parameter/ Description	PCL Code	Decimal Code Job
Inquire status			
Readback entity	Font	Ec*s0I	027 042 115 048 073
	Macro	Ec*s1I	027 042 115 049 073
	User-defined pattern	Ec*s2I	027 042 115 050 073
	Symbol set	Ec*s3I	027 042 115 051 073
	Font extender	Ec*s4I	027 042 115 052 073
Flush all pages	Flush completed pages	Ec&r0F	027 038 114 048 070
	Flush all page data	Ec&r1F	027 038 114 049 070
Free memory space	—	Ec*s1M	027 042 115 049 077
Echo	# = echo value	Ec*s#X	027 042 115 ### 088

TABLE B.3. PJL COMMANDS

COMMENT	@PJL COMMENT <words>[<CR>]<LF>
DEFAULT	@PJL DEFAULT [LPARM: personality] variable = value [<CR>]<LF>
DINQUIRE [<CR>]<LF>	@PJL DINQUIRE [LPARM: personality] variable
Response	@PJL DINQUIRE [LPARM: personality] variable <CR><LF>value<CR><LF><FF>
ECHO	@PJL ECHO [<words>][<CR>]<LF>
Response	@PJL ECHO [<words>]<CR><LF><FF>
ENTER	@PJL ENTER LANGUAGE = personality [<CR>]<LF>
EOJ	@PJL EOJ [NAME = job name][<CR>]<LF>
INFO	@PJL INFO read only variable [<CR>]<LF>
Response	@PJL INFO read only variable <CR><LF> [text <CR><LF>]<FF>
INITIALIZE	@PJL INITIALIZE [<CR>]<LF>
INQUIRE	@PJL INQUIRE [LPARM: personality] variable [<CR>]<LF>
Response	@PJL INQUIRE [LPARM: personality] variable <CR><LF>
value	<CR><LF><FF>

JOB [END = 1	@PJL JOB [NAME = "job name"] [START = first page] last page][<CR>]<LF>
OPMSG	@PJL OPMSG DISPLAY = "text" [<CR>]<LF>
RDYMSG	@PJL RDYMSG DISPLAY = "text" [<CR>]<LF>
RESET	@PJL RESET [<CR>]<LF>
SET [<CR>]<LF>	@PJL SET [LPARM: personality] variable = value
STMSG Response	@PJL STMSG DISPLAY = "text" [<CR>]<LF> @PJL STMSG DISPLAY = "text" [<CR>]<LF> key [<CR>]<LF><FF>
Universal Exit	<Esc>%-12345X
USTATUS Response	@PJL USTATUS variable = value [<CR>]<LF> @PJL USTATUS variable = value [<CR>]<LF> [text<CR><LF>]<FF>
USTATUSOFF	@PJL USTATUSOFF [<CR>]<LF>
PJL	@PJL [<CR>]<LF>

TABLE B.4. HP-GL/2 CONTEXT PRINTER COMMANDS

Command	Mnemonic	Parameters*
Dual context extensions		
Enter PCL mode	Esc#%#A	0 = Retain previous PCL cursor position. 1 = Use current HPGL pen position.
Reset	EscE	None

continues

TABLE B.4. CONTINUED

Command	Mnemonic	Parameters*
Primary font	FI	Font_ID
Secondary font	FN	Font_ID
Scalable or bit-mapped fonts	SB	0 = Scalable fonts only 1 = Bit-mapped fonts allowed
Palette extensions		
Transparency mode	TR	0 = Off (opaque) 1 = On (transparent)
Screened vectors	SV	(screen_type[,shading[,index]]]
Vector group		
Arc absolute	AA	x_center,y_center,sweep_angle]; [chord_angle];
Arc relative	AR	x_increment,y_increment, sweep_angle[,chord_angle];
Absolute arc	AT	x_inter,y_inter,x_end,y_end[, chord_angle];
Plot absolute	PA	[x,y ... [,x,y]];
Plot relative	PR	[x,y ... [,x,y]];
Pen down	PD	[x,y ... [,x,y]];
Pen up	PU	[x,y ... [,x,y]];
Relative arc three point	RT	x_incr_inter,y_incr_inter, x_incr_end, y_incr_end[, chord_angle];
Polyline encoded	PE	[flag[val]...coord_pair ... [flag[val]...coord_pair]];

*Parameters in brackets are optional.

Character group		
Select standard font	SS	
Select alternate font	SA	
Absolute direction	DI	[run,rise];
Relative direction	DR	[run,rise];
Absolute character size	SI	[width,height];
Relative character size	SR	[width,height];
Character slant	SL	[tangent_of_angle];
Extra space	ES	[width [,height]]
Standard font definition	SD	[kind,value ... [,kind, value]];

Command	Mnemonic	Parameters*
Alternate font definition	AD	[kind,value ... [kind,value]];
Character fill mode	CF	[fill_mode[,edge_pen]];
Label origin	LO	[position];
Label	LB	[char ... [char]]1bterm
Define label terminator	DT	[1bterm[,mode]];
Character plot	CP	[spaces,lines];
Transparent data	TD	[mode];
Define variable text path	DV	[path[,line]];

Polygon group

Command	Mnemonic	Parameters*
Bezier absolute	BZ	kind, x1_control_pt, y1_control_pt,x2_control_it, y2_control_pt,...
Bezier relative	BR	kind, x1_control_pt_increment, yl_control_pt_increments y2_control_pt_increments y2_control_pt_increments,...
Circle	CI	radius[,chord_angle];
Fill rectangle absolute	RA	x_coordinate,y_coordinate;
Fill rectangle relative	RR	x_increment,y_increment;
Edge rectangle absolute	EA	x_coordinate,y_coordinate;
Edge rectangle relative	ER	x_increment,y_increment;
Fill wedge	WG	radius,start_angle,sweep_angle[,chord_angle];
Edge wedge	EW	radius,start_angle,sweep_angle[,chord_angle];
Polygon mode	PM	polygon_definition;
Fill polygon	FP	
Edge polygon	EP	

Line and fill attributes group

Command	Mnemonic	Parameters*
Line type	LT	[line_type[,pattern_length [, mode]]];
Line attributes	LA	[kind,value ... [,kind,value]];
Pen width	PW	[width[,pen]];
Pen width unit selection	WU	[type];

continues

TABLE B.4. CONTINUED

Command	Mnemonic	Parameters*
Select pen	SP	[pen]; (required, 1 for black (recommended) or 0 for white)
Symbol mode	SM	[char];
Fill type	FT	[fil_type[,option 1[,option2]]];
Anchor corner	AC	[x_coordinate,y_coordinate];
Raster fill definition	RF	[index[,width,height,pen_nbr ... pen_nbr]]; (width and height must be less than 255)
User defined line type	UL	[index[,gap 1 ... gapn]];
Configuration and status group		
Scale	SC	[x1,x2,y1,y2[,type[, left, bottom]]]; or [x1,xfactor,y1,yfactor,2];
Input window	IW	[xLL,yLL,xUR,yUR];
Input P1 and P2	IP	[p1x,p1y[,p2x,p2y]];
Input relative P1 and P2	IR	[p1x,p1y[,p2x,p2y]];
Default values	DF	
Initialize	IN	[n];
Rotate coordinate system	RO	[angle];
Advance full page	PG	[n];
Replot	RP	[n];

TABLE B.5. SYMBOL SET VALUES

Symbol Set Name	Symbol Set ID	Kind 1 Value
ISO 60: Danish/Norwegian	0C	3
ISO 4: United Kingdom	1E	37
ISO 69: French	1F	38
ISO 21: German	1G	39
Greek-8	8G	263
Hebrew-7	0H	8
Hebrew-8	8H	264
ISO 15: Italian	I	9

Symbol Set Name	Symbol Set ID	Kind 1 Value
Microsoft Publishing	6J	202
DeskTop	7J	234
Document	8J	266
PS Text	10J	330
Ventura International	13J	426
Ventura US	14J	458
Kana-8	8K	267
Korean-8	9K	299
Line Draw-7 (Same as 0B)	0L	12
HP Block Characters	1L	44
Tax Line Draw	2L	76
Line Draw-8	8L	268
Ventura ITC Zapf Dingbats	9L	300
PS ITC Zapf Dingbats	10L	332
ITC Zapf Dingbats Series 100	11L	364
ITC Zapf Dingbats Series 200	12L	369
ITC Zapf Dingbats Series 300	13L	428
Math-7 (Same as 0A)	0M	13
Tech-7	1M	45
PS Math	5M	173
Ventura Math	6M	205
Math-8	8M	269
ECMA-94 Latin 1 (ISO 8859/1)	0N	14
ECMA-94 Latin 2 (ISO 8859/2)	2N	78
ECMA-128 Latin 5 (ISO 8859/9)	5N	174
ECMA-113/88 Latin/Cyrillic (ISO 8859/5.2)	10N	334
OCR A	0O	15
OCR B	1O	47
OCR M	2O	79
APL (Typewriter Paired)	0P	16
APL (Bit Paired)	1P	48
Specials	xQ	
Cyrillic ASCII (ECMA-113/86, ISO 8859/5)	0R	18
Cyrillic	1R	50

continues

TABLE B.5. CONTINUED

Symbol Set Name	Symbol Set ID	Kind 1 Value
PC Cyrillic	3R	114
ISO 11: Swedish for Names	0S	19
ISO 17: Spanish	2S	83[fo]

Laser Printer Hardware and Software Enhancement Products

LaserMaster WinJet 1200 Controller

Manufacturer

LaserMaster Corporation
6900 Shady Oak Road
Eden Prairie, MN 55344
(800) 365-4646

Application

1200x1200 DPI resolution enhancer

Description

LaserMaster has continued to set the standard for high resolution enhancement products for LaserJets and compatibles. With the introduction of the Hewlett-Packard LaserJet 4, LaserMaster has developed the WinJet 1200. This host-based, PostScript compatible card set includes 50 TrueType fonts, and a high-speed printer interface.

Shifting from their previous strategy of placing massive amounts of RAM and a coprocessor on their adapter cards, LaserMaster has used the computer's own processor and memory to implement the WinJet product. Although this does require that your application share the processor with the WinJet, it brings the full power of your computer's 386 or 486 processor to the printing job. As you increase the power of your computer by adding memory or upgrading the processor, you will also upgrade your WinJet 1200. By relying on your computer's memory and processor, LaserMaster is able to greatly reduce the cost of the WinJet 1200 as compared to previous models.

One of the major bottlenecks in printing from Windows-based products was the requirement that the printer controller—whether host-based or printer-based—needed to convert the Windows Graphical Device Interface (GDI) display into the native language of the printer—PCL or PostScript. With the WinJet 1200, LaserMaster has included a GDI rasterizer that translates Windows print requests directly. Although the LaserJet 4 has added high-speed parallel port support, the I/O ports still constrain performance in most circumstances. The WinJet's direct connection between the host-based rasterizer and the printer's laser printer engine enables it to skip the sluggish ports, and the need to store and rebuild the image within the printer, improving performance.

One of the complaints about previous LaserMaster products was the need for special drivers for each application. With the WinJet 1200, LaserMaster has addressed most of those issues. The WinJet 1200 supports three modes of printing. With Windows-based software, you can select the WinJet 1200's optimized Windows Direct Driver or the enhanced PostScript driver. The Windows Direct Driver produces up to 600 DPI resolution with the highest speed, and the enhanced PostScript driver can produce the full 1200 DPI resolution in TurboRes mode with only a slight performance penalty. The WinJet supports standard PCL 4 at 600 DPI when printing from DOS or the DOS compatibility box of Windows without application level PostScript support.

The proof of LaserMaster's resolution enhancement capabilities is in the looking. Figure C.1 shows a comparison of the LaserJet 4M printing at 600 DPI with RET on the left and the same image printed on a LaserJet 4 with WinJet 1200 installed. The continuity of tones and absence of staircasing produces a significantly improved image. Although for straight type, the difference is barely noticeable.

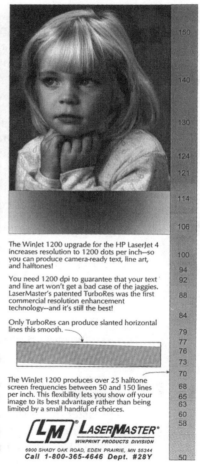

HP LaserJet 4M

This side printed on an HP® LaserJet® 4M using PostScript™ language at 600 dpi with RET.

Note the banding in the grayscale ramp. This is an undesired side effect of the HP LaserJet 4's Resolution Enhancement Technology (RET).

The RET processing tries to smooth the edges of the dots, but as the dot size changes, RET gets confused and alters the desired gray level.

Of course, you can always turn RET off, but then your text gets the jaggies—not a very desirable alternative!

RET is not very effective in eliminating the stairstepping in thin horizontal slanted lines like these.

Even at 600 dpi, the HP LaserJet 4M only provides six different halftone screen frequencies from 50 to 150 lines per inch.

© 1992 LaserMaster Corporation. The LM logo, LaserMaster, and TurboRes are registered trademarks, and WinPrint and WinJet are trademarks of LaserMaster Corporation. PostScript is a trademark of Adobe Systems Inc. HP and LaserJet are registered trademarks of Hewlett-Packard Corporation.

WinJet 1200

This side printed on an HP LaserJet 4 with a WinJet™ 1200 using the same PostScript–language file at 1200x1200 TurboRes®

The WinJet 1200 upgrade for the HP LaserJet 4 increases resolution to 1200 dots per inch—so you can produce camera-ready text, line art, and halftones!

You need 1200 dpi to guarantee that your text and line art won't get a bad case of the jaggies. LaserMaster's patented TurboRes was the first commercial resolution enhancement technology—and it's still the best!

Only TurboRes can produce slanted horizontal lines this smooth.

The WinJet 1200 produces over 25 halftone screen frequencies between 50 and 150 lines per inch. This flexibility lets you show off your image to its best advantage rather than being limited by a small handful of choices.

LM | **LaserMaster®**
WINPRINT PRODUCTS DIVISION
6900 SHADY OAK ROAD, EDEN PRAIRIE, MN 55344
Call 1-800-365-4646 Dept. #28Y

Figure C.1. WinJet 1200 Comparison.

How to Use

The WinJet is installed in an available slot on your PC and is connected to the Optional I/O port of the laser printer by a high speed cable. The installation process modifies your hardware configuration (PS/2) to recognize the new controller, and copies the controller software and font outlines to your hard disk. The software requires a 386 DX or a 486 processor and 16 megabytes of RAM on your computer.

After the WinJet 1200 is installed, you can boot up your desktop publishing system, reconfigure a document for the WinJet, and enjoy higher speed and resolution.

Comments

The LaserMaster installation routine is easy and well documented. The manual provides a fast track approach for advanced users and a comprehensive, step-by-step approach for less experienced users. The installation process requires almost half an hour from start to finish, but works flawlessly.

The output generated by the WinJet 1200 is ready for your print shop. After you adjust the print density on your LaserJet 4 and switch to a harder, brighter and smoother paper, the output is remarkable. Particularly noteworthy is WinJet's ability to generate very small and very large fonts. Very small (4 point) type was quite legible, and large type (36–120) points contained no annoying staircasing.

The speed of the WinJet 1200 was almost as impressive as the quality of the output. Compared to other enhanced resolution controllers and PostScript hardware and software emulators, the LaserMaster is in a category by itself.

Requirements

IBM PC or compatible using an INTEL 386 DX, 486 or compatible with 16 megabytes of RAM and an available slot, and a Hewlett-Packard LaserJet 4 or compatible.

Other Products

Although the WinJet 1200 represents the latest product from Laser-Master, it is not the only one available. LaserMaster offers resolution enhancement products for LaserJet II, III and compatibles. The WinJet 800 offers the same features as the WinJet 1200 up to 800 DPI, and the

WinJet 300 retains the 300 DPI standard of the printer for high-speed printing. Both of the lower resolution cards require a PC with at least 8 megabytes of RAM.

Hewlett-Packard PostScript Cartridge

Manufacturer

> Hewlett-Packard
> P.O. Box 3640
> Sunnyvale, CA 94088-3640
> (800) 538-8787

Application

PostScript add-on cartridge

Description

The two Hewlett-Packard PostScript cartridges add complete PostScript compatibility to LaserJet printers. LaserJet II series printers are supported by the Hewlett-Packard cartridge, and series III printers use the Hewlett-Packard Postscript Cartridge Plus. Unlike many other Post-Script compatible add-on cartridges, the Hewlett-Packard cartridges use a fully licensed copy of PostScript from Adobe Systems, Inc. and are fully compatible. They offer the standard 35 font families and support normal, bold, italic, and oblique styles. They also support reverse type, circles, arcs, patterns, rotation, and stretching, and are compatible with any software that has PostScript drivers.

How to Use

To use a Hewlett-Packard PostScript Cartridge, turn your printer off, remove any PCL cartridges from the left and right slots, insert the cartridge in either cartridge slot, and turn your printer back on. You now have a PostScript printer. Although the basic LaserJet III contains the minimum one megabyte of printer memory required for the Hewlett-Packard PostScript cartridge, Hewlett-Packard recommends that you have two megabytes. This requires the use of a memory expansion board. To switch back to PCL, you must turn your printer off, remove the Hewlett-Packard PostScript cartridge, and then turn the printer back on.

Comments:
Because Hewlett-Packard PostScript cartridges use a licensed copy of Adobe's PostScript, they are fully compatible and produce top quality results. The simplicity of *plug and go* is remarkable, although the inability to switch between PostScript and PCL modes without turning the printer off—available with some third-party PostScript emulator boards and cartridges such as the PacificPage—may be a problem for some users. As plug-in cartridges, they rely on the printer's microprocessor to scale the fonts as well as lay out the page. This can take a significant amount of time for complex pages.

The major drawback of the Hewlett-Packard PostScript cartridges is that, unlike some competitive products, including Hewlett-Packard's LaserJet 4 PostScipt SIMM module, they are not autosensing. To switch between PostScript and PCL, you must physically turn the printer off, remove the cartridge, and turn the printer back on, reversing the process to return to PostScipt.

Hewlett Packard LaserJet 4M PostScript Upgrade Module

Manufacturer
> Hewlett-Packard
> P.O. Box 3640
> Sunnyvale, CA 94088-3640
> (800) 538-8787

Application
PostScript add-in module

Description
Similar in concept to the PostScipt cartridges offered by Hewlett-Packard and others, the purpose of the PostScript module is to add PostScript language capability to the basic PCL version of LaserJet 4. Unlike previous upgrades, however, this module was designed to integrate with the LaserJet 4. It is much faster and easier to use than the plug-in cartridges and many of the other add-ins. In fact, you can order your LaserJet 4 with it preinstalled as model 4M.

The add-in module is easily installed into one of the SIMM slots on the right side of the printer. After it is installed, your printer is ready to accept PostScript print jobs. As an integrated element in LaserJet 4's design and in conjunction with the introduction of PJL, the PostScript module includes an autosensing feature and is available for explicit selection via PJL commands. In the default mode, the autosensing logic looks at the incoming print job and selects the proper language processor—PCL or PostScript.

Requirements
LaserJet 4

Hewlett-Packard LaserJet

Distinctive Documents I & Compelling Publications I

Brilliant Presentations I & Compelling Publications II

Other Cartridges

Manufacturer
> Hewlett-Packard
> P.O. Box 3640
> Sunnyvale, CA 94088-3640
> (800) 538-8787

Application
Scalable typeface cartridges

Description
Hewlett-Packard has added many new scalable typeface cartridges to their list of bit-mapped cartridges. These two examples of the scalable typeface cartridges build on PCL 5's ability to scale fonts on the fly, adding seven and eight faces respectively:

Distinctive Documents I & Compelling Publications I:

> Antique Olive
> CG Century Schoolbook
> CG Palacia
> ITC Souvenir
> Stymie
> Univers Condensed
> ITC Zapf Dingbats

Brilliant Presentations I & Compelling Publications II:

ITC Benguiat
CG Bodoni
ITC Bookman
Garamond Antigua
CG Omega
Shannon
Cooper Black
Revue Light

The fonts can be scaled from .25 to 999.75 points. They are available in medium and bold stroke weights, and regular and italic styles. Some of the fonts are supplied in special weights and styles; other cartridges and soft fonts add other combinations of faces. You should check with Hewlett-Packard about the latest list of available cartridges before you purchase one, because the number of combinations is always increasing.

How to Use

To use a scalable font cartridge, take your printer off-line by pressing the On-Line button and inserting the cartridge until it clicks into place. Press the On-Line button to bring the printer back on-line, and you are ready to print. You can access any of the scalable fonts from software that supports these font cartridges or by issuing the PCL commands to select the font you want by specification.

Alternatively, you can use the menu system to set one of the cartridge-based fonts as your default font. To do this, you need to first print out the font listing by taking your printer off-line by pressing the Print Fonts button or by selecting the PCL Typeface List menu option. The printout lists the font source and the assigned font number. Note that it also lists the required PCL command sequence for each font. Select the desired font and note its source and number.

To set a default font on the LaserJet II or III, access the LaserJet's menu system by taking the printer off-line and by pressing the Menu button. Press the Menu button again until the Font Source selection is displayed. Press the Plus or Minus button until the source for the font that you want is displayed, and press the Enter button to mark your selection. Press the Menu button again, and the Font Number selection is displayed. Press the Plus or Minus button until your selection is displayed, and then press the Enter button. You will be prompted to select a point size. Press the Plus or Minus button until your selection is displayed, and then press the Enter button.

To select the default font on a LaserJet 4, take the printer off-line and press the Menu button until the PCL Menu is displayed. Press the Item button until the Font Source item is displayed. Then press the Plus or Minus button until C is displayed, and press Enter. Next press the Item button until the Font Number menu is displayed, and press the Plus or Minus button until the number is displayed. Then press the Enter button. Finally, press the Item button until the Point Size menu is displayed and select the desired point size with the Plus or Minus button. When the proper size is displayed, press the Enter button.

Finally press the Reset button until the printer resets. Your selected font is now the default font. Note that your software may overwrite this selection if it designates its own default font.

Comments
The two scalable font cartridges offer a good value for most users. They provide a wide variety of font faces in any size and style. The fonts produced by these cartridges are top quality and the PCL 5 scaling system produces them quickly.

Requirements
LaserJet III or 4

Super Cartridge 3/ Professional Edition+
Manufacturer
IQ Engineering
P.O. Box 60955
Sunnyvale, CA 94088
(800) 765-FONT
(408) 733-1161

Application
Desktop publishing and other applications requiring a wide variety of scalable, high-quality fonts.

Description
The Super Cartridges 3/Professional Edition+ is a scalable typeface for LaserJet and PCL 5 compatible printers. It offers 35 equivalents of the PostScript font families. In addition, it offers IQE Garamond OS, Prestige Elite, and IQE English Blackletter. The Garamond face is a *classic publishing design*; the Prestige face is a fixed pitch font designed for business correspondence and financial use; and the Blackletter font is considered a formal *wedding* script. All of the fonts can be scaled from .25 to 999.75 in 1/4 of a point increments.

How to Use
Take the printer off-line by pressing the On-Line button. Then insert the Super Cartridge 3/Professional Edition+ into one of the cartridge slots on your laser printer. Press the On-Line button, and you will have the full battery of PostScript equivalent fonts at your disposal. The cartridge is shipped with font information files and custom drivers for the most popular software applications. The manual clearly spells out how to use the software included with the cartridge.

When you want to use one of the Super Cartridge 3 fonts as your default font, follow the preceding description under Hewlett-Packard's font cartridges.

Comments
The Super Cartridge 3 /Professional Edition+ offers an attractive alternative to PostScript boards. It is far less expensive than add-on Postscript Boards, it does not require any additional memory, and it is much faster than PostScript cartridges or software emulators. Most important, you don't have to give up PCL 5, as you do when you print in PostScript mode; the Super Cartridge 3/Professional Edition+ enables you to take advantage of the full power of your laser printer.

Requirements
A PCL 5-compatible laser printer.

UltraScript

Manufacturer

QMS, Inc.
Dept: USPC
P.O. Box 58101
Santa Clara, CA 95052-8101
(800) 845-4843
(408) 986-9400

Application

Software PostScript emulator

Description

The UltraScript software provides complete PostScript compatibility to your Hewlett-Packard LaserJet or compatible printer by translating the PostScript code generated by your application into code understood by these non-PostScript laser printers. It does this through the software and does not require any additional hardware, provided that your system meets minimum system requirements stated below.

How to Use

To use UltraScript, you need to install the software on your hard disk, modify your system configuration if required, and install a PostScript driver in your application—for example, with WordPerfect, you select the driver for the Apple LaserWriter Plus. You can treat your LaserJet as if it were a PostScript-compatible printer, and print from within the application if you have enough system memory. This is done by means of a RAM-resident portion of the UltraScript code that intercepts the print commands coming from the application software and converts them into a graphics image. The graphics image is then printed to the LaserJet in its native PCL mode.

When you do not have enough system memory, you can still use UltraScript, but you will have to create an intermediate PostScript print file from the application, exit the application, convert the print file, and then print it outside the application. Although this is more complicated, it enables the UltraScript system to work on less powerful or expensive systems.

Comments

The process of installing UltraScript is technically complex, but the comprehensive manual provided by QMS carries you through it step-by-step, even providing application specific instructions for most of the popular word processors and desktop publishing systems. After it is installed, UltraScript is transparent to the user.

Although you can run UltraScript on a 286-based machine with only 640 kilobytes of RAM, it is recommended that you do not. When you plan to print regularly in the PostScript mode, you will find it frustrating to enter and exit your applications, and wait for UltraScript to convert the print files. However, adding as little as one megabyte of extended memory enables you to print from within your applications.

When you are working with a 386- or 486-based system and have two or more megabytes of extended memory available, UltraScript outperforms many dedicated hardware solutions. By using the system's processor and memory, you get all of the advantages of a faster processor and more memory.

Requirements

IBM PC or compatible with a 286 or 386 processor; DOS 3.1 or above; 640 kilobytes of RAM, although two megabytes or more are STRONGLY recommended, and 4 megabytes of available hard disk space.

PrintCache

Manufacturer

LaserTools
1250 45th Street
Emeryville, CA 94608
(510) 420-8777

Application

Software print cache

Description

The PrintCache program increases the speed of communication between your software and your printer, and caches the print request in RAM or on disk. This enables you to return to your application when the print job is completed as a background task. PrintCache is one of the fastest print utilities around, and one of the most flexible. It enables you to select between regular memory, expanded memory, extended memory, or a disk drive as the cache location. It also enables you to specify the amount of memory to be assigned to the cache. The installation routine intelligently tests your hardware configuration and recommends the optimal solution. One of the advantages of PrintCache over its competitors is that it can be configured to use only 5K for the TSR portion when configured in extra memory, or 9K when you cache to your hard disk.

The latest release of PrintCache supports the new bidirectional port of the LaserJet 4. This enables the cache software to monitor the printer so that you can know the current printer status at all times when printing from DOS or Windows. When in Windows, the cache software will alter its icon to show the status and report the text of the message in the icon's title. If you have installed a sound driver in Windows, PrintCache will generate verbal messages as well. Although this is slick and does have some value for some users, you will soon turn this feature off when it becomes annoying. One feature that novice users will find quite useful is the PrintCache tie-in between Window's extensive help system and Hewlett-Packard's manual. When the printer reports an error or problem, the Windows-based cache uses the error message to provide context-sensitive help directly from the Hewlett-Packard manual. It not only tells you what is wrong, it tells you how to fix it.

How to Use

After it is installed, you can invoke the caching program by including it in your AUTOEXEC.BAT file, or invoke the program as required. After the program is invoked, the PrintCache program will intercept all print requests, divert them to the cache, return control to the application program, and print the report or letter as fast as the printer can operate in background mode. The PrintCache program is transparent to the user and most applications.

Windows needs to have its own caching program Print Manager turned off and the PrintCache program substituted in its place. When you install PrintCache, you can have it perform this step automatically. If you install Windows after you have installed PrintCache, you will have to follow the instructions to install PrintCache within Windows.

Comments

With so many application programs providing their own caching routines, an independent caching program would have to provide exceptional service to justify its additional cost. The PrintCache program clearly meets this criterion in terms of raw speed and minimal consumption of precious RAM. Its ease of installation and transparent operation are a bonus.

Requirements

IBM, or compatible; DOS 2.1 or higher; 7-20K of available RAM, and 500K disk space

The program will operate with a LaserJet II, III or compatible for standard operations, and a LaserJet 4 or compatible for bidirectional support.

TreeSaver

Manufacturer

Discoversoft, Inc.
1516 Oak Street
Alameda, CA 94501
(510) 769-2902

Application

Print compression software

Description

TreeSaver is a unique application that reduces the size of a printout as it is printed. This enables users to print up to four or more logical pages on a single sheet of paper. TreeSaver is installed as a memory-resident utility that intercepts jobs sent to the printer, and reformats them in smaller type that enables you to print one, two, four, or more logical pages on a single sheet of paper. It also shrinks graphic images.

How to Use

TreeSaver operates as a TSR application that sits in memory and intercepts all print requests sent to the printer. Depending on the setting of TreeSaver, it translates the print request into the requested new format. After it is installed and invoked, TreeSaver is controlled by a series of hot keys (Alt 1–9) in DOS or a Control Panel in Windows 3.1 that enables you to select full-scale pages or pages reduced to 1, 2, or 4 pages per sheet. You can also select special layouts, including

Tri-Fold, scaled to fit a particular sized paper—a daytimer—or multi-mode that enables you to set the number of pages up to 16. You can even control the TreeSaver mode by embedding special PCL-like codes into printer control strings. This would enable you to place the *Quad* mode command into your Lotus 1-2-3 setup string, print all of the spreadsheets in super-compressed, four-page-per-sheet mode, and leave all of the other programs in normal print mode. TreeSaver uses about 25K of RAM, unless you have expanded memory (EMS), in which case it uses less than 2K of DOS's 640K partition. TreeSaver can also be used in a nonresident mode by those who suffer from severe *RAM-CRAM*.

Comments
TreeSaver is a saver of paper and therefore trees. Even in the 27.27 pitch type, your reports will be highly legible without a magnifying glass. An additional benefit of TreeSaver beyond space reduction, is its ability to present four times as much information on a single page of paper or print a full page of data on a 3 1/2-by-6-inch slip of paper. You could print your entire address book on a single piece of paper and carry it in your wallet. Whether you are cost-conscious or environmentally conscious, TreeSaver is an extremely valuable laser printing tool.

Requirements
IBM PC, or compatible; DOS 2.1 or higher; and a Hewlett-Packard LaserJet PLUS or above printer.

TonerSaver
Manufacturer
Discoversoft, Inc.
1516 Oak Street
Alameda, CA 94501
(510) 769-2902

Application
Print density control software

Description
A natural complement to the TreeSaver software previously described, is Discoversoft's new Toner Saver software. By setting the printer to one of the internal patterns rather than pure black, it prints out text

and graphics with reduced print density and still retains its legibility. In addition, the Toner Saver software is capable of adding shaded overlays to your existing reports by using one of the internal patterns and adding lines, boxes, or text. You can use this to highlight standard reports with shading or add messages such as DRAFT or CONFIDENTIAL to your documents. (See Figure C.2.)

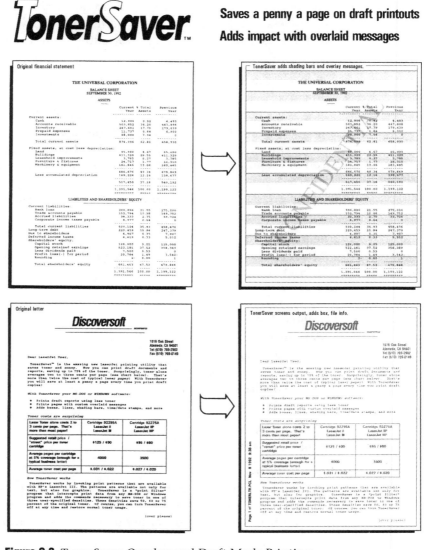

Figure C.2. TonerSaver Overlay and Draft Mode Printing.

How to Use

TonerSaver, like TreeSaver, works as a TSR application that sits in memory. It intercepts all of the print jobs sent to the printer, adding the code you need for the shading or overlays. As a TSR, you can adjust the settings with a series of hot keys, turning draft mode on or off, and resetting the density of draft mode. The program requires from 4 to 16K of RAM.

Comments

The draft output of TonerSaver is so legible that it is impossible to believe that you are using only 50 percent of the standard amount of toner. In fact, reducing the toner to the lowest setting—about 20 percent—still produces legible text. The overlay function is useful for some users, and the ability to date stamp and label print jobs will appeal to other users as well.

Requirements

IBM PC, or compatible, and DOS 2.1 or higher.

Draft mode printing requires a PCL 5-compatible printer—LaserJet III, 4 or compatible—and the overlay feature only requires a PCL 4-compatible printer.

4Print

Manufacturer

Korenthal Associates, Inc.
511 Avenue of the Americas, Number 400
New York, NY 10011
(800) 527-7647
(212) 242-1790

Application

Print comparison software

Like Discoversoft's TreeSaver program, 4Print reduces the size of a printout as it is printed. This application enables you to print two or three pages sideways on one side of a sheet, and four to six pages for double-sided printing. This program comes with a booklet-making utility called 4Book. 4Print is provided on the disk that accompanies this book as a DOS shareware version. (See Appendix D for further information about installing and using the program.) The retail version of the progeram has DOS and Windows modules.

How to Use

4Print uses landscape printing and small fonts to compress the size of the ASCII Text files. Commands are entered from the DOS prompt with a parameter for naming files, selecting fonts, and designating compression modes. Windows users can access a shell that eases the task of choosing print options. You can select one, two, three, or four columns of text per page, and normal, tiny or squashed fonts to print up to 242 characters per line. Double-sided printing enables you to maximize the amount of text printed on a sheet, and with a duplex printer—for example, the LaserJet IIID—you do not need to switch the sheet for reverse-side printing. The 4Book program that accompanies 4Print includes configuration files that enable you to customize the style of your manual. Special options let you choose different shadings and special effects for the cover, including sunbursts, eclipses, and a style called "Yech" that is designed to be ugly.

Requirements

Any Hewlett-Packard LaserJet or compatible printer equipped with a small, fixed pitched landscaped font.

LabelPro

Manufacturer

> Avery Dennison
> Consumers Services Center
> 20955 Pathfinders Road
> Diamond Bar, CA 91765-4000
> (800) 252-8379

Application

Label printing software

Description

LabelPro is a special purpose software package dedicated to printing Avery's standard labels in a variety of sizes, formats, and styles. It is menu driven and enables you to easily create repeating labels or merge text from WordPerfect or dBASE III or IV. You can even create your own database within the program. It also enables you to include a small graphic image in PCX format on each label. There is no version currently available for LaserJet 4 printers, but an upgrade is expected soon.

How to Use

The installation process is straight forward, and includes a procedure for calibrating your printer to ensure proper alignment. The menus enable you to easily design labels for any of the Avery labels and transparencies compatible with the laser printers. It also includes a variety of labels suitable for creating file lists for diskettes. Because the program knows the exact dimensions of each label and its positioning on the page, it easily handles the chores of justifying text of different sizes and fonts.

In addition, it contains a useful feature that enables the program to scan a database to see if any of the records will run over the edge of the label. After you have designed a label, you can use the design repeatedly by merging it with different data or updating dates, titles, label numbers, and so on.

Comments

The LabelPro software is easy to use and enables you to design a variety of formats. Its particular strength is its ability to work with databases merged from WordPerfect and dBASE. This feature enables users of those products to produce high quality labels easily. Be aware that the program only works with Avery label stock. That means you must have access to Avery products.

Requirements

IBM PC, or compatible with 512 kilobytes of RAM; DOS 3.0 or higher; and a LaserJet II, III, or compatible printer.

Windows Printing System

Manufacturer

Microsoft Corporation
One Microsoft Way
Redmond, WA 98052-6399
(800)227-4679

Application

High speed printer interface for LaserJet II, III, and compatibles

Description

The Windows Printing System is a hardware—cartridge—and software product that provides higher speed transmission and rendering of Windows print jobs on LaserJet II, III, and compatibles. It also provides bidirectional communication—similar to the LaserJet 4—and true WYSIWYG printing with TrueType fonts. The major source of speed improvement is provided by using the same Windows imaging language for the display and the printer. This avoids the need to translate the screen display to another language such as PCL or PostScript before printing. In addition, the Windows Printing System adds bidirectional communication between the computer and the printer, similar to the implementation on the LaserJet 4. This enables the printer to inform Windows about its status or needs. In keeping with the graphical interface of Windows, these messages are presented as text, and as an animated presentation of the printer and the paper as it travels through the printer. If you install a sound driver, the Windows Printing System also provides you with synthesized voice status reports. The system also enables you to control many of the printer's internal settings such as half-toning, brightness, and contrast. You can change the resolutions and turn RET on and off. Finally, it will collate multipage print jobs so that you can print on both sides of the page by manually reprinting each page in the proper order to create continuous two-sided reports.

How to Use

As with all Windows applications, the Windows printing system must be installed by Windows. After it is installed, the Windows printing system configures itself to both your computer and printer. If you ever change printers or computers, it dynamically reconfigures itself to the new environment.

Every time you create a print request within Windows, the print job is analyzed by the Windows Printing System that decides whether it would be faster to use the computer's memory and processor, the printer's processor to rasterize the image, or to send it to the printer for rasterization by the printer's processor. Because the Windows Printing System reconfigures itself to your hardware, it can accurately determine the fastest process and can provide an accurate estimate of the time remaining.

The Windows Printing System does not interfere with standard DOS printing on the same printer. It configures the printer whenever Windows is loaded and reconfigures the printer back to PCL when it is closed.

Comments

Although the new Print Manager and Windows Printing Display are the first items you will notice with the Windows Printing System, followed closely by the synthesized voice status reports, the true value of the system is speed and accuracy. The speed improvement will depend on many factors including the speed of your computer's processor, the amount of installed memory, and the complexity of your print jobs. The faster your computer and the more complex the job, the greater the improvement. The fact that the Windows Printing System uses the same TrueType fonts and rasterizing engine for the screen and the printer ensures WYSIWYG capability.

Requirements

Windows 3.1 and LaserJet Series II, III or compatible. Requires up to 5 megabytes of disk space.

PrinterFax

Manufacturer

Moonlight Computer Products
10211 Pacific Mesa Blvd
San Diego, CA 92121
(619) 625-0300

Application

Fax cartridge

Description

The PrinterFax cartridge is a Group 3, receive-only fax add-on for most Series II or III-compatible laser printers packaged in a standard plug-in font cartridge. It produces simulated 300x300 resolution plain-paper faxes using the laser printer alone. The computer does not need to be accessed during the printing processs.

How to Use

All you need to do is insert the fax cartridge into the left cartridge slot, plug it into a standard RJ-11C phone jack—T-connector included—configure it from the printer's front menu panel, and stand back to watch the magic. The Fax cartridge draws its power from the printer and requires no additional hand holding. It senses the incoming call, answers on the assigned ring, accepts up to 10 pages of incoming material (more if you add more memory), and prints the fax. It even has its own resolution enhancement—similar to RET—that prints the standard Group 3 fax's 200x200 fine resolution at 300x300, smoothing the jaggies as it goes. You can configure the printer for print only, fax only, or auto switching, the default.

Comments

The PrinterFax is a remarkable device. Its light weight and compact size make it a perfect *portable fax machine*. It is easy to install and you don't have to do anything to use it. Just leave your printer turned on—your computer can be off or on—and let it print your incoming faxes. It is inevitable that we compare the PrinterFax to standard PC-based fax modems. It outperforms any PC-based fax modem in every department except transmitting outbound faxes. The convenience, ease of use, and lower power requirements—you don't need to leave your computer on—make it an attractive product.

As an eminently portable device, it is convenient for the traveling businessman who can set up a fax machine wherever there is a laser printer and a phone line. Combined with an inexpensive, send-only fax modem, the FaxPrinter is a powerful tool.

Requirements

Hewlett-Packard LaserJet Series II, III or compatible. This product currently will not work with LaserJet 4, although a compatible product is in the works.

PacificPage PE/XL

Manufacturer

Pacific Data Products
9125 Rehco Road
San Diego, CA 92121
(619) 625-3576

Application
PostScript cartridge

Description
The PacificPage PE/XL is a PostScript-compatible emulator in a cartridge format. It provides full PostScript compatibility, including the capability for using the standard 35 typefaces. The model PE/XL also provides automatic language and port switching.

How to Use
Simply plug and play. Turn off your printer, insert the cartridge and the included memory card (if needed), and turn the computer back on. Load up the PostScript driver for your software and you are ready to print.

Comments
Pacific Data Products was the developer of the initial PostScript-compatible add-on cartridge, and the PacificPage PE/XL is the latest edition. The key improvements are automatic language sensing and switching, automatic interface switching and a new Intel i960 processor that improves rendering times. The quality of the output is excellent and the performance improvement quite noticeable. The automatic language sensing and switching is important in a shared printer environment such as a network. The multiple I/O port capability enables you to create primitive printer sharing by hitching one computer to the parallel port, and another to the serial port.

Requirements
Hewlett-Packard LaserJet Series II, III or compatible.

ShareSpool XL

Manufacturer
Extended Systems
P.O. Box 6368
Bozeman, MT 59771
(800) 235-7576

Application
Printer sharing

Description

The ShareSpool XL enables 8 users to share a single LaserJet 4 printer. Attaching to the optional I/O port of the laser printer, the ShareSpool card is linked to up to 8 individual PCs either via their parallel or serial ports. Each PC has access to the shared printer, and the job is spooled if the printer is already busy. In addition, you can locate individual computers up to 500 feet from the printer.

How to Use

Insert the card into the optional I/O port of your laser printer, attach the cables to your computer's adapter, and you're ready to run. As each print job is received, it is automatically queued and printed in sequence.

Comments

The ShareSpool XL is the latest in a long line of printer sharing hardware from Extended Systems. Its improved performance and solid construction make it the new standard in printer sharing devices. Other printer-sharing devices and network interface cards are also available from Extended Systems.

Requirements

Internal cards are available for all LaserJet printers. LaserJet compatible printers can use external cards fom Extended Systems.

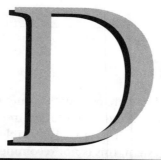

What Is on the Disk

The disk that accompanies this book includes two shareware programs that provide special printing features for LaserJet and compatible printers. The FONTEDIT program, by Alexander Walter, enables you to create and modify bit-mapped fonts that you can download to your printer. Also included on the disk is 4Print, a shareware version of a retail product created by Korenthal Associates, Inc. 4Print prints an ASCII document sideways on a page in compressed type, enabling you to reduce paper consumption up to 75 percent. 4Print includes a companion product called 4Book that enables you to print a document as a booklet.

The instructions for using the two programs follow. If you like FONTEDIT's custom font-building features or 4Print's document printing selections, you should register them with their distributors. By registering the products, you will ensure that you are kept informed about updates to the programs. You will also be helping to support the shareware concept of software distribution, that enables you to thoroughly test a program before buying it.

Using FONTEDIT

FONTEDIT will operate on any PC compatible computer with DOS 2.1 or above, a CGA or higher resolution monitor, and at least 256K of available memory. Although it is possible to run FONTEDIT on a floppy based system, this is not recommended as bitmapped font files tend to be quite large. FONTEDIT provides a wide variety of tools that enable you to import a font, to edit it letter by letter or as a complete set, and to modify individual characteristics all the way down to changing each pixel of a character. You can save your new font to a file and download it to your laser printer.

Getting Started

The FONTEDIT files are in a self-extracting file called FONTED.EXE in the FONTEDIT directory on the distribution disk. The files include the editor, documentation, and sample fonts. To install the program files on your hard drive, create a new directory with an appropriate name such as C:\FONTEDIT by using the following DOS commands:

```
CD \
MD FONTEDIT
CD \FONTEDIT
```

Place the distribution disk in your floppy drive and open the FONTEDIT files in the directory with the following command:

```
A:\FONTEDIT\FONTED
```

If the distribution disk fits into your B: drive, use the following command:

```
B:\FONTEDIT\FONTED
```

Place the distribution disk in a safe place and start the program.

Printing the Documentation

The complete documentation for the FONTEDIT program is located in a file called FONTEDIT.DOC distributed on disk. To print a hard copy of the documentation, use the following DOS PRINT command:

```
PRINT FONTEDIT.DOC
```

Starting FONTEDIT

To start FONTEDIT, move to the directory or disk containing the program and the file to be edited—or where a new file will be placed—and type the following:

```
FONTEDIT filename
```

File name is the name of the font file you wish to edit, or a blank if you want to create an entirely new font.The system will make a backup of the font with the .BAK extension and then present the first character of the font. You can use the Function keys alone or in combination with the Shift and Ctrl keys to access many different editing functions. (See Figure D.1.)

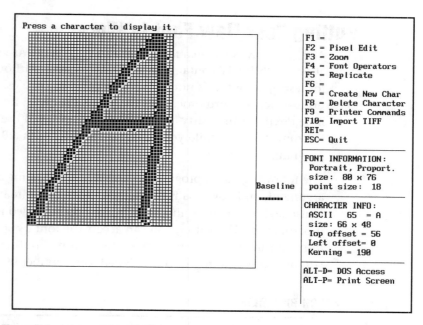

Figure D.1. A FONTEDIT Main Editing Screen.

The FONTEDIT program enables you to modify a font and it also has a built-in downloader—that enables you to download the font—a file printing function, and a temporary exit to DOS that enables you to run another program that will have access to the downloaded font.

The function of FONTEDIT is its font editing ability, by using the pixel editor in conjunction with the built-in graphics functions—cut and paste; ellipse, rectangle, polygon, and line drawing; reversing and inverting; special character features such as drop shadows and hollow forms, slant, rotation, and tilt changes, thinning and fattening, resizing; font features such as resetting baselines, underlining distances, and kerning values. FONTEDIT also enables you to control the detailed font characteristics including symbol set, Vertical Motion Index, point size, orientation, and cell height and width. You can do anything you want to create the perfect effect. You can even scan a sample into a TIF file and create a font from your own handwriting. The sample font shipped with the program was created in this fashion.

Putting Your New Font to Work

After you have created a font, how can you use it? As mentioned above, FONTEDIT contains its own downloader. Although this is fine for testing a font, it is not convenient for every day use. Most applications—such as word processors that use a variety of fonts—have integrated or third-party downloaders that you can use to download the font. You can build your own downloader with a Batch or BASIC program.

The following Batch program accepts a font file name as its only argument, and downloads the named file as the primary font to LPT1. It also assigns the font number 99 to the downloaded font and makes it permanent. Thereafter, you can access the font by specifying the font's feature features, the primary font—until another is named by you or your software—or the assigned font number 99.

BATCH PROGRAM

Program code	Comments
ECHO _*c99D >LPT1:	Declare a font ID number
COPY /B %1 LPT1:	Download the specified file
ECHO _(99X >LPT1:	Make font 99 the primary font
ECHO _*c5F >LPT1:	Make font 99 permanent

The _ character is the Esc character. To create the _ character in DOS EDIT, press CTRL-P and then hold down the ALT key when you are typing 027 on the numeric key pad. This batch file is called DL.BAT and you can find it on the distribution disk.

After you have downloaded your sample font, you can verify that it has been properly installed by printing a test sample or by requesting the PCL Typeface List, an option on the Test Menu. Because the downloaded font was specified as a permanent soft font, it will be included on the list.

Registering FONTEDIT

When you enjoy the power and features of FONTEDIT, register the product with Alexander Walter with a check for $30. Registered users will be kept posted about new updates to FONTEDIT.

The program's author can be reached at the following address.

Alexander Walter
182 Iler Drive
Middletown, NJ 07748

Phone support is available at 908-949-0507 or 908-671-5080.

Using 4Print

4Print from Korenthal Associates, Inc., is a paper-saving utility for Hewlett-Packard LaserJets and compatibles. 4Print prints two or three fully readable pages of text sideways across the page. By printing on both sides, it can yield four, six, or even more pages of text on each sheet.

4Print enables programmers to view four pages of source code at a time, writers to read four pages of text, and spreadsheet and database users to print wide reports all the way across the page. 4Print can reduce paper consumption and paper costs.

4Print's printing features include single- or double-sided page printing on any LaserJet or compatible, one- to four-page printing across a sheet; up to 242 characters per line, reverse order printing to eliminate the need for manual collating, and compression of blank lines and page breaks.

A utility called 4Book is included with 4Print. This companion program enables you to print precollated booklets by folding the printed pages in half. You can customize the cover and title page to create your own special style.

Getting Started with 4Print

To install the shareware version of 4Print from the disk included with this book, create a subdirectory on your hard drive called 4PRINT, change to that directory, and then run the self-extracting program 4PRINT#.EXE from the disk. This will load the program and documentation files in the 4PRINT directory. Type the following DOS commands to install the program:

```
CD \
MD \4PRINT
CD \4PRINT
```

When the distribution disk is in your A: drive, type the following:

```
A:\4PRINT\4PRINT#
```

When the distribution disk is in your B: drive, type the following:

```
B:\4PRINT\4PRINT#
```

To access 4Print from any drive or directory on your computer, you will need to add the 4PRINT directory to your DOS search path. The DOS Edit or Edlin programs can be used to change the path statement in your AUTOEXEC.BAT file.

Printing with 4Print

Included with 4Print is a help file that contains the options that you can use to print an ASCII text file. To begin the program and browse through the command choices, type the following at the DOS prompt:

```
4PRINT
```

You can use the PgUp and PgDn keys to look at the command choices, that are preceded by a hyphen on the command line. Options that can be selected include text centering, reverse printing, word wrapping, a choice for paper trays, and dozens of others. The help screens show many of the most common command usage statements.

To print a document, you need to follow the 4PRINT command with the name of the file and any options you want to use. For example, you can print the README.DOC file included with the program in a single-sided format by typing the following command:

```
4PRINT README.DOC -s
```

To print the document in a double-sided format, eliminate the "-s" option. For duplex printers such as the LaserJet IID and IIID that can print on both sides of a sheet in one pass, replace the "-s" option with "-d." Unless you are using a duplex printer, 4Print will pause between passes and ask you to reinsert the paper in the paper tray to print the reverse side.

To see what the 4Book program does, try creating a booklet using a small text file. To print the README.DOC file, for example, type the following command:

```
4BOOK README.DOC
```

The program will pause after it scans the file and prompt you to press "Y" to print the booklet. 4Book will call 4Print with the name of the file and any options that you have specified. Unless you have a duplex printer and you have included the "-d" option on the command line, 4Print will pause after the first pass so that you can reinsert the sheets in the paper tray for reverse side printing.

When you are printing a double-sided document, you may find that you need to to rearrange the pages before reinserting them to insure that the page order is correct. 4Print provides two reverse-order printing options to eliminate the need for this manual collating. To determine which combination of these options are appropriate for your printer, run the Testprin program in your 4PRINT directory.

Registering 4Print

The version of 4Print that comes with this book is provided at no charge for evaluation purposes only. When you like 4Print and want to continue using it beyond the thirty day trial period, you should register the product. The file REGISTER.DOC in your 4PRINT directory includes a registration form. The DOS version included on this disk costs $49.95. A DOS and Windows version is also available for $69.95.

Korenthal Associates, Inc. can be contacted at the following address:

Korenthal Associates, Inc.
511 Avenue of the Americas, No. 400
New York, NY 10011

You can register by phone by calling (800) 527-7647, or (212) 242-1790 outside the U.S. Fax orders can be directed to (212) 242-2599. Payments can be made by credit card, personal check, or bank check. Shipping and handling costs are $5 for the U.S. and Canada, and $10 for foreign orders.

I

Index

A

B

C

D

E

F

Q—R

S

The Laser Printer Reference
REPLACEMENT ORDER FORM

Please use this form when ordering a 3.5-inch disk or a replacement for a defective diskette.

A. If ordering within thirty days of purchase

If a diskette is reported defective within thirty days of purchase, a replacement diskette will be provided free of charge. *The back of this card must be totally filled out and accompanied by the defective diskette and a copy of the dated sales receipt.* In addition, please complete and return the Limited Warranty Registration Card.

B. If ordering after thirty Days of purchase but within one year

If a diskette is reported defective after thirty days, but within one year of purchase and the Warranty Registration Card has been properly filed, a replacement diskette will be provided to you for a nominal fee of $5.00 (send check or money order only). *The back of this card must be totally filled out and accompanied by the defective diskette, a copy of the dated sales receipt, and a $5.00 check or money order made payable to Simon & Schuster, Inc.*

C. If ordering 3.5 inch replacement disks

If you wish to order 3.5-inch disks for this product, please complete the back of this card and mail it with your original 5.25-inch diskettes along with a nominal fee of $5.00 to cover shipping and handling (send check or money order only). In addition, please complete and return the Limited Warranty Registration Card.

The Laser Printer Reference
LIMITED WARRANTY REGISTRATION CARD

In order to preserve your rights as provided in the limited warranty, this card must be on file with Simon & Schuster within thirty days of purchase.

Please fill in the information requested:

NAME _____ PHONE NUMBER ( ) _____

ADDRESS _____

CITY _____ STATE _____ ZIP _____

COMPUTER BRAND & MODEL _____ DOS VERSION _____ MEMORY _____ K

Where did you purchase this product?

DEALER NAME? _____ PHONE NUMBER ( ) _____

ADDRESS _____

CITY _____ STATE _____ ZIP _____

PURCHASE DATE _____ PURCHASE PRICE _____

How did you learn about this product? (Check as many as applicable.)

STORE DISPLAY_____ SALESPERSON _____ MAGAZINE ARTICLE_____ ADVERTISEMENT_____

OTHER (Please explain) _____

How long have you owned or used this computer?

LESS THAN 30 DAYS_____ LESS THAN 6 MONTHS _____ 6 MONTHS TO A YEAR _____ OVER 1 YEAR _____

What is your primary use for the computer?

BUSINESS_____ PERSONAL _____ EDUCATION _____ OTHER (Please explain)_____

Where is your computer located?

HOME_____ OFFICE_____ SCHOOL _____ OTHER (Please explain) _____

1-56686-050-4

Get the Spark. Get *BradyLine*.

Published quarterly, beginning with the Summer 1990 issue. Free exclusively to our customers.

☐ Check here to begin your subscription.